HOUSEBOAT CHRONICLES

NOTES FROM A LIFE IN SHIELD COUNTRY

JAKE MACDONALD

M&S

National Library of Canada Cataloguing in Publication Data

MacDonald, Jake, 1949-
Houseboat chronicles : notes from a life in Shield country / Jake MacDonald.

ISBN 0-7710-5403-3

1. MacDonald, Jake, 1949- – Journeys – Canadian Shield. 2. Canadian Shield – Description and travel. I. Title.

FC75.M393 2002   917.1   C2002-902352-1
F1017.M33 2002

We acknowledge the financial support of the Government of Canada through the Book Publishing Industry Development Program for our publishing activities. We further acknowledge the support of the Canada Council for the Arts and the Ontario Arts Council for our publishing program.

Typeset by M&S, Toronto
Printed and bound in Canada
This book is printed on acid-free paper that is 100% ancient forest friendly (100% post-consumer recycled)

McClelland & Stewart Ltd.
The Canadian Publishers
481 University Avenue
Toronto, Ontario
M5G 2E9
www.mcclelland.com

1   2   3   4   5   6   06   05   04   03   02

For Ann

A blank landscape.

My hand, holding a Laurentien coloured pencil in Emerald Green, pauses at the lower right-hand corner of the page. What should I draw? All around me, kids are hunched over their desks. Grumbling, furtively farting, whispering to each other, humming softly as they work at their own pieces of art.

It's hard to concentrate because the teacher is somewhere in the back of the room. This is Sister George Mary's Grade 6 class, and there's no tomfoolery permitted. When Kenny Richard catches my eye from across the aisle, pulls a booger from his nose, and pretends to flick it in my direction, Sister George launches towards him.

Sister George wears a hooded head cowling and floor-length black skirt, and glides up the aisle like a condor. Bending over, she hisses in Kenny's ear and writes his name on her clipboard. He's earned another five points in The Minute Club. Ha ha. He gives me that look, like he's gagging. Every time one of us gets caught communicating with a classmate, Sister George fines us five minutes. Every two weeks, you have to stay after school and work off the fine. After four detentions, you get the strap. When someone takes the long walk down to the principal's office, accompanied by the teacher, the entire school gets as quiet as Sing Sing prison during an electrocution. Everyone sits there, exchanging anticipatory monkey grimaces, waiting for the sound of the leather belt to come echoing up the waxed hallway.

St. Ignatius School is in the south end of Winnipeg, at the corner of Stafford Street and Corydon Avenue. Just a few blocks north of the school is the genteel, wooded neighbourhood of River Heights, where the large century-old homes are occupied by lawyers, doctors, and judges, many of whom are Anglican or United Church and are unfortunately going to Hell. South of the school is the poorer, working-class neighbourhood of Fort Rouge, where the crooked old wood-frame houses are filled with large Italian immigrant families, many of whom are rosary-clutching church-goers going to Heaven. Or at least the women are.

When it's my turn to serve 6:45 mass I walk to church in the bitter cold, sharing that desolate time of morning with the frozen elms, a million stars, and perhaps a furtive wild creature or two – a cottontail rabbit darting through the fresh snow, pausing to perk its ears and look back at me – and when I get to church those Italian mothers are always there in their black veils, kneeling. They're praying, no doubt, for their wayward sons, my enemies. Their sons tend to be thin sulky boys who smoke cigarettes and fight with their feet, dancing around like fighting cocks. One of the worst is Raymond Cantafio, who weighs about eighty pounds, stands about four foot ten, and has hair like a matinee idol. Many times I've seen Raymond Cantafio slap the faces of boys twice his size, slap their faces back and forth, trying to goad them to fight. And once, while walking home, I had the grave misfortune of running into Raymond Cantafio in a back lane. For an entire city block I edged along backwards, walleyed with terror, while Raymond hissed and feinted at me like a ferret.

Boys like Raymond and his friends make certain streets into no-go zones. But like the cagey citizen of some bombed-out European city, I know safe routes through the various enclaves. Some of my friends are rich, from Yale Avenue, and some are poor, from Garwood. Some are feeble and some are tough. Some are good in school and some are so dumb that you have to wonder if they're retarded. (Danny Barton, for example, shot himself in the leg with a .22 pistol to impress a girl.) I'm sort of in-between. I'm not the most uncoordinated boy in the school yard, nor am I an athlete who gets picked first for baseball teams. My father is a senior bureaucrat with the city, so he makes a good salary. But my parents are raising a family of seven kids, so we're kind of poor anyway. We live in a tract-house neighbourhood seven blocks west of the school. The post-war economy is humming, and my street, Mulvey Avenue, is sort of a suburban battery farm – long rows of temperature-regulated boxes churning out small human beings like me.

It's Sister George's task to whip us into shape, but art class is not high on her list of educational priorities. Art class can only encourage us to screw open the lids of our fetid little minds, and what good can come of that? She'd rather have us do something useful, like long division. Or, if she's in a good mood, she'll permit a spelling bee. Today, she's definitely not in a good mood. I have a bruised lip to attest to that. At lunch hour, when we were all stampeding back to class, I stopped for a drink at the water fountain. Sister George glided up and whacked me in the back of the head, driving my upper lip into the chromium steel of the spigot. "Woe betide," she exclaimed, "if you're not back to class in one second." I should have known better, trying to drink water after the bell had rung. But Sister George's bloody willingness to always ratchet up the tension one more notch fills most of us with a fearful respect. This is a woman who, without too much provocation, would probably drive spikes through our heads and cook us for dinner.

On Sister George's desk at the front of the room, a plastic desk radio issues the rackety piano music of the CBC's weekly Manitoba School Broadcasts. The announcer has the sweet maternal voice of Miss Roma Harpell, the hostess of a television show called *Romper Room*. I don't think it's actually Miss Roma, but it sounds like her. She sounds like the sort of woman who thinks that children are bunnies, full of bright ideas and sweet affections. As Kenny would have it, she's fucked in the head. But I'd rather spend the next hour listening to Miss Roma than Sister George. So I cooperate with all of Miss Roma's instructions. As the piano murmurs gently in the background, her cooing voice issues our marching orders. *Now children, put your heads down on your desks and close your eyes. That's right, nice and tight! Now just be very quiet . . . and dream that we're drifting in the vast darkness of space. Look at that lovely blue planet over there! How pretty it is! Look at the many green continents, so magical and different! What faraway lands will you visit today?*

Somewhere behind me a yardstick whacks a desk. "Close your eyes!" bellows Sister George.

It's the same battle in every art class. The girls close their eyes. The boys refuse. We cooperate to the extent of laying our heads on our arms, but closing your eyes is for sissies. If Sister George prowls past, I scrunch my eyes shut, but open them again as soon as she's past. Sneakily, with my head down, I peer out the window and try to decide what faraway land I'm going to visit today. Outside, the snow is falling, a grey winter afternoon somewhere in the long march from Christmas to Easter. As long as Sister George doesn't catch me, I can spend long minutes thinking up my magical land, lulled into a dream by the hypnotic motion of the falling snow.

You're allowed to sit up straight when you're ready to start drawing. Having selected my destination, I draw a green wavy line across my blank sheet of paper. Using the sides of the pencil, I fill in the contours with olive greens and smoky blues, creating a prospect of distant hills. Above the hills, a hazy sky. With a check mark I create a cruising eagle. I'm fairly serious about art class. If I had my choice, this is what I would do all day. All my textbooks are disfigured with little sketches. With the money that my aunt gave me for Christmas, I sent away for a book called *Learn to Draw with Jon Gnagy*. I've learned some tricks from Jon Gnagy. For example, he's got this trick where you can draw any animal with a series of interlocking circles. But constructing animals from circles is not as interesting as dreaming up a picture – staring at a blank page, then scrawling a horizon line, a pale sky, a drifting eagle. You feel as if a new world is coming to life under your fingertips. It's like being God.

Actually, it's not like being God. You can burn in Purgatory for thinking like that. In my desk I have a comic book called *Chuck White, Catholic Boy*. Each issue tells a story about a dilemma in Chuck's life and how he solved it. The latest issue talks about Purgatory, and all the good works Chuck performs whenever he catches himself thinking sinful thoughts, like comparing himself to God. As every Catholic knows, there are two types of punishments awaiting sinners in the afterlife. Purgatory is the penalty for venial sins, like coveting your neighbour's bicycle or thinking impure thoughts. If you act on your thoughts – steal your neighbour's bicycle, for example, or feel up a girl – you commit a different class of offence, a mortal sin, and get sent to Hell, which is a maximum security institution from which there is no escape. *Chuck White, Catholic Boy* doesn't talk much about Hell, because what's to say? Hell is like a big penitentiary, full of screaming people who are on fire. Hell is a conversation-stopper. The only insurance against going there, after committing a mortal, is to get yourself immediately to Confession. But that doesn't always work. Chuck had a friend who French-necked with a girl, and on their way to church they were run over by a cement truck.

Chuck reduces his earned time in Purgatory by performing good works, which earn rewards, called indulgences. Indulgences can be applied to one's own Purgatory sentence or transferred to someone else's. They're like Old Dutch points. The black-veiled Italian ladies who attend 6:45 mass every morning are earning major indulgences, which they transfer to their no-good sons. The biggest indulgence of all is called a Plenary Indulgence, and it pretty much buys you a permanent licence to commit mortals. Whenever Chuck feels a gnawing worry that he's building up a lot of Purgatory time, he performs good works and keeps track of his indulgences with an easy-to-use reward schedule at the back of his Holy Catechism book. Let's say he attends first Friday mass for a year. Right away, he can look it up on the chart – *One Year of Attending Mass on First Friday – 412 years off.*

Still, it's probably easier to avoid blaspheming God in the first place by comparing your art-class drawings to His mighty works. Choosing a pencil of Mediterranean Blue, I grind the tip in my little pencil sharpener and set to work creating a lake in the foreground, and a red canoe. Two people are paddling the canoe across the lake, a boy and a girl. They're not thinking impure thoughts; they're just paddling a canoe. Choosing my trusty green pencil again I create a foreshore, and a yellow cottage. From force of habit I draw a ribbon of white smoke slanting up from the chimney. The CBC lady has conducted her invocation well. Scribbling madly with the coloured pencil, I'm no longer sitting in Sister George's class. It's not winter any more. It's a warm summer afternoon, and I'm walking through the meadow to our cottage. I can feel the prickly grass under my bare feet, and I can smell the lake.

∾

My father built the cottage a few years ago. He built it at Laclu, a small community by a lake that played an important role in the romance between him and my mother.

When he was young, my dad studied graduate level economics at the University of Toronto. He roomed on Spadina Avenue with his buddy Frank Pickersgill. It was the late 1930s, and the Spanish Civil War was underway. My dad and Pickersgill were fellow Winnipeggers and avid lefties. They would spend their weekends sitting in swanky restaurants in hotels like the Royal York, arguing about politics and ordering crusty rolls and coffee. They would eat crusty rolls for about two hours, then leave without ordering dinner. As they walked out, they'd wave at the head waiter. Sorry, we changed our minds! For fun, they'd sneak into examination halls and try to pass the tests for courses they weren't enrolled in.

After university, my dad got a job with the Winnipeg Electric Company, a utility that ran the streetcars. There weren't a lot of people in the office with postgraduate degrees from the U of T, so he was groomed as senior management material. He stood six foot two, had blue eyes and an athlete's graceful saunter, and the secretaries liked him. But he was awkward around women and wasn't suited to small talk. He could talk for hours with men, but couldn't think of three words to say to a woman. He told the secretaries he had a fiancée in Toronto named Frances, meaning Frank.

One of the clerks in the payroll department was an Irish Catholic girl named Peggy Monahan. With her shoulder-length dark hair and dark eyes, she looked like the teenaged Elizabeth Taylor in *National Velvet*. My father kept dropping by her desk to scrutinize memos, and finally confided that he didn't really have a fiancée, and would she like to go to a movie? They went to the Capitol theatre and watched *The Light That Failed*, starring Ronald Colman. On their second date he showed up at her front door with a cardboard box containing a puppy. Her mother was infuriated at his nerve, but Peggy christened the collie pup Eubie, after the Baltimore jazzman, and kept it at the foot of her bed. When the puppy fell ill with distemper a few weeks later, her mother knit him a yellow sweater and nursed him through the crisis.

Donald Ian MacDonald and Peggy Christine Monahan were married in June 1941 and went on their honeymoon to Laclu – a pretty lake in the Canadian Shield, a hundred miles from Winnipeg, in the western part of Ontario. They rented a cottage and explored a different uninhabited lake every day, hiking the portage trails with a canoe and Eubie galloping up the path to check for bears. It was an unusually cold and stormy June, and the lakes were so rough they had to be careful traversing the big stretches, keeping to the lee shores and making Eubie lie down when they headed into the heavy waves. At night, they curled up in the cottage and listened to the radio, and caught up with the bad news coming from Europe. Swastika flags were flying above Paris. The Americans hadn't joined the war yet, and Britain was preparing to make a last stand against Operation Sea Lion, a massive German invading force that was expected to arrive on their beaches during the next full moon.

At the same time they were exploring the lakes around Laclu, a crew of German sailors was ploughing a monstrous new German battleship named the *Bismarck* through the heavy seas of the Denmark Strait. The *Bismarck*'s battle plan was to cruise down into the shipping lanes of the north Atlantic and prey on Canadian convoys hauling supplies to the doomed England. An RAF Spitfire spotted the *Bismarck*, and warships of the King's Royal Navy set off to engage the battleship. In the murky predawn light of May 24, a British heavy cruiser named the *Hood* caught sight of the *Bismarck* and challenged him (the Germans referred to their warships as males) from sixteen miles away. The *Bismarck* swung broadside, fired one salvo from its terrible huge guns, and hit the *Hood* amidships. The explosion literally blew the *Hood* out of the water, and it sank in less than a minute. Three English sailors survived; 1,415 died.

The *Hood* had been the pride of the Royal Navy, and the news that she'd been destroyed delivered yet another devastating blow to British morale. With bulletins like this coming over the CBC radio (courtesy of the announcer Lorne Greene, whose grave delivery earned him the title "the voice of doom"), my father knew that it was just a matter of time until he wound up in uniform, so after their honeymoon at Laclu he volunteered, and ended up a lieutenant in the Royal Canadian Navy. His friends all volunteered too. His best buddy, Frank Pickersgill, spoke fluent French, so he volunteered for the intelligence service and parachuted into occupied France. As soon as he arrived, he was caught by the Nazis, thanks to an informant, and was sent to Buchenwald, where he was tortured with piano wire at Block 17, then hung on a meat hook cemented into a wall. According to German camp documents that became available after the war, the only words his torturers could extract from him were "Long live free France, long live Canada." After the war, my father kept his war stuff and Pickersgill's letters in the top of his closet. My brother and I would take out my father's Navy gas mask, a rubbery-smelling thing with squid-like eyes, and chase each other around the bedroom.

Laclu therefore held a special place in the hearts of both my father and mother, and in 1954 they bought two acres of land on the north shore of Laclu lake. When summer came, we all piled into the car and went to see the property. We had seven kids in the family by then, plus my parents, plus my beloved white-haired grandmother, so we needed a big car, and a big car we had. My dad was a General Motors man, and his latest car was a lime-green Buick with chromium exhaust ports and doors as big as the loading bays on a Halifax bomber. Ten people, however, made a full load even for a car that size, so it was a long ride. That particular day, it was fantastically hot, as only southern Manitoba can be in July. I drank too much grape juice and fell asleep with my head tilted drunkenly askew in the direct blast of the sun. When I awoke, with a wretched gurgle of the stomach, a purple column of vomit spewed out of my mouth and arced across the back seat onto my brother Danny, who looked at the vomit on his shirt and immediately threw up on Sally, who threw up on Babe, and so forth. In short order, the crowded back seat was a vomitorium, and we all had to change into fresh clothes on the side of the road. But somehow we made it to Ontario, turned off the highway, drove along a winding gravel road for a few miles, and parked in the middle of nowhere.

We got out of the car and milled around in confusion, blinking in the heat. Where are we? Where's the lake? Can we go home now?

We were surrounded by nothing. On the right side of the road was a thick forest. On the left side of the road was a rolling hayfield. The sky was empty and there wasn't a building any-where. Led by our intrepid parents we hiked through the hayfield, over a knoll, and down towards the lake. There wasn't much to look at, really. Just high grass, and a few wooden stakes pounded into the ground to mark our property line. We walked around for a while, looking at the stakes, then one of my sisters screamed – wood tick.

Back at the car, we had to strip down to our underwear and pick off the ticks. My brother and I wanted to burn them to death but my mother wouldn't allow it. My mother is the sort of human being who won't kill even a bee. She traps them alive in a wad of tissue paper and releases them outside. So that was our first visit to the vacant lot that would soon become our cottage site. The following summer, we returned to Laclu and rented a cottage at Webbs' Camps. My father worked on the cottage and we hung around Webbs'. There was an enormous amount of work to do, but that wasn't our problem. Our job was having fun. Every day my mother would do her laundry, her cooking and cleaning, and every day my father would build the cottage. When he came back at night, he'd be all filthy and banged up from the construction work, and we'd exclaim, "Show us your splinters!" He'd sit down and display his big hands, impressively damaged by the day's work.

It couldn't have been much fun for either of them, but they kept at it. Over the next couple of summers the cottage began to take shape – a big wooden box on stilts. It had a stepladder for front steps and no roof. The site was strewn with scrap lumber, and the hayfield was full of bloodthirsty ticks. But every time we arrived the place looked a little better. The farmer who sold us the land came and mowed the hay, using his tractor to pull the hay-rake, a scary-looking contraption with scissor-action teeth. When he was finished, the lawn was as spiky as tooth-picks. But at least it no longer harboured wood ticks, and after a few days, the grass got softer and we could walk on it bare-foot without mincing.

Finally my mother decided to spend a whole summer there, with us kids. My dad worked in the city, and every Friday night he drove up to the lake. We walked down the road to meet him. My brother and I wanted to toughen our feet so we walked bare-foot. The whole family made a game of estimating how far we would make it along the road before my dad's lime-green Buick came gliding over the hill.

Danny and I met some other kids. Every morning, we convened for the purpose of adventure. Some mornings we walked to Webbs' and went swimming. Other mornings we caught frogs, snakes, and turtles and gathered them in large menageries. Sometimes we armed ourselves with hatchets and home-made spears – hunting knives lashed with twine to the end of a pole – and went off to explore the woods. We'd cross the big hayfield and venture into the deep woods. We never went very far. Maybe a hundred yards, close enough to the road that we could still hear the rip of cars going past, but far enough that we could feel the great palpable Presence of the wilderness.

∾

Towards the end of summer the cottage was roofed in, plumbed, and wired. And one Saturday morning my father announced that he was taking the day off.

People who don't own vacation properties might assume that the whole point of owning a cottage is to have a place where you can relax, enjoy nature, and take the day off. But there were seldom moments when my parents weren't working. The drone of a lawn mower, the swish and gurgle of the wringer washer, the distant growl of my dad's curse as he whacked his thumb with the hammer – this was the sound track that should have accompanied my drawing. Every day, my mother was either making meals, cleaning up after meals, or getting ready for the next meal. Every morning, my dad would eat his standard breakfast of bacon and eggs, then go out into the yard and set up his sawhorses, unfurl his extension cords, and get to work. Their days consisted of work, dawn to dusk, seven days a week. But every once in a while, perhaps twice during the summer, they'd take a day off to enjoy themselves.

In northwestern Ontario, something quite dramatic occurs around the fifteenth day of August. The mornings are still lush and warm, but there's something in the air, or more accurately, something missing from the air. You wake up one morning, step outside, take a curious look at the lake, the emerald dew-covered lawn, and realize with a vague uncertainty that something has changed. The sun is still strong, but it seems hazy and fixed at an odd angle in the sky. And the forest seems different. What is it? You can stand there for minutes before you realize what it is – the birds have stopped singing.

All the various flowers, insects, and songbirds go through intense, dramatic breeding cycles that last only weeks, or even hours. Once the birds have raised their young, their chatter ceases. And you realize, with a surge of sadness, that summer is ending. Undoubtedly, it was a recognition like that that caused my father to announce one day over breakfast, "Mother, let's take the day off."

It always surprised me to discover that my parents had lives of their own. Sometimes they expressed their independence by going for long car drives together or, in Winnipeg, going to the monthly Sneak Preview at the Gaiety Theatre. We didn't mind when they went out on these dates. It gave us the chance to have the house to ourselves. We could eat what we wanted, jump on the beds if we wanted, and if our older sisters, who were in charge of us, ended up in a hair-pulling brawl, so much the better. On nights when they announced their intention to go out on a date, my mother would have a bath, change into her slip, then sit at the vanity table in their bedroom, powdering her cheeks, putting on her lipstick, and taking the better part of an hour to get ready. Her emollients and creams filled the room with the scent of flowers, and my brother and I would sit on the edge of the bed, watching her brush her hair.

We hadn't yet developed any real routines at the cottage, so when my father made his announcement that he was taking the day off, we weren't sure if that included us. I don't think he was sure either, because he and my mother conferred in the kitchen for a while, then came out and suggested that we all go fishing. My sisters had been hoping that we'd go to Kenora, and they didn't seem much interested in a fishing trip. That left my little brother Danny and me. So we packed a lunch, went to the Webbs' store, and bought some fishing tackle. (I knew every lure by heart. The Mud Puppy had a beautifully illustrated cardboard box that showed an enormous gape-jawed muskie bearing down on the hapless Puppy. The yellow Five of Diamonds spoon cautioned buyers to "stand behind a tree" when fastening the lure to their fishing line, lest the fish jump right out of the lake and grab it out of their hand. To my distress, my father ridiculed these advertisements, telling me they were "meant to catch fishermen, not fish.")

After stocking up on lures, minnows, and soft drinks, we drove up the winding gravel road, heading north. The road was an offshoot of the Trans-Canada Highway that passed through Laclu, then wound through heavy forests and swamp country. I loved driving up this road, because it got narrower and rougher as you went, and you never knew when you might see an animal. My father was in a good mood, and he drove with his window down and listened to the news on the radio. It was 1960, and John Diefenbaker was the prime minister of Canada. In Hamburg, Germany, the Indra Club was rocking every night to the tunes of a teenage band called the Beatles. And in Canada, the farthest north you could drive, in this part of Ontario, was a muddy little parking lot at Rosena Lake. From Rosena Lake onward, if you wanted to keep going, you had to climb in a canoe or a float plane, or start walking. There wasn't another road or power line all the way to the North Pole. So in effect, when we pulled into the parking lot, we'd arrived at the edge of civilization, the edge of the world.

Here lived a trapper named Carl Mueller. A rusty old pick-up truck was parked next to his ramshackle cabin, and his backyard was filled with scrap lumber, discarded appliances, plywood hide stretchers, bed frames, rotting boats, stacks of mouldy firewood, and half-dismantled outboard motors. Past the beach, the blue waters of Rosena Lake glittered in the sun. I knew that my dad had fished here with his buddies prior to the war. I'd seen the old black and white photographs – young men in leather jackets and tweed motoring caps, holding up impressive stringers of fish. So my brother and I were excited. Clambering out of the car, we dashed down to the lake to explore the shoreline.

The half dozen boats pulled up on the shore were flat-bottomed rowboats, full of scummy water that swarmed with tiny waterbugs. After making a rental agreement with Carl, my parents came down to the shore toting tackle boxes and fishing rods. My dad bailed out one of the boats and got its little Johnson Sea Horse running. He put some dry boards in the boat so that we didn't have to walk on the slimy bottom. We climbed in and headed off on our adventure.

When we reached the fishing spot, my father shut off the motor, opened his tackle box, and assembled an intricate series of swivels, lead weights, clips, and something he called a June Bug spinner, which was a red and white blade that fluttered in the breeze like a bangle earring. Reaching into the metal bait bucket, he extracted a live minnow and threaded the hook through its mouth, out its gills, and through its midriff. He then rigged up rods for my brother and me. Starting the motor again, he trolled slowly along the shoreline while we paid out line from each of our rods, careful not to let out too much line lest we snag our lures on the bottom.

A few minutes later my brother shouted the alarm. His rod began dancing and we all shouted conflicting instructions. He avidly cranked at the handle of his reel and soon a fish appeared at the side of the boat. My father scooped it up with the landing net and laid it, flipping crazily, in the bottom of the boat.

I'd never seen such a fish. Its skin was textured like hammered brass, and its jaws snapped open and shut as it writhed in the wet net. Sharp spikes protruded from its back and its white eyes were as large as marbles. My father said that it was a pickerel, the best type of fish, and we'd save it for dinner. He clipped a chain stringer onto its jaw, lowered it into the water, and smiled. "All right, let's catch another one."

He explained that pickerel travel in schools, so once you catch one, you should troll back over the same spot. This time it was my father who caught one. After catching a few more – which my father released because they were too small – we carried on, and the lake got wilder and more desolate-looking. On one island we heard dogs barking, and as we drew closer we saw some huskies chained up along the shore. They looked like slant-eyed, half-starved wolves, and they yelped angrily at us as we puttered past. "Those are the sled dogs for Carl's trapline," my father said. "He keeps them here all summer, and throws them a fish now and then."

"It's so cruel to keep them chained up," my mother said. "Look at their ears."

My father nodded in agreement. We could see the bloodied stumps of their ears. Each dog had a halo of tiny flies buzzing around its head. My dad liked people well enough, but he saved his unconditional affection for dogs. Even hostile dogs rated a kind word. If a chained-up dog barked at him, he would scold it for being such a grump, let the dog sniff his hand, and soon enough it would wag its tail. These huskies looked like they hadn't eaten in weeks. I half-expected my father to go ashore and give them our lunch.

A little farther on, we trolled into a bay that was full of lily pads and sunken trees. From inside the long grass, a blue heron suddenly popped open like an umbrella, croaked, and laboured away with great wing-beats. Looking down into the murky water, I could see schools of minnows darting through the down-slanting rays of light. Near the shore, a snapping turtle sunned itself on a rotted log. The monstrous creature's shell was as large as a slab of rock, covered with bony ridges and dried algae, and as we trolled past, its snakelike head swivelled towards us.

Just after we passed the turtle, I felt a violent jerk at my lure and the rod doubled over. Realizing that I'd hooked a whopper, my father ordered my mother and brother to reel in their lines. He instructed me to let it run, but I didn't have any choice in the matter. I was using a nickel-plated Pflueger Akron reel, loaded with black line, and the hub of the reel was spinning so quickly that it burned my thumb. In no time, the fish peeled off so much line that my father had to chase it with the boat.

When we got into deeper water, the fish headed straight down. If we'd been a group of Nantucket whalers in Melville's novel, we'd have said that the fish had "sounded." The momentum was brutal and irresistible. It was like my fishing lure was attached to an anvil. I wasn't worried about losing the fish as much as by the possibility that I would never see it. I devoutly wanted to see it. I knew that it had to be a fish, but I kept imagining that it was something else, I didn't know what. This was such a wild, spooky place – this weedy bay, this desolate lake with its pre-historic turtles and crazed dogs – I wondered if it was possible that I'd hooked onto something else: something nameless, an underwater creature that would amaze us when it surfaced.

With so little line left on my reel, I clamped both thumbs down on the spool and held on with all my strength. My father shouted a warning, but I wasn't about to let the beast escape. The rod bent terrifically, then the line snapped.

What?

I couldn't believe that the fish was gone. Hoping against hope, I cranked the reel until the frayed end finally emerged from the water. "What did I do wrong?" I whined.

"Nothing," my father said.

"Do you think it'll come back?"

He just chuckled, as if such foolishness didn't deserve an answer.

"How big do you think it was?"

"Who knows," he said. He started the motor and shifted into gear. No one could accuse my dad of coddling his kids. He came from a long line of jocular but unsentimental Scots. His solution to bad luck was simple – take it on the chin and move on.

We motored to another spot and caught more pickerel. Some we kept, and some we released. By mid-afternoon, we had nine or ten fish on the stringer. I'd caught a few keepers myself, which had helped me to recover from the loss of my big one. As we trolled back to the trapper's place, my dad pointed out a winding marshy creek that led, he said, to the next lake to the north. He said that Rosena was part of a chain of lakes that went on forever. There were thousands of lakes, so many lakes that most of them didn't even have names. I thought this was amazing. "What do they call this place?"

"It's called the Precambrian Shield."

"Why do they call it that?"

He shrugged.

"But why do they call it that?"

"Because scientists aren't very good at naming things."

"But really, why do they call it that?"

"Because it's a big plate of rock, shaped like a shield."

I looked at the broken cliff along the shore. It didn't look much like a shield to me. "But if it's made of rock, why is it covered with so much water?"

He gave the rod a twitch. He was wearing a white T-shirt and his big arms were resting on his knees. He was so accustomed to boats that he drove them with a kind of detached air, steering with a nudge of his knee or elbow. He wasn't a man who relished conversations conducted at the Grade 5 level. It wasn't that he was bored by my questions. He had an encyclopaedic mind and enjoyed talking about things. But I had a short attention span, and often he'd get halfway through an explanation and I'd interrupt him with another question. On long car trips, I'd stand in the back seat of the car, elbows propped against the seat back, interrupting him with questions until he refused to answer.

So when I asked him about the Precambrian Shield, he was quiet for a minute, as if hoping I would lose interest in the subject. But I really wanted to know the answer. I wanted to explore this place. It felt both mysterious and forbidding, two qualities that were near irresistible to my ten-year-old brain.

"Answer him, Don," my mother said. She believed we would all become brilliant scientists one day.

"In a country called Wales," he said, "they once discovered rocks that came from a very ancient time, when life on earth was just beginning. The nearest town was called Cambria, so they named the period the Cambrian period. Precambrian rock is even older. It comes from a time before there was life on earth. You see that smooth rock along the shore? That's Precambrian granite, and it's almost as old as the sun."

This seemed incomprehensible, and I was silent for a moment, absorbing it.

"The Shield is covered with lakes," he continued, "because granite doesn't soak up water. When the rain falls, it gathers in these big pools, these lakes."

"So is this water really old too?"

He thought about this for a moment. "I'll show you a book about the water cycle sometime. In the meantime, there's the trapper's house. So reel in your lines."

I reluctantly brought my lure in, reeling slowly, hoping that some big fish would take advantage of one final opportunity to gobble my bait. When the lure came up beside the boat, I leaned over the gunwale and watched the gold blade spinning lazily in the water. This was the part I loved, the nose-to-nose examination of the big mystery. Below the lure, columns of sunlight slanted through the water and disappeared into the purple depths. Rippling on the surface of the water was the reflection of my face.

∾

The Spanish essayist Ortega y Gasset once wrote, "Tell me where you live and I'll tell you who you are."

If a substitute teacher had come into our class one day and asked us to write a paragraph introducing ourselves, I probably would have written down my name, my height and weight, and the names of my family members. I would have described the house where I lived, the bedroom that I shared with Danny, the paint-by-numbers portraits on the wall of the two dogs we called Inky and Stinky, and the view from our bedroom window of the white houses, freshly laid streets, and skinny trees of our neighbourhood. I would have described the seven-block walk to school, the back alleys where the bullies lurked, the stores where you could buy licorice whistles, and the classroom where I spent most of my waking hours. I would have described the wet-sheepdog smell of the cloakroom where we kept our coats and boots, and the gravel school yard where Kenny and I spent recess, running back and forth like dogs liberated from a kennel.

That was all I knew. My entire world was defined by the ten square blocks where I lived. Years later, when I grew up, I acquired an Econoline camper van and used it to explore far-flung parts of Canada. I clambered hand over hand down a crumbly red-sand cliff in Prince Edward Island, stripped off my clothes, and swam in the cold Atlantic. On the west side of Vancouver Island, I clambered down yet another precipitous cliff, stashed my clothes, and swam in the cold Pacific. Along the arctic sea coast of northern Manitoba, I walked the ice-scoured granite shoreline and wondered if I was going to blunder into a polar bear. And one time, in the wooded valley of the Battle River in Alberta, I cooked dinner over a fire and watched a big harvest moon rise in the east while distant coyotes yipped and howled.

These experiences weren't exceptional in any general sense. But I regarded them as exceptional because they happened to me. When you see a place, when you walk its roads and listen to its birds and crickets, when you kneel down on its earth and smell the aroma of its mouldy topsoil and feel its wind on your face, it leaves an impression that never goes away. The land becomes part of who you are. In the same way, thanks to the woods and the fields around Laclu, my brothers and sisters and I developed an expanded sense of the possibilities that the world offered. We went Indian, as they say. We became water babies. We swam all day, built rafts, explored the lake by canoe, and played on the beach at Webbs'. There was a rickety swimming raft at Webbs' with a three-level diving tower. There was deep water all around the diving raft and it was kind of scary, swimming out to it, feeling the slippery weeds brush your legs. We'd cannon-ball off the top tower or swim underneath the raft. It was dark and creepy underneath. There were vacant compartments with no flotation barrels and the sunlight bladed down through the floorboards, illuminating the water with a green glow and making our voices echo as we ducked under the greasy planks, wondering if we could make it back out again without drowning. The scariest part was feeling the cold water beneath you. The lake was so deep, so mysterious and frightening and beautiful at once. If you could move through this environment without flinching, it was like defying death.

When summer finally ended, we weren't happy about returning to our old selves. We pulled into the city on a Sunday night. It was a beautiful late-August evening, and the melodramatic sunset made it seem even crueller that we were going home. The suburban homes looked neat and well-kept. Sprinklers chattered on the lawns, and the sweet aroma of new-mown grass hung in the air. My siblings and I were disgusted. "Look at all these cars!" my sister Wendy exclaimed, holding her nose. "Can you stand this pollution?"

Back at school, my new teacher was Mrs. Laviolette, a civilian teacher who had a metal brace attached to her leg and walked with a limp. She seemed to like kids, so I liked her more than the nuns. But I wasn't pleased to be cooped up in her classroom. I kept to myself and spent the day drawing. In the margins of my school books, I drew pictures of birds and animals. My textbooks didn't have a single patch of habitat that wasn't occupied by a turtle or red-winged blackbird. In my imagination, I was still at the lake.

At home, my father had fixed up the basement and filled the shelves with books and long-playing records of music from America's jazz age. Prior to the post-war housing boom of the 1950s, our neighbourhood hadn't existed. Meadowlarks and jackrabbits had populated the wide-open prairie, and horses grazed in the alfalfa field across the road. Now our neighbourhood was a warren of tract housing, and our particular home was a two-storey, stucco-covered white box that looked like every other house on the street. But my father turned the basement into a sort of shrine, or museum, filled with old stuff that counteracted the newness and sameness of the neighbourhood. He covered the walls with varnished pine half-log siding that made you feel like you were in a log cabin. There was a brick fireplace in the centre of the room, and an ancient wooden cabinet clock that marked the hour with heavy, London-style echoing bongs. There were oil paintings of Brittany hunting dogs, two or three shotguns hanging on the wall, and an antique piano. Not very often, perhaps once a month, my mother would go down to the basement and play the piano. She liked playing when no one else was in the room, and we'd hear the sweeping melodies of her favourite composer, Hoagy Carmichael, come echoing up the basement stairs.

My best friend, Kenny, didn't have a cottage at the lake, and he'd never been to Laclu. But he'd somehow latched on to the

same obsession with the wilderness. He lived in a small bunga-
low deep within Little Italy, and since he was lucky enough to
come from a small family, he was often alone in the house. On
Friday nights I would buy a large bag of potato chips and bicycle
down to Kenny's house, keeping a weather eye peeled for
Raymond Cantafio and his merry band of foot-fighters.

When I arrived at Kenny's house, we'd heat the potato chips
in the oven – a recipe we'd devised ourselves – then retire to the
living room, where there was a low-slung, walnut-panelled
Eatonia hi-fi along one wall of the living room, and if you pushed
on the front panel, it swung open to reveal a record compartment
inside. The long-playing albums all belonged to his father, so we
had to be careful about leaving no evidence. Wiggling his fingers
like a safecracker, Kenny would delicately withdraw a record and
hold it up for my approval. His dad had good records – Bobby
Darin, Duane Eddy, Carl Perkins, and of course our favourite,
Johnny Horton, the Singin' Fisherman from Noonday, Texas.*

---

* They called Johnny Horton the Singin' Fisherman because he made up his
songs while he was out by himself for weeks on end, fishing in the Everglades.
He was at the peak of his career, that year, and he'd just married Billie Jean
Williams, the capricious beauty who'd driven Hank Williams into an early
grave and had been the subject of many of Hank's songs ("Hey, Good
Lookin'"). Like so many other young singing stars of that era, Johnny Horton
was marked for death. On November 5, 1960, he was scheduled to drive to
Dallas in the pre-dawn darkness and meet his buddy Claude King ("Wolverton
Mountain") for an early-morning duck hunt. After the hunt, he planned
to carry on into Dallas and have lunch with Ward Bond, who wanted him to
appear in an upcoming episode of *Wagon Train*. But a drunk driver crossed the
centre line of the highway and collided with Horton's car, killing him instantly.
Later that morning, on his way to meet Johnny Horton for lunch, Ward Bond
died of a heart attack. So it was a bad day all around for people who like
cowboy hats.

After removing the glassine sleeve, Kenny would lay the Johnny Horton record on the turntable, turn on the power, and delicately lower the needle onto the opening grooves. A thunderous hissing filled the room, followed by the whack of a drum and a male choir hooting the ghostly refrain "Way up north."

In no time, Kenny and I were up on our feet, marching around the room and singing "North to Alaska." The carpet became a field of snow, the walls a forbidding range of mountains. Wolves howled, the northern lights flamed overhead, and the spooky chanting of the back-up singers completed the hallucination. My favourite part was crossing that huge expanse of frozen lake, popping our whips at the labouring dogs. Like all great singers, Johnny Horton had vocal techniques that he only hinted at, and when the song warranted, when the lyric rose to dramatic summits that called out, indeed begged, for some kind of passionate emphasis, he threw in a slight yodelling, glottal yip that made our blood run cold.

The movie *North to Alaska* had also just been released, so we eagerly rode the bus down to the Lyceum to see it. We paid our twenty-five cents, took our usual seats in the front row, and completed the usual security precautions with our popcorn (each of us sticking a kernel up our nose, smearing it with nasal fluid, then shaking it in with the rest of our box to ensure that the other guy wouldn't snatch a handful when he'd finished his own).

The movie starred John Wayne and Fabian, and it was the usual overblown star vehicle, with the Duke sauntering into every scene, reciting his lines, then grinning at the audience as if to let us know that he didn't take it seriously either. The movie's version of Alaska didn't look like our version. There were no frozen lakes and jagged mountains, no glittery-eyed timber wolves baying at the cruel stars. These prospectors spent most of their time in some red-velvet saloon, slurping down mugs of beer and fighting over the waitresses. By the end of the picture John Wayne had cowed the bad guys, taught Fabian a few lessons about life, and walked off with the sexy starlet on his arm. But as disappointing as the story was, it was reassuring, somehow, to see that Hollywood had gotten it wrong. The ghostly wind of the north still muttered through Kenny's living room. And I could continue to dream about the secrets buried at Rosena without worrying that someone had already taken them.

~

I realized that if I was going to explore the Precambrian Shield, I was going to need equipment.

Since we were now cottage people, my mother enrolled me in Saturday morning swimming classes at the downtown YMCA. But after taking a swing through the locker room at the Y, I decided that it wasn't my kind of place. There are probably all kinds of ten-year-old boys in this world who don't mind spending their Saturday mornings in a locker room full of fat guys with hairy asses, but I wasn't one of them.

Instead of going to my swimming class I surreptitiously hung around a store called Sydney I. Robinson, which was right across the street from the YMCA. Sydney I. Robinson was a wilderness store. It didn't cater to the fashionable urban nature-lover crowd. It catered to rustic people who lived in the woods. Besides being a prairie city, Winnipeg is also a gateway to the north. For centuries, northern firms have been based here. The Hudson's Bay Company, which was once the largest company in the world, is headquartered in Winnipeg. And because of its ongoing association with modern resource industries – commercial fishing, mining, pulp and paper – Winnipeg was the perfect location for a store like this: a bustling, crowded warehouse where you could see guys with plaid shirts and work boots shopping for peavey poles, snowshoes, and beaver traps.

I could easily dispose of an hour walking around Sydney I. Robinson. There was a fur-buying section in the back, hung with racks and racks of fresh animal pelts, and nobody seemed to mind if I strolled up and down the aisles, running my fingers through the silky pelage of timber wolves, mink, and otter. The fur was plush and aromatic. Unlike people, animals don't seem to develop bad body odour, although you'd think they would. They smell great, even when they're dead. The red fox smelled like ginger, and the black bear hide, which was stiff as plywood and hung on the rack from its eyehole, smelled like wild hay.

Instead of hanging around the Y, learning to tread water, I spent my time watching trappers haul their wares through the loading door, carrying in bundles of fur they'd brought down from the north. A grader in a leather apron took charge of the pelts and laid them out on the table for pricing. Trappers kill animals by the thousands, so you'd expect them to be unsavoury types. In Hollywood movies they're always unshaven thugs with French-Canadian accents and whisky on their breath. But the trappers at Sydney I. looked kind of pleasant to me. You'd see some strong-looking sixty-year-old Metis guy come walking in with his plaid shirt, suspenders, wool logging pants, high-top leather boots, and a bundle of muskrat pelts. He would have an old-style pencil-thin moustache, and he'd flash a big smile as he joshed with the fur grader. Watching him, I would be tempted to

ask a few questions, He'd no doubt learned a few things, spending his life in the bush. But I never summoned the courage to
walk up and introduce myself.

The tools of his trade were displayed in the next aisle.
Sheaves of steel traps hung from the wall. Most of them were
Oneida Newhouse long spring leg-hold traps, a type invented in
a backwoods commune over a hundred years ago. The members
of the Oneida commune renounced private property and marriage, and vowed to share all work, assets, child-rearing, and
sex. Since there was no welfare or unemployment insurance in
those days, they had to rely on their own wits for making money.
After experimenting with various types of small manufacturing,
they decided to make steel traps and sell them to local woods-
men. They recruited a local trapper named Robert Newhouse,
built a metal forge and a steel fabrication shop, and began experimenting with trap designs.

In 1852, Robert Newhouse stumbled upon a scientific tem-
pering process that made his trap resistant to temperature
change. Until then, most of the traps on the market stiffened up
in extreme cold weather. But the new mainspring on the Oneida
Newhouse trap worked fine in bitter cold, and within five years,
the commune's leg-hold steel trap captured the market in Russia
and Canada, where the cold climate produced the richest furs in
the world. The commune eventually split up over bickering and
sexual jealousy, but their patented steel trap dominated the
Canadian fur industry for over a century. Hanging in bunches by
their chains, the Oneida Newhouse traps at Sydney I. Robinson
were displayed according to size, ranging from No. 2 muskrat
traps, which cost only $1.50 and were small enough to put in
your pocket, to huge forty-five-pound bear traps, which had

steel fangs welded onto their jaws and were powerful enough to break a man's leg.

Next to the trap display, shelves were stacked with skinning tools and hide stretchers and bottles of obscure potions, lures, and scents. Each scent was brewed up for a different animal. I knew that asafoetida was apparently so awful-smelling that if I opened the lid for even a second, I could probably clear the store. Other bottles contained female wolf urine, skunk scent, and extract of beaver testicle. Animals themselves may not smell bad, but they relish foul odours. A bottle of fish entrails, left to cook in the sun for several weeks, produces a violent and horrific-smelling residue that supposedly spells sheer lust to bobcats and lynx. As a substitute, trappers sometimes use Chanel No. 5 perfume, which you wouldn't think would have much in common with the oily residue of fetid beaver testicles, but in the deep woods, they supposedly both connect to the same primitive nerve in the limbic brain.

In other parts of the store there were rows and rows of axes, tents, ice augers, dog sleds, and guns. There were so many guns that I may as well have been walking through the armoury of the Royal Winnipeg Rifles. The guns weren't sequestered up on walls behind the salesman's desk or locked up with lengths of plated chain. They were stacked in the open, row upon row, and everywhere you looked, men were testing their heft and balance as they might hockey sticks, racking the authoritative actions and pointing them across the store at a moose head on the wall.

I knew that some people regarded guns as nasty things. But in Winnipeg even non-hunters tended to regard them as symbols of the outdoorsy life that everyone wished to have. In the pine-panelled basements of my friends' homes, they were displayed as a rustic design motif, like a dartboard or beer sign. Usually their owners didn't even use them. They regarded them as conversation pieces, or symbols of a rural life that their grandfathers lived, many years ago, and to which, in daydreams, they imagined returning one day. There were no legal restrictions on buying guns, and most people would have thought it downright unpatriotic to imagine that there ever would be. It wasn't really a crime issue, because criminals knew better than to use guns in Winnipeg. If they did, the city's cops – most of whom were gigantic, foul-tempered Scotsmen – would seize them by the scruff of the neck and given them a licking they wouldn't soon forget.

The current law stipulated that you had to be only fourteen years old to buy a gun. But I was just ten, so I had to content myself with browsing the air rifles. The best air rifle in the store was a Daisy Scout BB gun. It looked like the lever-action Winchester that the cowboys use. And it was powerful enough to punch a hole in a can, break a bottle, or do other kinds of damage, which I felt was important. Lifting one off the rack, aiming it at the poor old moose on the wall, I could easily imagine keeping it handy while I canoed up the winding creek that leads north out of Rosena. I knew I would need a lot of things when I eventually made that trip. I would need a BB rifle, a good compass, a hatchet, and a few bear traps. And to get them, I would need money.

To that end, I acquired a paper route. My bundle drop was at the corner of Cambridge and Corydon. Every night after school, my chain-smoking district manager pulled up in his *Winnipeg Free Press* panel van and threw down a hefty bundle of eighty papers, my allocation, for which I signed my contract. Stuffed into my canvas bag, the papers made a heavy load; heavier still on Thursdays, when they included flyers, and on Saturdays, when they included comics and classifieds. Most days, the bag weighed about forty pounds, and since it was a good seven-block hike to the beginning of my route, I ran the strap across my forehead, like the "tumpline" employed by voyageurs to haul massive bundles of pelts across the old portage trails that connected one lake to the next.

Bent over, with my load balanced on the small of my back, I could walk a long way without tiring. And it wasn't so bad, in any case, to surrender to the pure mindlessness of a long walk, to soak in the world without really looking at it; to walk out of summer's end and into autumn's beginning. I saved my money in a hollow Porky Pig, and with each passing month the pig filled up with more dimes, quarters, and crumpled dollar bills. I had no idea what it cost to buy a compass, axe, belt knife, BB gun, or a grizzly bear trap. But I was beginning to feel rich. My mother was impressed because I was doing so well with my swimming lessons. And my father was impressed because I was a news-paper carrier. It was a job that he seemed to idealize, given the long perspective of adulthood and the fact that he was an ex-newspaper boy himself.

During Sunday dinner, he sometimes hinted that I was fulfilling an important social task. After all, I wasn't delivering junk mail; I was delivering the news, hauling not just a bunch of paper but forty pounds of the truth. He admired newspapers, and people in the newspaper business. One night after Sunday dinner he asked me if I knew who John Dafoe was. "John Dafoe is the editor of the *Free Press* and probably the best journalist in North America," he said. "And he's your boss." He retrieved a book from his library and thrust it into my hands. "Read this."

The book was called *The Unknown Country*, by a journalist named Bruce Hutchison. It was a book about Canada. In it, the author devoted a chapter to Dafoe, the "huge roughcast figure, the shaggy head of reddish hair, the carved-stone face."

> For nearly fifty years Dafoe has been doing a large part of Canada's thinking. Day in, day out, he has sat down in his littered office and slowly, with the stub of a pencil, has scrawled his closely reasoned and documented editorials. What Mr. Dafoe said today will be said all over Canada tomorrow, echoed in other newspapers, stolen by scores of journalists, voiced in Parliament, often denied by the government and quietly incorporated in government policy. In his own field, Dafoe has been more influential than any corresponding journalist in the British Commonwealth.

Hutchison liked Winnipeg too, which made me hopeful, since I was stuck here.

> This was the ideal place for him. Winnipeg largely gave him his character. His character has largely made the mental climate of Winnipeg. . . . The spirit of Winnipeg is the true hope of Canada – the forward look, the broad, world-wide feeling, the pioneer spirit, the willingness to gamble. It is no accident, therefore, that Canada's best thinking in the last twenty years has come out of such a place.

The newspaper's publisher, Sir Clifford Sifton, was no slouch either. He owned both *The Winnipeg Free Press* and *The Toronto Globe and Mail*, and for many decades, one covered the east and the other covered the west. You couldn't follow national affairs without reading both. He was also smart in the way he structured his business dealings with his front-line troops – the paper carriers. Under Sifton, we weren't employees; we were "contractors." We bought our newspapers on consignment and resold them to our customers. It was our job to collect our bills. If we couldn't collect from a certain troublesome customer, it came out of our share, not the newspaper's. We never questioned the arrangement. We thought it was the way of the world, and it was.

My route stretched along five blocks of Grosvenor Avenue. It was an old neighbourhood, with big trees and large turn-of-the-century homes, and my customers were reasonably affluent. But collecting my money was sometimes like going through one of those trials of character from medieval literature. There were three or four dogs on my route that came after me the moment I entered the yard. One of them was a monstrous German shepherd. It wore a leather muzzle, so it couldn't actually bite, but it made little whining sounds as it thumped its snout against my legs – a display of impotent fury that the owner watched from the window with amusement.

Another one of my customers was a middle-aged woman who was missing half her hair. The entire front portion of her head was bald. I didn't know much about cancer or chemotherapy, but I knew there was some terrifying problem here. And every time I showed up at her door, I prayed that she wouldn't invite me in to share her story. I also ran into problems at 1123

Grosvenor. It was a big stone house with the faint whine of an electric guitar coming from inside. I would ring the doorbell over and over again, shifting back and forth to keep warm in the winter darkness. Finally a lanky, mop-haired teenager would come to the door with his Gretsch guitar strung over his shoulder and a slightly peeved look on his face.

"Collecting," I said, showing him my little receipt book.

"Mum's not home," he mumbled. You could barely hear him. He was one of those teenagers who mumbled not because he was shy, but because he was sixteen years old and couldn't be bothered wasting valuable time talking to people.

"When will she be home?"

"I dunno."

"Later on tonight?"

"I dunno."

This was a recitation we conducted every two weeks at his doorstep. He sometimes played with his rock band at our CYO[*] dances. This, and the fact that his mum was a minor celebrity on CBC television, made me hesitant to press the issue, and to this day, I believe Neil Young owes me $2.40.

Along with the paper route, I earned money shovelling snow or working as a bartender. My bartending job was not a real job. My dad belonged to a poker club that sometimes convened at our house. They played in the pine-panelled room in the basement, where they guffawed at their own jokes and filled the house with cigar smoke. My dad's circle of chums included a man who ran the neighbourhood Esso, the mayor of the city, a biologist who spent his life studying mosquitoes, a hard-drinking Irishman

---

[*] Christian Youth Organization.

who lived in a half fallen-down barn and rented riding horses for three dollars an hour, and a man whose line of paperback romance books had made him the largest publisher in Canada. For Danny and me, poker night was a major event. Dressed in our pyjamas, we loitered in the kitchen, periodically nipping downstairs to take orders. Playing bartender wasn't complicated, because my dad's friends always ordered the same drink – "I'll have another rye and Seven there, junior." In eastern Canada, men drink scotch. But on the prairies, the patriotic liquor was rye whisky, made from number one western wheat.

When we delivered the drinks, the men generally passed us a quarter and ignored us, this being the contemporary and normal way to treat children. Grown men of that era didn't like to get too friendly lest it erode the sense of deference children needed to become good citizens. Even after my dad's chums had a few drinks, they never did much more than wink at us or crack a joke at our expense. No matter how rowdy the party became, my brother and I never addressed them by their first names or spoke to them without being spoken to first.

The only one whom we addressed by his first name was Ned Jordan. Physically, Ned was an imposing figure – a tall, broad-shouldered gypsy with a swarthy face and a hooked nose. He worked part-time at the racetrack, which you could tell by his sheepskin coat, which exuded a strong aroma of whisky and cigars and horse manure. My dad was working his way up the ladder at the city bureaucracy, and Ned was one of his right-hand men, a supervisor at the Transit Department. Ned drove around in a Transit patrol car and kept an eye on the buses, making sure there were no foul-ups moving citizens from one end of the city to the other. It was probably a mundane job, but

Ned made it look dire and mysterious. He wore an old cowboy hat, and whenever he happened to cruise past in his Transit patrol car, he lifted his paw in a stately wave, and my brother and I shouted a fervent greeting.

During the poker games, Ned always asked Danny and me how we were doing in school, how many goals we'd been scoring in hockey, and so on. During one of these conversations, I mentioned that the clutch of quarters in my hand was going straight upstairs to my piggy bank, to be hoarded for the eventual purpose of acquiring a tent, axe, compass, hunting knife, and of course a BB gun. Ned must have listened with some amusement because a few weeks later, with no advance warning, his Transit car pulled up to the house and he climbed out with two long cardboard packages under his arm.

My mother rose from the dinner table and greeted him at the door. She liked Ned and this excused him from a variety of missteps. So even though she probably knew what the packages contained, she smiled and thanked him. Without pausing to visit, Ned raised his arm in his trademark cowboy salute and walked back to his car.

Ripping open the boxes, my brother and I howled in ecstasy. Daisy Scout lever-action BB guns! We were armed! Cocking one of the guns, I raised it to my shoulder and aimed at a vase. The gun made a *whap* and fragments of glass flew in all directions. My sisters screamed. Oh brother, I thought, I didn't know it was loaded. My father roared in dismay and seized the guns on the spot, promising to keep them until we learned to use them safely. Later, when he cooled down, he explained that he wasn't blaming us. We just needed to learn the basics, which he would teach us next summer, at the lake.

This was cruel punishment. I couldn't believe that we had to wait until next summer to use our new guns. So I gave him a few days to cool off, then brought up the case of my friend Kerry, who owned not only a gun, but a real gun, a Mossberg .22 rifle. And he was allowed to shoot it in the city. In fact, he was not only allowed to shoot it in the city, he was instructed to shoot it in the city, by his dad, who hated squirrels. The squirrels nested in their attic and chewed the insulation. Sometimes Kerry's dad even shot the squirrels himself. On Sunday mornings, when the squirrels woke him up with their chewing, he would go out into the backyard in his pyjamas, swearing his head off, and shoot at the squirrels. One time he winged a squirrel and followed it halfway down Oxford Street, blasting away at it while it scrambled along the trees and did flying Tarzan leaps between the telephone wires.

I used this story to demonstrate to my dad that the city provided excellent hunting opportunities, as long as you exercised reasonable caution. But my dad wasn't impressed. He told us we couldn't shoot our BB guns until we got to the lake, and that was final. Anyway, he pointed out, Kerry's dad had a special permit to discharge a firearm inside the city limits from his golfing buddy, George Blow, the chief of police.

∾

People who grow up on the prairies usually display a few subtle quirks, one of them being a preoccupation with the weather. They know what sundogs are, and they know what kind of winds presage the arrival of a cold front. Our local TV sports commentator, Cactus Jack Wells, opens his newscast in typical fashion. "Well, folks, it turned out nice again."

Like the landscape, the local weather gets inside us, and becomes part of who we are. Coexisting with twelve months of prairie weather is like living in a family of twelve strong-willed individuals. There's no choice but to try to get along. January has the worst reputation, but in my opinion, January in Winnipeg is not as bad as everyone thinks. January has a stillness that comes with stable weather. The polar air mass has established itself over the northern Great Plains, and there are few storms or even cloudy days. The air is fiery cold, but the snow is pure white and the noon-hour sky is as blue as a flag. After a fresh snowfall, it's so silent that the only sound is the steamy huff of your breath and the squeaking of the snow underfoot.

February feels different.

At sunrise it might be twenty-six below zero, but when you walk to school you can feel the tentative but noticeable warmth of the early sun on your face. Sunrise comes a few minutes earlier every day. And if you have a daily routine as I do, trudging down Jessie Avenue with schoolbooks and my frozen peanut butter sandwiches under my arm, the sun is higher each morning above the smoking chimneys. Nobody talks about spring yet. After all, the hockey and curling seasons are in full swing. But the faint warmth of the sun in early February is the first palpable hint that this winter, too, will pass.

My dad has probably felt the difference in the weather, because he's taken on a new project. On cold February nights, after dinner, he puts on his coat, hefts his toolbox, and goes outside. If you peer out the frosted windows, you can see a light burning in the garage. Intrigued, my brother and I go out to spy on him.

A little baseboard heater grumbles in the corner. The wires on the convex face of the heater glow fiery-red in the dark, but it's still so cold in the garage that my father's breath rises like smoke as he saws, hammers, drives the long brass screws into the oak brackets. The muscles of his forearm jump as he turns the massive screwdriver. The project sits propped up on two sawhorses. It's sixteen feet long and resembles the skeleton of an upside-down beluga. The ribs are frayed with wood splinters that need to be sanded off, and the spine is caked with drops of malodorous red glue. Watching him drive the screws into the skeleton's pelvis, we ask no questions, and he offers no explanation. The noticeable thing about fathers is not what they tell you, but what they keep to themselves. We don't know where he got the plans, or how he learned to do any of this. All we know is that he's building a boat.

By early March the blue skies and doldrums of midwinter give way to unsettled winds from the south. The sky turns white and the high prairie wind begins to blow. This is humid air from the south, and nights are turning mild. The sidewalks are caked with frozen slush, and the wind, as I'm walking to the hockey rink at night, carries a pungent reek that evokes rain and dreams, faraway places. It smells like the ocean. If they didn't put so much salt on the streets of Winnipeg and Regina, maybe all those prairie boys wouldn't be so quick to join the navy.

Now that spring is in the air, I'm collecting other critical items for my survival kit. I've purchased a beautiful brass compass, with a flip-up crosshair sight. And I've bought a book called *I Live in the Woods*: an excellent Canadian manual filled with techniques for building rudimentary shelters, cleaning swamp water with sand, and starting a fire with nothing but dry sticks. You can't study this stuff without developing an enormous respect for the Indians. They're the masters of the wilderness.

They were authentic hunter-gatherers. Each native hunter carried about twenty-five pounds of stuff with him. Anthropologists have studied hunter-gatherer societies all over the world and discovered that they all stick to the twenty-five-pound rule. If they exceed the limit, they throw something away. It explains why they didn't own a lot of things. Who wants to carry a Spanish Colonial bedroom suite over a three-mile portage? They perfected the use of the natural materials around them. If they put a hole in a birch-bark canoe, they fixed it in a few minutes with materials from the forest. If you had given them a modern, expensive aluminum canoe, they probably would have thrown it away. What good is a boat you can't repair?

When I grew up, I met a man named Tommy Duck[*], a Chipewyan hunter from northern Manitoba. Tommy is one of the most impressive human beings you could ever meet. In his hockey jacket, baseball hat, and heavy-framed Masters of the Universe sunglasses, Tommy resembles a swarthy Anthony Quinn going incognito.

In the bitter cold of a January afternoon in Churchill, Manitoba, I once stood on a street corner talking to Tommy Duck. No matter where you travel in the north, you'll run into Tommy Duck. He's everywhere, like Zelig. I asked him what was new in his life, and he mentioned that he was leaving for Yellowknife the next day. I asked him how he was getting there. "I just walk," he said.

I thought he was pulling my leg. Yellowknife was almost 1,000 miles to the west, across a trackless wilderness riddled with frozen lakes. It was minus 34 with a stiff wind. Walking

---

[*] Who has a relative, no surprise, named Donald.

from the Seaport Hotel to Penny Rawlings' Trading Post was like getting your face massaged by a belt-sander. But Tommy Duck wasn't pulling my leg. The arctic landscape didn't frighten him. He said he made the journey often, with a small backpack, a sleeping bag, and a .22 rifle. "But what if you get lost?" I asked.

He shrugged. "How can an Indian get lost when he's already home?"

❧

My birthday comes in the month of April, so the weather on that day is cemented like a survey stake into my memories of spring.

On the morning of the big day there's usually a bit of snow in the shade of the house, and the sodden lawn has frozen overnight. But the sidewalks are bare, the streets are covered with sand, and the flag-blue sky echoes with the beagle-like yelping of migrating geese. The polar air mass is falling back, falling back, retreating to its refuge in the high north, and the tropical air mass is sweeping into southern Manitoba. By the end of April, the days are sunny and warm and mint-green leaves are emerging from the elm trees. By early May, we're making plans to return to the lake.

My dad has finished the boat. With its broad rear end and deep midsection it's designed for hauling a family, but it has a dashing aspect too. It's red and white and there's a bold lightning strike down its side. Just as the invention of the airplane opened up a whole new world of the sky, this boat will take us on into a new state of evolution. We'll become emperors of the water.

Once spring arrives, there isn't a person in the city who isn't walking with a bounce in their stride. The citizens of "Winterpeg" tend to feel defensive about their city, as if the sub-zero temperatures were their idea. But when the month of May arrives, everyone feels vindicated. Winter is over, and now this prairie outpost is on its way to becoming one of the best places in Canada instead of one of the worst.

With the bush country only an hour's drive away, there are thousands of pristine wilderness lakes where city people can go camping and canoeing. And because of the abundance of inexpensive vacation property, Winnipeggers have the highest rate of cottage ownership in the country. When the Victoria Day weekend arrives, it's generally assumed that anybody with an ounce of sense will be heading "down to the lake." Two days before the appointed day, my mum has already done the shopping, my dad has filled the boat with freight and tied it down under a tarpaulin, and Danny and I have packed our clothes, comic books, and BB guns. On the morning of Friday, May 18, my parents issue strict instructions – come straight home from school, no dawdling, so we can get a jump on rush hour.

Everyone in the city has the same plan. Once we load the car and get underway, it takes half an hour to creep through heavy traffic into St. Boniface, where the great slaughterhouse and its awful smell mark the edge of the city. The highway is so choked with vehicles that we might as well be refugees fleeing Budapest with the Germans blowing up bridges behind us. My mother sits in the front seat of the Buick with Mary Kate, the squalling baby, on her lap. Nanny sits beside her, with Peter the toddler squished in between her and my dad.

Our family has gradually somehow become what Zorba the Greek described as "the full catastrophe." Despite all the theories about kids being products of their environment, every human being in this car is different. When he grows up, Peter will become an orthopaedic surgeon, with hands as graceful as a blackjack dealer's, but right now he can't seem to get a glass of orange juice anywhere near his mouth without dumping it all over his shirt. Mary Kate will become a judge when she grows up, but right now she is having a major fit because she's lost her pacifier. The other five – my brother Danny and I and our three older sisters – are crammed into the back seat, threatening each other in furious whispers. When Sally grows up she will become a pediatrician, but right now she is acting like a bit of a child herself, elbowing Babe, the future ethics professor, who is unethically sitting on a paperback copy of *Bonnie Prince Fetlar, The Story of a Pony*. The missing book belongs to her sister Wendy, who is frantic, because she loves the book and loves horses more than anything else on earth, even though she is allergic to them. We have to fight silently, because only one person in this car is allowed to make a sound, and that's my father who, as he creeps through traffic, regularly thumps the steering wheel with the heel of his hand and grumbles about the "bloody idiots" he's sharing the road with.

We arrive at Laclu at sundown. The cottage looks a bit faded and neglected after the long winter. Some of the young apple trees have died, and the soggy lawn smells like a collie. After hauling our bags into the cottage and dropping them beside the fold-out couch on the veranda, my brother Danny and I sprint down to the shoreline to look at the lake. It's always the first item on the work list when we arrive at the cottage – we have to run down the hill and look at the lake.

The water looks the same, black and cold, and the dock has survived the winter. My dad built the dock with timbers, rocks, and rough lumber. The challenge around here is building a dock that will make it through the spring, when big rafts of ragged ice come drifting down the lake, tearing out buoys and docks, and pushing big rocks up onto the shore. Ice-out usually happens in a few hours, and if the wind is from an unfavourable direction, the ice destroys everything in its path. It's a final pointless gesture of hostility from winter. Our dock is bent and heaved slightly, but it escaped major damage. Walking up and down, testing it with our weight, we judge it sound. My brother elbows me and points across the darkening lake to a necklace of delicate yellow lights moving along the far shore. It's the Canadian!

Every Friday night the Canadian arrives and stops at the little railway station alongside the lake. I've never ridden on a train. With so many kids in our family we can't afford it, but Danny and I love watching the Canadian stop, toot its whistle, and then slide off again. Its dome cars and myriad lights reflecting on the glassy water evoke some romantic postcard image of old-time Canada.

When it's gone we continue our inspection. The water is tea-coloured and barren, devoid of life; not even a minnow has survived the winter. We skip a few stones, then explore the tangled woods along the shore, where we discover a dead thing secreted in the underbrush, a great malodorous sodden hump of black and white feathers. It's probably a duck, or perhaps a loon. It's been lying under the snow all winter, and now it's rotting like a thawed mammoth. We poke it with sticks a few times, then walk back to the dock, where we listen to a celebratory yodel echoing across the lake. Another loon has evidently survived and is announcing to the world that it's ready to take a go at life.

ᖆ

The next day my father puts the new boat in the water. We kids have been exchanging whispered speculation about whether it will actually float, and when my father backs the trailer into the lake at Webbs' beach we're horrified to see water flooding into the scuppers. Our new boat is sinking!

My father is unconcerned. He says that all wooden boats leak for the first couple of days until the wood joints swell up. The outboard motor, a 10-horse Johnson, sits in the trunk of the car. My dad lifts the motor out of the car and climbs into the boat.

The combined weight of a motor and a two-hundred-pound man makes the boat tremble, but my dad steps lightly down the row of seats and lowers the motor onto the transom. Now comes the start-up procedure. He opens the air vent on the gas cap, clips the fuel line onto the motor, and squeezes the rubber bulb until it's full. Then he flips out the choke and yanks the cord effortlessly, yanks it again, and again, with the engine coughing and sputtering as if in alarm. Then suddenly a concussive report detonates inside the motor and it bursts into life. He fiddles with some settings, closes the choke switch, adjusts the Lean-Rich dial, and a great cloud of delicious smoke pours out across the clean water. What excitement! My sisters are applauding. My brother and I are exchanging punches. And Spike the cocker spaniel, a local mutt who doesn't really belong to us but hangs out at our cottage anyway, barks in agreement.

At my dad's order, we all climb into the boat and grab a seat. My dad gives the motor some gas, and moments later we're roaring down the lake with big waves unfurling off the transom. Spike stands wide-legged on the prow of the boat, with his chest puffed out and his ears flapping in the wind.

Since this is the boat's maiden voyage, none of us have the nerve to ask my dad if we can drive it. But the following weekend my sisters start lobbying for permission. Soon enough, they're moving the boat from one side of the dock to the other, using it to pick up a life jacket that has accidentally blown into the lake, or volunteering to take the boat to the store to pick up a quart of milk for my mother – an errand that seems to require the better part of an afternoon. By the beginning of summer holidays Danny and I have launched our own lobbying campaign, and my father is growing increasingly grumpy about the subject. He takes the position that he put a lot of effort into building the boat. And the more kids start using it, the more likely it is that someone will crash into a rock and wreck it.

It's a good point. But this is a large family, with the kids spaced only two years apart, and the sheer number of siblings produces a random, ever-evolving fog of disinformation that works in our favour. My parents almost need a chart on the wall to keep track of curfew times, allowances, and the types of movies each of us is allowed to attend. This is complicated by the fact that my dad is a libertarian who doesn't like rules and likes obeying them even less. So when he's obliged to issue a decision, he assumes that we'll respect the reasonableness of his point of view and conduct ourselves accordingly. He doesn't realize that we're going to come at him with one appeal after another. And when that happens, he can't quite remember what he said in the first place.

After my older sisters have been driving the boat for a few weeks, Danny and I try appealing to the notion that it's inherently unfair to let Sally drive it when she's just a girl. This doesn't sway him, so we try arguing that most of the kids our age are driving boats, which is hard to respond to when he doesn't know if it's true.

So he meets us halfway and permits me to drive, by myself, and Danny when he's with his older sisters. After a couple of lessons, he decides I'm qualified to take the boat to Webbs' for a carton of milk. It's exciting to have such a powerful vessel under your personal control. But sometimes I wonder if my dad is right, and this is too dangerous for someone my age. When I walk to the dock and sit down to face the motor, my gut twists with apprehension. The green Johnson Sea Horse has a lurking, hostile quality. The muscular bulges of its cowling are smeared with grease. And its many mysterious dials carry labels that I don't understand. What, for example, is the High Speed Mixture Adjustment? Does it make the boat go faster? I'm particularly shocked by the faded label stuck to the faceplate of the motor – *Failure to Comply With Operational Guidelines May Result in Serious Injury or Death.*

There's no going back, so I take a deep breath and grasp the pull cord. Some people prefer to start the motor from a sitting position. My sister uses both arms and plants her foot against the motor. I prefer to stand wide-legged so that I can exert full body force. But when the motor backfires, the cord yanks so hard it almost pulls my arm off. After two or three unsuccessful pulls, my gut begins to fill with dread. What if I flood the motor? My father always cautions me against flooding it. I don't know what flooding the motor means, but if the smell of gasoline begins to penetrate the air I know I'm in trouble. When you flood it, you have to unhook the fuel line and pull the cord fifty or sixty times, then hook up the gas line and start all over again. I'm strong enough for only a couple of dozen pulls. So the smell of gas is like the smell of fear.

If I screw up, I can always walk up the hill and get my dad to help. But when I'm at the store, flooding the motor would be a disaster. Girls my age are often suntanning on the dock there. They wear feline dark glasses and maintain an air of haughty scientific detachment as they watch the boats come and go. They're in charge of determining who's a loser and who isn't. If the motor defeats me while they're watching, I might as well go back to the cottage and spend the rest of the summer curled up on the couch sucking my thumb. So whenever I sit down like this to prepare the boat for a quick trip to the store, the fear inside me is not only fear of personal injury, but also fear of the total collapse of my worth as a human being.

Even if I manage to start the motor and get it running, dangerous things can happen. Once, when I was coming back from the store by myself, it suddenly issued a wild, terrifying roar, as if it had abruptly decided to destroy me in an act of ritual sacrifice. I frantically shut the motor off. And since the cottage was only a few hundred yards away, I paddled back to the dock where, thankfully, no one had witnessed the incident. It never happened again, and I had to assume it was just another one of those unexplained, bizarre things that machines do when you lower your guard for a moment.

One day at Webbs' our friend Larry climbed into the boat to "give her a try." For some reason Larry felt that his casual friendship with Danny and me entitled him to drive our dad's boat. And for some reason we agreed with him. Untying the ropes, Larry got into the boat and neglected to check the throttle grip on the motor. It was set at full-speed, and as soon as he pulled the cord the boat lunged forward. This is the precise scenario by which numerous fishermen, every year, get thrown overboard and killed. It's a curious fact that an empty boat will inscribe a near perfect circle. If the steering handle is tilted over at a gentle angle, the circle will be a large one. If the steering handle is tilted acutely, the circle will be tight and ferocious. But either way, the boat eventually comes back over the same spot and strikes the person in the water. The victim can sit there treading water for a full minute, watching the far-off boat go through the clubhouse turn, knowing that it's coming back to get him. What's the best thing to do? Ducking underwater at the last minute takes coolness and athletic coordination, two qualities that aren't common to situations of primal terror. Fully dressed, in boots and maybe a life jacket, you won't find it easy to get far enough underwater to avoid the charging propeller. So if you ever get thrown out of your boat, good luck. You probably have only a few moments to live.

In Larry's case, the steering handle was tilted all the way over. So the boat slewed around and started cutting crazy tight circles with its bow pointed straight up and its engine roaring. Larry lay upside down in the back of the boat, his hands clawing for purchase, his eyes white with shock. The boat went around and around, making extraordinary gyrations. And although we were only a few steps away, standing on the dock, we were powerless to stop it. For perhaps twenty or thirty seconds the boat tore around in tight circles, flinging Larry back and forth like a kid strapped into a Tilt-o-Whirl. Then the boat suddenly straightened out and rammed into the shore, stalling the motor. We pushed it off the rocks and Larry climbed out, tearfully swearing. In situations of stress, Larry usually blamed his older brother ("That goddamn Brian . . ."). But we weren't worried about him. We were worried about the boat.

Fortunately, my dad had built the boat with a hefty strip of brass on the prow, which absorbed most of the impact. We never mentioned it to him, but it was a good lesson anyway – preadolescent self-confidence getting to know billion-year-old granite.

∾

Gun training takes place at a gravel pit down the road.

My mother comes along. She stands in the background, saying nothing as my dad lectures us on the responsibilities of gun ownership. My brother and I stand straight as soldiers. My dad, with the Daisy BB gun in his hand, walks us through the rules. What's the first thing you do when you pick up a firearm?

"Point it in a safe direction," my brother recites. "And check to see if it is loaded."

"Once you're sure that it is unloaded, how do you handle it?"

"It's always loaded," I respond.

"What do you mean?"

"You always assume it's loaded, and keep the muzzle pointed in a safe direction."

My father nods. He's throwing us trick questions, and it's a good thing that we're catching them. Every couple of minutes he reiterates that if he catches us handling our guns in an unsafe manner, he'll take them away.

It's a clear Saturday morning in May, with new leaves fluttering in the poplar trees and ravens arguing in the woods. A good day for establishing dominance over Mother Nature. The sun is cold, and my mother is holding her white cardigan sweater to her throat. If this country plans on producing a summer, it's got a lot of work to do. My dad searches around in the dead weeds and finds an empty Rothmans package. He mounts it in the fork of a sapling and steps back, loads the BB gun, and holds it up to his shoulder. He pulls the trigger and the gun issues a sharp asthmatic *thup*.

We walk up to the tree and look at the package. Wow. He hit it dead-centre!

My brother and I are next. We take turns shooting at the package and missing it. Every once in a while the cardboard flinches, registering a hit. Normally my brother and I would be razzing each other, but today we're on our best behaviour. No crude comments in the presence of my mother. We're responsible gun owners.

On subsequent weekends we get more training. My father walks us along the lake, drilling us with the rules. The rules are complicated, with innumerable clauses and sub-sections dealing with everything from gun etiquette to ballistics. If we break the rules, he'll take the guns away.

Once we've passed the safety module, he teaches us which living creatures we're allowed to shoot and which we're not allowed to shoot. Birds are definitely off limits. We probably could have figured this out on our own – the walls of our cottage are covered with framed bird pictures, and the yard is full of birdhouses. All winter long he builds birdhouses, and once we're at the lake, he nails them up in the crooks of trees. Needless to say, if we shoot a bird, he'll take our guns away.

We know that Dad goes duck hunting in the fall, so we diplomatically introduce the notion that we could perhaps use our BB guns to bag a mallard or two.

"You can't shoot a duck with a BB gun," he says. "You'd just wound it."

"What if we shoot it in the eye?"

My father pauses for a long moment. Maybe he's sending a mental note to Ned Jordan. "Look . . ." he says. "You don't hunt ducks in the summer. They're raising their young. What if you crippled a mother duck?"

This seems a bit melodramatic. Does he really think we're going to provide child support for every duck in the neighbourhood? But we don't debate the point, or he might take our guns away.

He also prohibits us from shooting hawks, on the grounds that they control mice; barn swallows, on the grounds that they control insects; and frogs, on the grounds that it's just a stupid idea. "Why in god's name would you shoot a frog?"

"Okay, rats," my brother proposes.

"There are no rats in Laclu."

"But if we find a rat, can we shoot it?"

We agree to all his rules, and the next morning he allows us to take our guns when we go exploring. Soon we run into some boys who also have BB guns. Without a word of discussion we immediately understand that we have to form a gang – five or six rebel boys in bathing suits and flip-flops. We master the art of waving at our parents, looking boyish and harmless as we walk away. As soon as we meet our fellow gang members, we get down to the gunplay proper.

Adults have rules, but gangs have rules too. One of our rules is "If it flies, it dies." We shoot at crows, hawks, blackbirds, or anything that moves. A hundred BBs cost only a nickel, and we shoot so much, day in, day out, that soon we're handling our guns with an offhand and lackadaisical expertise. We speed-load our guns by pouring a whole package of BBs into our mouths, like Apaches, and spitting them into the magazine. Cocking the gun with a quick stroke of the lever, we can hit a dragonfly on the wing or shoot a thrown soup can without even raising the gun to the shoulder. In a good breeze, we know how much windage you need to hit and shatter the glass insulator on a tele-phone pole. And we know the various distances at which it is acceptable to shoot a human being. If your brother is wearing jeans, for example, you can put one into his rear end at sixty paces without actually injuring him. He'll just wheel around and give you the thumb – a gesture that we've accepted as the ulti-mate put-down. But if you shoot him at that distance when he's wearing a wet bathing suit, the sting of the BB will be wicked enough to make a welt, which will cause him to yell in pain, and maybe even threaten to tell Mum, who will then tell Dad, who will take our guns away.

∾

All winter long I have been looking forward to exploring the wilderness. Now that school has adjourned and we've moved to Laclu for the summer, I'm keen to get back to Rosena Lake. I've decided that I want to be an Indian. My father has given me Ernest Thompson Seton's book *Two Little Savages*, and I can't wait to make a bow and arrow, a buckskin vest, and a birch-bark canoe.

I've told the other members of my gang about the Precambrian Shield. I've told them about the snapping turtles, the giant fish that broke my line, and all the thousands of name-less lakes that lie just beyond it. I've told them we could do some serious hunting up there. We could build a teepee.

"Where are we gonna get a teepee?"

"I've got the plans. We'll use my dad's tarpaulin."

"Okay, so what's this lake look like?"

"Lots of dead trees, cliffs, and swamps."

"Cool. Is there quicksand?"

For some reason, quicksand plays a big role in our determination of whether a place is interesting. I didn't see any quicksand at Rosena, but I tell the boys I'm pretty confident that we could find some if we put our minds to it.

"Okay, this columbian shield of yours," says Dennis, sucking thoughtfully on an ice cube. "What's the best way to get there?"

"We'll take canoes," I say. "We'll take the creek from Laclu into Bell Lake, and then take another creek into Rosena."

Dennis points out that Danny and I are the only gang members with a canoe. "One canoe won't carry all five or six guys."

"I could get my mum to drive us," says Randy.

Dennis groans. He's a bit older than we are and thinks that getting driven places by someone's mother defeats the whole purpose of being in a gang.

I tend to agree with him. Now that my dad has shown me the way to the Shield, I want to try exploring it without the benefit of parental supervision. "Why don't we walk?" I suggest.

"How far is it?"

"About four miles." I have no idea how far it is, but four miles sounds about right.

So it's agreed – we'll hike to Rosena. Once we get there, we'll do some scouting and find a good campsite. After a preliminary scouting trip we'll return with pup tents, fishing rods, hatchets, and gasoline. With a good campsite, we'll be independent of adult interference. We'll stay up late, play poker, and smoke Cameos. During the day we can shoot things and roll giant boulders off the cliffs. We can go around smeared with soot from the fire, wearing feathers in our hair and animal skins for loincloths. We can build an Apache war drum and use the gasoline for making torches. Soaked in gas, held aloft, a burning cattail will illuminate the eyes of any hostile predators circling our stronghold.

For the next few days we refine our plan. Our general meeting place is Webbs'. People come to Webbs' to buy groceries or gas. We like to watch them buy gas. Sometimes the gas pump is the most interesting show in town. It's an archaic contraption with a glass fuel globe on top. When motorists fill their tanks, air wobbles up through the clear brown gasoline like murderous thought-bubbles rising in a Martian's brain. When they're finished buying gas, they purchase groceries inside the store, which is a large rustic building divided into two sections. One half of the building makes up the store, and the other half is a large dance hall with varnished log walls. High on the wall of the dance hall there's a stuffed bull caribou that was shot on the lake in the winter of 1923. A moth-eaten northern pike the size of a railway tie hangs above the fireplace. There's a bandstand at the back end of the room, and a lunch counter at the front. After our afternoon swim, in which we furtively try to overturn the diving platform, we gather at the lunch counter. Johnny Webb, the owner of the place, never seems particularly happy to see us, perhaps because he suspects that we're the unknown parties who have been releasing garter snakes in his store. But he tolerates us enough to accept our grimy fistfuls of warm change, which we barter for chocolate bars and packages of BBs.

While we sit at the counter, we debate various aspects of the trip and make lists of the things we're going to need. Because I've been to the Precambrian Shield already, and because I'm basically the promoter of the trip, I more or less chair the meetings. My fellow gangsters are full of questions, and although I don't necessarily have the answers, I use my experience based on an afternoon of fishing and a winter's worth of book research. In our planning sessions, Rosena Lake gradually rises to grandiose stature. It's not just a picturesque lake where we plan to camp out and do a little hunting. It's a place where we will unravel the mysteries of life and become men.

We spend so much time planning that I begin to worry we're going to spend the whole summer talking about it instead of actually doing it. Every morning, I wake up in a general condition of optimism, wondering if this is going to be the day for our wild trek. Danny and I sleep on the eastward-facing veranda, and our bed is flooded with sunlight by five-thirty in the morning. We thrash around a bit, clamp pillows over our heads, but by six o'clock it's so bright we can't sleep, and we're stumbling outside to take a pee in the grass. Being a kid, I'm not formulating what you'd strictly call a "plan" for the day. But I'm thinking about it. Once you get half a dozen boys together, then add in weather, family chores, and the chaos theory, it's quite an accomplishment that we're even planning something.

After breakfast we fill our backpacks with apples and peanut butter sandwiches and set out to meet the boys. Will this be the day we go to Rosena? It's hard to know, because there are many temptations between there and here. Two boys walking barefoot along a dewy gravel road with Daisy Scout lever-actions have no trouble finding distractions. It's an absorbing world, in the early morning, with the hieroglyphics of tiny animal footprints in the sand, the incessant chatter of unseen birds in the woods, and the macabre spiders spinning their gossamer webs in the cool gloom of the undergrowth. Our meeting place is a derelict wooden church that stands at a crossroads a little way north of our cottage. When we approach the church early in the morning, I sometimes feel like it's an emblem of my fallen religion, a ruined building with the morning sunlight playing on its blanched siding and broken windows. Just beyond it is the backdrop of the wilderness, the dark swamps and forbidding woods.

The roadside ditch alongside the church is filled with stagnant water, and the high grass beside the ditch is filled with leopard frogs, good-sized ones, which leap into the water with a loud splash when you stalk through the grass. Once a frog jumps into the water, it thinks it's safe, and it floats there, its arms akimbo, staring up at you. The other boys like to shoot frogs, and I shot a few myself the first time I carried my BB gun – just to see how it worked on them – but it feels mean, to kill them for no reason. My affection also extends to turtles, with their general all-around helplessness and their good-natured willingness to trudge for hundreds of yards on crooked legs. Snakes I like too. Cold and unblinking, they're like living strings of code. And while I understand why people might recoil from snakes, it seems craven and sissified to snap their backbones in jest, as I've seen my buddies do.

So while Danny keeps a lookout for the other boys, I usually check out the interior of the church. The churchyard is overgrown with hip-high weeds and Russian thistle. Making your way around to the back stairway, you have to watch your step because of all the old boards with nails sticking out of them. If you step on a rusty nail you get lockjaw, and they have to pull out your teeth in order to pipe water into your mouth so you won't die of thirst. The stairs themselves are rotted and falling apart. Climbing up the stairs, you enter a porch and then a little office. It's probably the Lutheran equivalent of what Catholics call the sacristy, where the priest dons his vestments and prepares for mass. It's a little room with old wine bottles on the floor and rain-buckled girlie magazines in the drawers. When I first arrive in the sacristy I spend a little time looking for hidden contraband or new writings on the wall. Because of my reasonable fear of rabid animals, I never go into the church until my gang arrives.

How many dark winter mornings have I spent in rooms like this? The priests I always worked for never spoke while they dressed. Their glittering rayon vestments rustled in the silence. The only sound came from the main hall of the church, where you'd hear an occasional cough or the bang of a kneeler as the old Italian ladies filed into the pews. I'd pull on a black cotton cassock, and over that, a blowsy white surplice with short sleeves. The priest never talked when I prepared his candles and filled his glass wine cruets. Some priests wanted only a dollop of wine. Others wanted the chalice full to the brim, and we had to know the difference. While preparing for mass, you knew there were things you could touch and things you couldn't. It was like working in a laboratory. Touch the Host, for example, and you were doomed. My friend Kenny once got the flesh of Christ stuck to the roof of his mouth and pried it off with his finger. It was a spur of the moment decision, but he's probably going to Hell for it.

Above the cheap little plywood desk with its cupboards, there's a church service schedule and some ancient birth and death notices pinned to the wall. The names are mostly Swedish. Or maybe they're Icelandic. Whoever they are, they arrived in

Canada late, after the best agricultural land had already been taken, and the Federal Land Office convinced them to try farming in northwestern Ontario. The rolling hills, lakes, and verdant forests around Laclu must have looked attractive when they first arrived, and quite a few farmers – including Gunnar Sigurdson, the man who sold us our cottage property – slaved half their lives trying to make their farms work. They cleared forests, built barns, and raised pigs and dairy cattle. Their kids went to a one-room schoolhouse just up the road, and on Sunday mornings, the families gathered here for church. But this country is hell on livestock. The winters are so cold that animals have to be kept inside, like prison inmates. The sweltering hot and thunderstormy summer days produce hordes of biting flies that can drive a thin-skinned dairy cow mad. So eventually the farmers lost everything. And the only reminder that Laclu was once a bustling little farming community is this derelict church with its old announcements pinned to the wall.

Once my crew finishes up with the frogs and comes up the stairs into the sacristy, we move into the church proper, cocking our guns and keeping an eye peeled for hydrophobic skunks. You can tell a skunk with hydrophobia because it trails long gobs of drool from its fangs as it staggers towards you, wanting to accomplish just one last thing in its miserable life and that's to kill, kill. We've already got a tactical plan worked out for our first encounter with a rabid skunk – who shoots first, who shoots backup, etc. – but if one of us gets bitten we know what happens next. Our parents would never admit it but we know the truth: they chain you to a stout tree. Doctors arrive, but they don't actually touch you. They push food and water towards you with a stick until they find out if you're going to turn rabid.

That's all right. If you're going to venture into the woods, you have to take the good with the bad. We know that during any one of these patrols one of us might get caught in quicksand, step in a rusty old Oneida Newhouse bear trap, or get attacked by a crazed furbearer. Still, a ruined church is too powerful a lure to pass up. This is a place where adult society has no writ, and it fills us with reverent silence. We communicate in whispers as we pad up the aisles, past the shattered stained glass windows and empty pews, stepping over the animal turds and broken glass with our guns at the ready.

Near the back of the church I spot the skeleton of a dead animal lying on the buckled linoleum floor. Kneeling down, I examine the skeleton, probing it with the muzzle of my gun. It's the remains of a bird, I think. The bones are slender and delicately tethered, like the ribs of a broken kite. Above me is the stained glass window where the bird beat itself to death, trying to escape. If it had had a larger brain, it could have flown right up through the roof. High overhead, there's a rent in the ceiling, a hole laced with rafters where you can see the blue sky. A big puffy white cloud drifts across the opening. Its escape route was right there. It's like what the life-saving manuals always advise. When you're drowning, kick free and head for the light.

∾

After we satisfy ourselves with a thorough exploration of the church, we descend the stairs and get moving again.

The morning is well advanced by now, and the sun is hot on our bare arms as we move up the road. Cars occasionally roar past us, stirring up clouds of dust, and we wave at them with our thumbs out.

No one seems interested in picking up six barefoot boys with BB guns. I've calculated that it's probably about a two-hour walk to Rosena Lake, and it's a constant challenge to keep my fellow hoods focused on the mission. Squirrels lope across the road, provoking fruitless pursuit. Glass insulators need to be shot. Or sometimes it's a big wasp nest. Wedged in the crook of a tree, like a lady's hat, a wasp nest is a provocation that can't be ignored. When the first BBs hit the nest, the wasps come boiling out. It takes them a few moments to determine why little holes are being punched in their structure. But then they send out scouting parties, and even if you're a hundred feet from the nest, you're going to be sorry when they find you.

Farther on, there's a bend in the road where, many years ago, someone spilled a trailer load of rotted lumber or plasterboard. Instead of loading it back onto the trailer, he just flung the trash into the ravine. Eventually that particular bend in the road became an accepted place to jettison garbage and is now known as the dump. There's no official sign indicating that this place is a dumping site. But when you get within about fifty yards, the bad smell floating up from the ravine lets you know you've arrived.

The dump is such a compelling spot that our mission to Rosena gets delayed while we check it out. It's usually deserted, with no signs of life except a few ravens flapping around in the pit. With our guns resting in the crooks of our arms we stand in silence on the lip of the pit for a few moments, soaking up the atmosphere. A few garbage bags are lying on the very edge, left there by people who are too frightened of bears to walk to the edge and throw them in. We throw the bags two-handed to get maximum destruction as they crash down the slope. Then we climb down after them. The sun is high overhead by now, and the motionless, super-heated air of summer is so fouled with the smell of decomposition that we have to screw up our faces to breathe.

Down in the ravine the ground is drenched with chemicals, pools of green fluid scummed with dead insects. Ravens fly overhead, croaking in alarm. Walking around, we look for things to shoot. The dump is a target-rich environment, littered with unbroken windows, whisky bottles, and tin cans. The best target of all is the Franklin's ground squirrel. The Franklin's is a tough and resilient little animal, and a direct hit in the body isn't enough to disable one. They know us, and it's hard to get a shot at them because their sentries issue a shrill warning call as soon as they spot us. As we stalk through the ravine, the gophers scold us from their hiding places, making high-pitched hysterical titters.

All summer we've been trying to bag a gopher. Sometimes we encircle the dump in a pincer movement, communicating with each other with birdy whistles and hand gestures. The suspense heightens as we draw closer, belly-crawling through the rusted cans and straggly weeds. At the very edge of the crater, we mount our guns and scrutinize the detailed walls of the pit, watching for any tell-tale movement that might, with the blink of an eye, magically transform itself into the slinky body of a foraging gopher.

Inevitably, something goes wrong. In the relationship between hunter and prey, the odds overwhelmingly favour the prey. According to my library books, wolves have the devil of a time bringing down a moose. African lions fail nine times out of ten. Human hunters are even less effective, and feminist anthropologists like Adrienne Zihlman have proven that hunter-gatherer cultures relied less on hunting, which is done by men, than on gathering, which is done by women. The Indians who used to live around here probably wouldn't have wasted their time hunting at all if an occasional kill didn't yield such a bounty of protein. Five hundred pounds of moose meat, cut into thin strips and dried in the sun, would feed an extended family for months.

Even gophers exceed our ability as hunters, and most of the time a snapped twig or an incautious whisper triggers a mad chorus of warning calls. Our stalks fail in curious and hard-to-predict ways, and the manner in which they fail is almost as interesting as the stalk itself. On one occasion, for example, we make it all the way to the garbage pit without triggering a warning call. With anxious hearts, we take up sniper positions on the edge of the pit and lie in silence, waiting for an unsuspecting gopher to show itself.

Finally, on the garbage slope below me, a gopher slinks out from underneath a broken railway tie. Standing upright in that oddly serpentine way, it searches the area for danger. As I carefully take aim and squeeze the trigger, a paper wasp – probably one of the same wasps whose nest we destroyed a week ago – lands on my neck and decides to sting me. As the wasp pumps venom into my skin, I'm slowly pulling the trigger. The BB is already travelling down the barrel at 450 feet per second when the pain receptors in my neck light up. The barrel twitches and the BB flies a few inches astray and strikes the railway tie head-on. The tiny metal spheroid pushes into the tar-saturated fibre of the railway tie for a millisecond or two, rebounds, then flies back towards me at near-full velocity, striking me in the centre of the forehead.

Yelping in pain, I clutch at both injuries, on my neck and forehead. The forehead wound is worse and produces a wee spot of blood. If the pellet had hit me an inch or two lower, it would have embedded itself in my eye and blinded me for life, a fact that everyone in the gang finds hilarious, including me.

∾

Finally, we make a kill.

My sniper's position is down in the bottom of the dump, behind a tipped-over refrigerator. It's a humid mid-summer afternoon and my underarms are slick from the heat. The silence is threaded by the steady oscillating drone of hornets and bluebottles. Above me, the steep rumpled slopes of garbage and heaped grass clippings are trapping the sun's heat like a solar panel. The flattened mud beneath my sandals is saturated with some kind of lime-green engine fluid, and its molecular formula is rising in my nostrils. As the minutes pass, there's ample time to sink into non-thinking awareness. This is what hunters spend most of their time doing – nothing. Everyone thinks that hunting is aggressive, but actually it's passive. You sit and wait, and wait. All the white noise of civilization – interior monologues and radio chatter and annoying snippets of the latest songs – gradually fade out, giving way to the awareness of your steady breathing and the complex texture of the physical world.

To relax my eyes, I occasionally cut my gaze off towards the far end of the dump where the strewn garbage gradually gives way to grass and foliage. A few plastic bags flutter from the low willows. Beyond that is a forest of aspen trees, then a high dark jungle of evergreens. That's the edge of the northern forest, right there, and it's one of the reasons this dump is such an intriguing spot. It's a two-hearted kind of place in between civilization and the wilderness. Black bears come here. We've seen their blue-berry-speckled crap, and sometimes even a footprint. Bear tracks add a whiff of danger, and we're regularly checking the forest fringe to make sure that one of them doesn't come walking up behind us.

Shifting my focus back to the garbage heap, I'm startled to see a large gopher emerge from a gutted sofa and perch on the armrest. It's just a few yards away, and it doesn't see me. I take careful aim at its head. We've learned that a lightweight metal BB can't penetrate their furry skin. On past occasions, when we've managed to hit one in the body, it's just taken off, bucking up and down like a bronco whacked with a lariat. This time I squeeze the trigger carefully and the BB hits it right in the fore-head. What happens next is a bit horrifying.

Every mammal's legs and arms are controlled by spinal reflexes. They're called "reflexes" because they're capable of independent action. If you step on a sharp piece of glass or get stung by a hornet, your muscles don't wait for instructions. They automatically jerk your limb away from the pain stimulus. The next time you're walking barefoot through your house and you step on a discarded staple, notice how your leg automatically buckles, refusing to accept your full weight. That's a reflex deci-sion. The limbs of the body are like remote provinces, with their own local powers, and sometimes they choose to run the show on their own. The whole system seems to work just fine until you remove the central governance of the brain.

When my BB strikes the gopher in the forehead, the animal's brain temporarily shuts off, and in the sudden absence of neural guidance, all the various squabbling reflexes take control. This results in what a scientist – if we'd had a scientist in our gang – would call "inappropriate motor response," that is, scrambling, back-flipping, frantically running on the spot, and so on. Even the hard-core members of our group are shocked by this performance. Right before our eyes, the gopher starts flipping, whirling, and somersaulting through the garbage, looking like it's possessed by demons. At moments like this, we realize that we're staring deep into a world that's scarier than we imagined.

Dennis, however, is more seasoned than the rest of us. He has an inky coil of Bobby Curtola hair dangling from his forehead, and keeps a pack of Cameos stuffed down the front of his pants. He's seen some things, in his day, and doesn't let a little thing like a freaked-out gopher bother him. While I just stand there, stunned, watching the gopher doing its dervish-dance, Dennis sprints down into the garbage pit, grabs a stick, and whacks the gopher until it's dead.

He lifts it by the tail and shows it to the group. Everyone cheers. It was a team effort, and now we're the proud owners of one dead gopher. Once we realize it's dead, a subtle mood of anticlimax settles on the group. We like to think of ourselves as subversives, but now that we've succeeded in killing an animal, we can't remember why we did it. Dennis hands me the gopher, and I examine the little feller. It has neat black claws and a tiny drop of blood oozing from the tip of its lacquered nose. It has tiny footpads. Under different circumstances, we might have been friends, this gopher and I. Stroking its handsome fur, I reflect that it could have perched on my hand, eating the crusts of my sandwiches. But it's too late now. Holding it up by the tail for one last admiring glance, flicking off the tiny red lice that are trying to climb my wrist, I pass the gopher to the next guy.

Being a fallen Catholic, I'm always trying to keep the boys cognizant of the various ethical dimensions of our crimes, and since I've killed this gopher myself, I feel duty-bound to treat the

corpse in some kind of ceremonial way. We devote a considerable amount of time arguing about what we're going to do with
the body. Everyone has an opinion. One of the boys suggests
that we tie a rock to the gopher's tail and drown it in the lake. A
dissenter points out that you can't drown something that's
already dead. Grant suggests that we douse the corpse in gasoline and set it on fire. But Grant is going through a phase where
his solution to everything is to set it on fire. I'm in favour of skinning it. I argue that we can collect a number of hides and sell
them at Sydney I. Robinson. Everyone thinks this is a good idea,
so we head for the tree house.

Our tree house is located in the woods behind the church.
It's a rickety platform of lumber and plywood nailed into the
crotch of a big tree. We borrowed our dads' tools to build it and
scavenged old lumber from the ruined church. Nailing stubs of
two-by-four to the bole of the big poplar tree, we built a ladder
that allows us to easily climb up to the platform, which sways
minutely in the breeze and affords a distant, foliage-screened
view of the church steeple with its old rugged cross.

With the boys gathered around me in the tree house, I
conduct an autopsy. Slicing open the gopher's belly with my dull
pocket knife, I draw out the spaghetti entrails and tiny multicoloured organs, and organize them in neat rows on the sun-lit
plywood floor. Observing this, my colleagues argue over which
is the stomach and which is the heart. Cutting off its feet, removing its tiny claws for a necklace, I carefully skin the animal and
nail its hide to a board. One of these days we'll have to return
these tools. The other day my dad was in quite a temper, looking
for this hammer.

Once the hide is stretched out it looks official and satisfying,
like a miniature bear rug. It's not always pleasant, killing things,

but a man has to make a living. Once the skin is properly converted into leather by the sun, I'll take it back to Winnipeg, to Sydney I. Robinson, and do some haggling with the fur buyer. If they don't offer me a fair price, I'll keep it for a trophy. With a border of red felt, it would look nice up on my bedroom wall.

Propping the little board up so that the gopher skin absorbs the direct rays of the sun, I follow the boys back down the ladder. We then adjourn to Webbs', to celebrate our victory with a 7-Up float. There's an old kerosene tank behind Webbs' store, with high grass growing up beneath it. We always hide our guns under the tank. Like a frontier salon keeper, Johnny Webb has a no-guns policy in his establishment.

A few days later, I return to the tree house to retrieve my gopher hide. Unfortunately, the bluebottles have found it, and the fur is seething with maggots. To dispose of it, I have to climb down the ladder and toss it in the bush, holding my nose to stave off the gag reflex.

∾

Summer is drawing to a close.

The early part of August has delivered two solid weeks of rain and thunderstorms, and now the wind has turned around to the north. The sky is low and shaggy. The lake is corrugated with whitecaps. Every morning when we wake up there's rain drumming on the roof, and nobody feels like going exploring.

My dad has been trying to dig a septic field. But with all the rainy weather, he's running out of time, so he decides to hire a contractor to help finish the trench. My dad doesn't usually seek outside help. He comes from a tradition of self-sufficiency, where men own their own tools and solve their own problems.

But every once in a while he encounters something he can't handle by himself, and that's when he calls Cliff Harrison.

Cliff lives year-round at Laclu and drives a ramshackle '49 Fargo pick-up truck. His truck has so many loose parts that after breakfast, we can hear it clapping and banging long before it comes into sight. Cliff is a jack-of-all-trades. He does plumbing, wiring, carpentry, and garbage hauling. He drives your honey-wagon and he traps your nuisance skunks. He has a backhoe for digging holes, and when his truck comes into sight, his orange backhoe is bounding along behind it.

Climbing out of his truck, Cliff spits a wad of tobacco into the grass and greets us with a modest wave. He wears a striped railway engineer's hat and tattered coveralls, and his face is as dark as an old leather boot. Johnny climbs down from the tractor and swats away the various neighbourhood dogs. Johnny and his dad are a physical mismatch, the two of them. Whereas Cliff is thin and tall, Johnny is chubby and tragically short. He's short enough that it's easy to imagine that when he grows up his shortness will become a sort of infirmity. As Cliff would have it, they built the sidewalk too close to Johnny's ass.

Climbing up into the back of the truck, Cliff organizes his tools. Johnny doesn't say anything. He just leans against the truck. While we wait for my dad to come up from the dock and direct the project, Danny and I grill Cliff about his tractor, his truck, his trapline, his hunting dogs, his guns, and whether he's shot any bears lately. "Just that one the other day," he allows.

Ah yes, that one. Johnny Webb had spotted a bear on his property and called Cliff. Everyone in Laclu knows what to do when bears venture onto the property – you blow them to kingdom come. Cliff showed up an hour later and drove around looking for the bear. Finally a kid on a bicycle flagged Cliff down and told him the bear was just down the road, dismantling a garbage bin. When Cliff showed up, the bear was standing in the driveway with a milk carton in its mouth. Without even getting out of the truck, Cliff rolled down the window and put a bullet in its chest.

When the gun went off, Danny and I were swimming at Webbs' beach about three hundred yards away. A few minutes later we spotted Cliff pulling up to the pump in his old Fargo truck. We grabbed our towels and ran up to see him. "What's going on, Cliff?"

"Just shot a bear," he casually remarked, gesturing towards the back of the pick-up.

We scrambled to the back and looked inside. It was the first time I'd seen a dead bear. I've always expected that a real bear, close-up, would be some enormous beast with slobbery jaws and a head the size of a sofa. But the animal in Cliff's truck didn't look much bigger than a badger. It had small ears and a narrow wedge-shaped head, and it was slumped face down on the hard metal. The leathery nose was no bigger than a dog's, and its front legs were splayed stupidly akimbo, as if it had been whacked on the head. There was a slick of syrupy blood on the ribbed metal truck bed. Carrion flies with green jewel-like tails had somehow already found it, and were crawling all over its face. "Is it a baby?" my brother finally asked.

"Hell no," said Cliff. "Three or four years old, probably."

"What are you going to do with it?"

He shrugged. "Throw it in the dump."

This seemed like a waste, throwing away a perfectly good dead bear. I considered asking him if we could have it. It seemed to me that if you had a dead bear, you should keep it around for a while and give everyone a chance to enjoy it. I reasoned that Danny and I could borrow a wagon and pull it back to the cottage, and keep it in the tool shed for a few days. But I knew that my parents would think it was a dumb idea. We asked Cliff if we could join him the next time he shot a bear. But he pointed out that bears don't keep to a schedule. Still, we decided to keep tabs on Cliff's activities. And when he showed up in our yard that morning, I asked him what jobs he'd planned for the day.

"I'm gonna dig this trench."

"Then what are you going to do?"

"I'm going up to Rosena Lake to check on some minnow traps."

Danny and I looked at each other. "Can we hitch a ride?"

"Why?"

"We want to go camping."

"Well . . . ask your father."

We ran down to the dock, where my dad was gathering his tools. We asked him if we could go camping overnight at Rosena.

"Ask your mother."

∾

An hour later, we're speeding down the gravel road in the back of Cliff's pick-up truck.

What an adventure! My dad offered to drive us in the Buick, but we've leapt at the chance to go in Cliff's truck, which not only affords a better view of the passing countryside but has the added benefit of being dangerous. Five of us are in the truck – Dennis, Larry, Randy, my brother Danny, and I – and we've loaded so much gear into the back that we have to perch on the rails, grasping at whatever handholds we can find to avoid being thrown out.

My dad has agreed to let us take the red canoe, and it's among us, tied down with a cat's cradle of yellow ropes. Alongside the canoe there are piles of sleeping bags, life jackets, fishing rods, BB guns, Coleman coolers full of soft drinks and wieners, and various cardboard boxes stuffed with chocolate chip cookies, ripple chips, marshmallows, and other survival gear.

We couldn't have picked a better day for our expedition. It's a warm day in mid-August with signs everywhere that summer is ending. The hayfields are high and ripe, tawny now instead of green and powdered with dust from the passing traffic. The aspen trees alongside the road are showing patches of yellow. In another week we'll all be heading home, to the dreaded prospect of a new school year. We couldn't be happier than to be swooping down this gravel road in the back of this old Fargo truck. But our happiness is informed by the knowledge that our days of freedom will soon be over.

With each passing mile, the road gets narrower and rougher, as if the contractors gradually lost enthusiasm for pushing much farther north. By the time we arrive at Rosena the foliage is leaning overhead and slapping against the fenders of the truck. Cliff pulls up to the boat launch next to the trapper's cabin, and although there's a dog barking inside the house there are no other signs of life on the property. For us this is an adventure, but for Cliff it's just another chore. He's always got lots of work to do, so we hurriedly remove our stuff from the truck.

Finally the supplies are laid out on the beach. Cliff makes sure that the truck is empty, and pauses to take one last look at us. "So you're all right? When is your dad coming to pick you up?"

"Tomorrow at four o'clock," I answer. We wanted to stay out here for a week, but it took some lobbying just to persuade our mothers to agree to a single overnight. My mother was disappointed that we preferred to catch a ride with Cliff, rather than my dad. But the whole point of going camping is to do it on your own.

"You sure you got enough stuff?" he asks, glancing at the mountain of supplies on the shore. He's kidding us, I know, but it's remarkable how much equipment you can assemble when you're trying to keep things to a minimum. "Is your tent rain-proof?"

"Yep, but the forecast is for nice."

He scowls and looks up at the sky, which is starting to look a little hazy. "Looks like rain to me. But anyway . . . good luck." He waves and climbs into his truck.

We get busy loading the canoe. The shores of Rosena Lake are fairly easy walking, a long open expanse of granite lightly wooded with jackpine, and our plan is to conduct a two-pronged foray into the wilderness. We'll use the canoe as a sort of freight barge for our supplies. One guy will paddle it, loaded to the brim, along the shoreline while the exploration party pushes forward on foot.

This seems like a good idea, in theory, but after we launch the canoe, with me paddling and the others proceeding on foot, the foot patrollers soon run into a swampy bay that's fringed with cattails and marsh grass. They can't get across it, so I come ashore and ferry them across the bay, one guy at a time, with the canoe so overloaded that I can barely move without tipping it over. The deerflies are bad today, and the guys who are waiting on the shore keep yelling at me to hurry up. It's an arduous process, going back and forth. But finally we're on the other side of the inlet, pushing on, pushing on past the island with its barking huskies, past the bay where I hooked and lost my monstrous fish, past the lily-pad bay where we saw the big snapping turtle, and towards the creek mouth which leads farther north, into the secret heart of the wilderness.

Just as Cliff predicted, it's getting cloudy. We're not afraid of a little rain, but we'd like to find a campsite and get our stuff inside. So at the mouth of the creek, I beach the canoe and we get organized. While we're unloading the canoe and hauling stuff up to the campsite, the first serious mishap occurs.

Along with the firecrackers and potato gun, we've brought along a gallon jug of gasoline. Gasoline is essential for making bonfires, bottle bombs, cattail torches, and other camping equip-ment. An average cattail fits snugly into the mouth of the jug, and once you've soaked five or six of them with gasoline and mounted them in a circle around the tents, it makes the campsite look like a village in a Boris Karloff movie. But while Dennis is carrying stuff up to the campsite, the glass jug slips out of his grip and smashes on the rocks. The gasoline runs down through the undergrowth to the lake, where it produces a rainbow-hued slick on the water. This is rotten luck, but there's nothing we can do. So after grumbling a bit, we continue unloading the canoe. Then we encounter another problem – how are we going to pound plastic tent stakes into bare granite?

Various solutions are proposed. Can we anchor the tent with big rocks? This doesn't seem workable. What if we use big logs and some nails? This sounds a little more promising, but we forgot to bring nails. So we stand around for a few moments, thinking it over. Dennis fishes a Cameo out of his pocket and lights it, tosses the wooden match over his shoulder. It lands on the moss and the hillside explodes.

The fire is ferocious and silent. The flames are chin-high and stretch all the way down to the water's edge. For a moment we stand frozen, then come to the same instant conclusion. Let's get the hell out of here! Grabbing our tent, groceries, and sleeping bags, we run down to the shore and toss them into the canoe. I leap in and madly paddle after the boys, who are wasting no time galloping down the shore, through the woods, up and down granite humps and ledges, putting space between them and the fire. We're not afraid of being burned alive. We're afraid of getting in trouble.

Paddling like a man possessed, I feverishly review excuses – it wasn't us; it was an accident; some big kids made us do it, etc. Deep in my heart, however, I know we're sunk. We've just started a forest fire. In another twenty minutes this whole place is going to look like a preview from *Walt Disney Presents* – towering flames, stampeding animals, and teams of forest rangers swooping down in helicopters. The other boys have out-distanced me by now. They're about two hundred yards ahead of me, waving and shouting. I'm paddling as fast as I can. But they keep pointing, so I pause to look back.

The fire has gone out.

Is it possible? I can see a faint wisp of white smoke rising from the campsite, but even now it drifts on the wind and dissipates. Turning the canoe around, I paddle back to the campsite, where we all review the damage. The moss is scorched and blackened. The willow bushes along the hillside are denuded of their leaves, but the fire has gone out. All the rain we've been having for the last few weeks has apparently rendered the woods uninflammable. Walking up and down the hill, we stomp on a few wisps of smoke and pour water on anything that looks like it might start burning again. But if flames taller than our heads won't do the job, I don't think we have to worry much about embers.

What now? If we stay here, an adult might come along. If he sees all these charred bushes, he'll probably try to blame it on us. So we decide that we'd better find a new spot. Just down the shoreline we find a little peninsula covered with scrubby oak trees. The ground is rough and knotted with roots. There aren't many places large enough to pitch our big tent. But at least there's enough dirt to hold tent pegs. So we get to work.

Erecting the tent takes about half an hour, and involves the usual bickering and Laurel and Hardy teamwork, tripping each other with guy ropes, etc. But finally we step back and admire our work – a sway-backed hump of canvas that actually resembles a tent.

We're still covered with soot, so we decide it's time for a swim. It's always a bit intimidating, swimming in an unfamiliar lake when you happen to know that snapping turtles and other flesh-eating creatures swim in its depths, so after changing into my suit, I stand on the shore for a while, gazing down at the chilly-looking water for signs of trouble. Finally I decide there's no point in drawing out the torture, and I suck in a deep breath and jump. The water erupts all around me, as I sink into the shocking cold and darkness. Planting my feet on the greasy rocks of the lake floor, I push upwards, break into daylight. The other guys are looking at me from the shore, waiting for my report. With an effort to keep my voice steady, I say, "You're not going to believe how warm it is."

As they run towards the water and take flying leaps, I shout, "Suckers!"

࿇

As we're cooking dinner, someone shouts an alarm.

I'm down on one knee, tending the fire. Looking towards the east, I see a dome of red light bulging up through the trees – a full moon.

We're making a dinner of roasted wieners, marshmallows, and Kool-Aid. After dinner we retire to the tent for an evening of poker, with wooden matches of various lengths representing ten-, twenty-, and hundred-dollar poker chips.

The moon floods the tent like a headlight. Whenever I go outside to take a pee I'm unprepared for the brightness of the night landscape. The lake is paved with hammered silver and the granite shoreline is creamy pale. It reminds me of the night scenes in the old cowboy movies. While I pee, I keep hearing crackly noises in the forest. I can't imagine camping in these woods alone. Frankly, it's not bears I'd be worried about, but tall frog-men with clawed hands and seaweed dripping off their shoulders. Inside the tent, I feel safe. There's courage in numbers. We've got belt knives, hatchets, and machetes, and any creature short of a legionnaire of the damned is going to have his work cut out, tackling us.

Dennis has brought along a little transistor radio, and it's hanging from the tent pole. As the walls of the tent luff and sway in the wind, the little radio turns minutely on its strap, rotating like a radar dish. It's difficult to pick up radio stations around here. The nearest town, Kenora (pop. 15,000), has a radio station that supposedly plays the Top 40. But you can't pick up its signal from more than a few miles away. Radio stations from the United States are more powerful. One of the best is WLS in Chicago, the power station, 890 on your dial. Call in and win, baby; WLS is gonna make you a rich bitch. Thanks to the full moon, WLS is coming in strong tonight, bringing us songs that come drifting through the crackle and static like messages from an alien planet. Right now the radio is playing Del Shannon's "Runaway." I love the opening scene in the song, where he's walking down the road in the rain. And I like it when he loses it and starts stuttering and the organ takes over and does the singing for him, erupting into the wild chorus that sounds like the howling of a ghost.

Sitting cross-legged in the circle, slapping my bets down and drumming my fingers to the baying organ, I feel liberated from my grim future, at least for tonight. As soon as I get back to the city, it'll be time to face another school year. It'll be time to face newer and crueller schoolteachers (I'm probably going to get Sister George, the dragon slayer), bigger school-yard thugs, colder winter nights, tougher homework assignments, and better-looking girls who are even less interested in me than they were last year.

The other guys are facing the same fate. We're a bunch of rejects, every one of us. I have such a sore back that I could barely lift the canoe. Randy stutters. And Larry has a dick the size of a peanut. It probably wouldn't hurt to talk things over. But that would be unmanly. We just let Del Shannon's organ do the talking for us.

☙

In the early morning the lake is a mirror. With my fishing rod I walk along the rocky shoreline, feeling the stiffness in my back dissipate as I move around a bit. When I come to a little rocky point, I tie a River Runt on my line and cast it towards some off-shore lily pads.

As I reel it in, the lure swims brightly, wagging its sexy rear end from side to side. Suddenly the water erupts in a boil and the lure disappears. It's a fish! I've got a fish! The rod bends over, and a strange power comes vibrating up the line. A second later a three-pound bass leaps out of the lake, shaking its head furiously. The boys come running out of the tent. "Don't horse him!" they yell. "Don't horse him!"* After a valiant battle, the bass weakens, and I drag it onto the rocks and the boys cheer. They run and get their own rods, and within an hour, we've caught three bass, two pike, and a small pickerel. We've filleted them, lit a fire, heated the frying pan, and the delicious aroma of birch smoke, fried fish, and sizzling bacon is floating on the morning air.

After breakfast we fill our backpacks with supplies and strike off on a hike. Dennis carries the potato gun – a bazooka-like weapon we built in his tool shed, and Larry carries the ammunition. Larry's mother didn't have any potatoes, which make the best ammo, so he brought a sack of onions instead. We hike along the shoreline to a high cliff at the end of the lake, where everyone decides to set up the cannon and do some artillery practice. I'd prefer to keep moving. I want to do some serious exploring, but Dennis is insistent upon setting up the cannon

---

* It's an accepted fact among us that you're guaranteed to lose a fish if you "horse" it, whatever that means.

and firing off a few volleys. "I see an enemy force headed our way," he says, gesturing towards a group of seagulls riding the waves perhaps two hundred yards away.

Larry gathers some good-sized rocks and builds an emplacement for the cannon. The potato cannon is a piece of plastic pipe three feet long, two inches in diameter. We learned how to make it from Richard Johnson, the local hot-rodder. The day we learned about the potato gun, Danny and I were walking barefoot down the gravel to Webbs', and Richard Johnson came thundering past with his buddies. He hit the brakes and backed up. "Hey . . . where's your sister?"

"Don't know."

"Where are you going?"

"Nowhere."

"Have a smoke," he said. Richard had been influenced by the thoughts of Duane Eddy and kept a pack of Pall Malls rolled up in the sleeve of his T-shirt.

Danny and I each accepted a cigarette.

Richard reached out the window with one muscular arm and flipped the top off his Zippo. Holding the flame to each of our cigarettes, he watched as we lit up. "You have to inhale."

I inhaled a big lungful of smoke and coughed so hard I almost retched. Inside the car there was a chorus of laughter from Richard's hoodlum buddies.

When we finished coughing, Richard pulled a piece of plastic drainpipe out of the back seat and brandished it in our faces. "Want to see something?" He aimed it at a road sign, pushed a red button, and the pipe banged like a gun. An object of some kind caromed off the road sign.

"Holy cow," Danny exclaimed. "What's that?"

"Potato cannon," Richard Johnson said. "Play your cards right, I'll show you how to make one."

It was an idle promise, intended most likely to enhance his standing with our older sisters. But we took him at his word. And whenever we saw him at the gas pump at Webbs', we badgered him for instructions. Finally he whipped out a pencil and drew us the plans on the hood of his car. We knew the basic stuff. Like most boys, we already had a working familiarity with most types of home-made artillery. In Winnipeg, we'd built light, practical cannons from dismantled bicycle pumps. The explosive charge was a four-inch blockbuster, dropped down into the tube. The projectile was a crab apple, a rounded slug of modelling clay (which made an impressive blue splatter when it hit a stucco wall), or a jumbo marble. Loaded with a big cat's eye marble, that baby kicked like a shotgun.

Richard Johnson's potato cannon, however, opened up a whole new world of personal artillery. We built the barrel and combustion chamber out of plastic pipes, elbows, and screw-off drain caps that we scrounged from our dads' tool sheds. Instead of using expensive firecrackers for propellant, we used WD-40, a common lightweight lubricant easily liberated from any tool shed. Instead of using a flammable wick, we used the standard push-button igniter found on any barbecue. And instead of crab apples, we used cooking potatoes for ammo, which we rammed down the muzzle with a stick.

Our first prototype didn't work. We discovered that you have to take care while ramming the projectile home, or you push the potato down into the combustion chamber and the charge of WD-40 doesn't have the correct fuel-to-air ratio required to make an explosion. You can't use too much WD-40 either, or you flood the combustion chamber and you have to take the whole thing apart. But we experimented, built a ramrod with a notched marker that drove the potato to the perfect depth, and toyed with varying concentrations of WD-40 until we found the perfect mixture (three careful squirts, left to vaporize inside the combustion chamber for the count of ten). Finally, after many failures, we tried firing it and to our shock the gun barked like a tailpipe. The shell, a hefty white sebago, shot skyward with such velocity that we couldn't even pick it out with the naked eye until it was two hundred yards distant, a miniature dot curving down from the bright blue like a golf ball whacked by Gary Player.

We used a vacant hayfield for a firing range, and stacks of cardboard boxes for targets. After lots of practice, we could visualize the potato's soaring trajectory even before we fired the trigger. Once the various complexities of muzzle velocity and distance wore a groove into our neural pathways, it became difficult to see the world in the same way. I could no longer look across an expanse of driveways and private yards and see a barbecue standing alone without thinking, hmm, nice target. I couldn't watch a speedboat go past without calculating the windage and elevation required to drop an Idaho red into its cockpit. Potato artillery was fascinating at first. But as soon as you acquire a new body of expertise, you quickly lose respect for it. So I'm feeling a bit impatient about interrupting our hike while the gang nestles the cannon among the rocks and makes ready to fire on the hostile gulls.

Selecting an onion, Dennis rams it home, then squats down and peers along the barrel, making tiny adjustments by shifting the rocks supporting it. He unscrews the plastic cap and injects three squirts of WD-40. Silently counting to ten, he nods towards Larry. "Fire in the hole."

Larry pushes the button and it clicks. Nothing happens. He pushes it again. Click, click, click. It's a misfire.

Dennis unscrews the cap of the combustion chamber and trouble-shoots the system, wiping off the lighter switch, cleaning out the residue of WD-40, and screwing the whole thing together again. This time, the cannon makes a healthy *whack*, and the projectile soars out in a faint arc and throws up a plume of spray fifty yards shy of the enemy birds. "Who brought these stupid onions?" Dennis asks, scowling at Larry, his gunnery corporal. "We might as well be shooting bran muffins."

Dennis tries a larger onion, but it jams in the barrel, and Larry declines to push the button, a cowardly refusal which Dennis feels is rather selfish, given that we're supposed to be working towards a common goal. No one else is willing to take the risk of having the gun blow up in his face, so Dennis has to take the cannon apart again. This is getting a bit tedious, so I make some impatient noises in the background. Dennis probably shares my feeling that all this bluster, tomfoolery, and ineffectual fist-shaking in the direction of Nature is starting to look a bit pathetic, because after fussing with the cannon for a few minutes he suddenly stands up, holds the length of plastic tubing in his hands as if seeing it for the first time, then flips it over his shoulder and says, "Fuck it. What's next?"

I hook my thumb over my shoulder. "Let's head north."

We forge on, following an old portage trail that winds through the woods. For half an hour we follow the trail, which may have been pioneered by buckskinned Montrealers two hundred years ago, or maybe even stone-age Indians a thousand years before that. We enter a spruce bog, a place that even in daylight seems spectral and gloomy, full of gnarled spruces shaped like medieval candle sconces draped with cobweb. The muskeg underfoot is so yielding and bosomy that we hop warily from hump to hump, fearing that we'll get caught in the warm muck, burdened with heavy backpacks, and get horribly sucked down while the others shout advice and offer flimsy sticks. On the other side of the bog the trail zigzags up the flank of another cliff. And when we reach the crest we have to cast around, looking this way and that, until we find some trees with healed-over axe cuts that mark the trail.

Now we're on a high ridge, heavily wooded, and the trees around us are great tall monsters that creak like rigging in the wind. The ground is carpeted with pine needles, and as we follow the faint imprint of the trail I feel that we're making progress, advancing the quest, following this pathway into the past, into our childhood dreams, back into the dreams, too, of the voyageurs, ancient hunter-gatherers, and rough ice-age beasts that must have slouched down this path thousands of years ago.

Sometime in the last few years – I don't know exactly when – I lost my belief in religion. I've come to the conclusion that the stories in the Bible are just fables, like the adventures of Sinbad the Sailor. I don't believe that the Red Sea actually divided in two when Moses raised his staff, or that it rained frogs in Egypt, or that the Apocalypse will be announced by four skeletal riders on pale horses galloping out of the clouds. I've decided that my school-age religious instruction was just a package of far-fetched scary stories to make us behave. Now that I've thrown away my religion, I've got nothing to replace it.

It's like being lost and having no compass. I no longer know where to go, or what the truth is. But by a process of elimination, I've worked my way through the places where the truth isn't. I know, by now, that you won't find it inside a priest's sacristy at six-thirty on a winter morning. I know that you won't find it with a piece of home-made plastic artillery, or inside a gopher's multicoloured entrails. So far, the only place that seems promising is this pathway into the wilderness.

Finally we arrive at a lake that is too big to walk around. Standing on the crest of a huge granite promontory, we gaze out at a great vista of wrinkled water and islands, and a faraway opening that might be the mouth of a river or a creek.

"Looks like a dead end," announces Dennis.

The wind is filled with the peaty scent of the lake, and the water is green and rough, slopping against the rocks far below. That far-off narrows might be a river mouth, in which case it would be worthwhile to bring the canoe next time.

"We should climb a tree," I suggest. "Get a look at the far end of the lake."

Dennis sits down. "You climb one, major."

We have a rotating system of command. The others guys criticize you until you get crabby, and then someone else takes over. I'm not a very good climber. But sometimes doing the dirty work is the price of holding office.

The big white spruce has stout branches that are spaced like ladder rungs. And without much strength or climbing expertise, I am able to climb to a frightening height. I climb so high that I can feel its monstrous trunk stirring in the wind. The branches open like windows on the lake, and I can see that the far-off opening is definitely a creek mouth. Bordered with lime-coloured marsh grass, it winds sinuously out of sight. With a stout branch serving as a seat, I sit up there for several minutes, feeling the tree sway, and feeling the clean wind. I can hear the boys shouting at me but I ignore them.

They can climb up here and see for themselves. Maybe someday I'll come back here without them. Maybe when I get older I'll have a girlfriend, and she'll enjoy exploring the wilderness too. We can paddle up that river and find out where it leads.

ꙮ

Three drawings are completed now.

I've got them in a neat pile on the corner of my desk. There's one portrait of our yellow cottage on a summer day, one of a giant snapping turtle hauled out on a log, and one of Big Sam crossing a treacherous, half-frozen river with his dog team.

When we're finished with our drawings, Sister George will stuff them in the garbage. Schoolteachers haven't yet become "educators," and they're not in the habit of praising their little darlings' work and mounting it on the walls. My parents have been better supporters of my artwork, and last year my dad took me to meet Dick Sutton, the curator of the Manitoba Museum. Dick Sutton is quite a wildlife artist, and he showed me some of his own pencil sketches, and some paintings in the museum by different artists. My favourite Canadian painter is a guy named A.Y. Jackson, whose cold lakes, rocky ridges, and gnarled jack-pines remind me of the landscape around Rosena. Sister George isn't quite as keen on art, and she usually throws our stuff away as soon as the class is over. So Kenny and I usually try to compare our pictures when her back is turned.

Catching Kenny's eye, I display my portrait of Big Sam and carefully pass it over to him. Kenny scrutinizes the picture. He'll probably add something, like a wolverine crouching in the branch of a tree, getting ready to pounce on Big Sam's head. We sometimes do this – pass the same picture back and forth, layering on plot twists like dime novelists complicating a mystery. We're not defacing each other's work. We're trying to work within the realistic possibilities of the scene. If Kenny challenges me with a wolverine, I'll have to counter the threat. Perhaps I'll sketch Fabian into the background, bringing up the rear in his own dog sled, drawing his Colt revolver as he spies the looming threat from the pugnacious little member of the weasel family.

Kenny shoulder-checks, then shows me his own picture, a fine landscape of a clear morning on an island in the south Pacific, circa August 1942. In the foreground is a flat sandy beach and some ratty palm trees. It looks like an island in the Solomons, perhaps Guadalcanal. We attend a lot of war movies, and we're pretty much up to date on our Pacific battle sites and aircraft recognition. He's drawn a Japanese Zero dive-bombing out of the sun, hosing hot lead at a squad of American Marines. They're galloping down the beach, but they can't outrun a pair of drum-fed Mitsubishi wing cannons. Body parts are flying in all directions, smeared with lurid Crayola splashes of blood and liquefied brain matter. Walking past Kenny's desk, Sister George looks at his drawing and just shakes her head. Miss Roma would probably be shocked by the mayhem that issues from our imaginations, but Sister George, in her discouraging way, knows us better than anyone.

There's still ten minutes left in the class, enough time for me to create one more scene. Sharpening my blue pencil, I stare across the room, watching the snowflakes feather past the windows. Where should I go? Mathematics class comes next, so this is our last few minutes of happiness. While I ponder my choices, Sister George opens the door and walks across the hall, confers with Sister William, who teaches the adjoining class. Both doors are open, and I can see into the other room.

This gives me an opportunity to catch a side view of Teresa, a pretty blond girl who sits in the other Grade 6. Like us, they're listening to the CBC Manitoba School Broadcast, and Teresa's face is clenched with concentration as she works at her sketch. Upright as a quail's topknot, her blond ponytail quivers as she leans over her page, scribbling furiously. I can't see what she's working on, but it seems to be a large piece, with paper drooping off the sides of her desk. She's wearing a bulky turtleneck sweater, a pleated skirt, and her long thin legs are all intertwined beneath her desk.

Teresa is a good subject, so I begin planning a wilderness scene in which she's a central figure. For me, human beings are difficult to draw. I can produce an excellent sketch of a leaping fish or a galloping horse. But my human beings end up looking like they were drawn by Picasso during his eye-in-the-forehead phase. Faces, in particular, defeat me. There are dozens of muscle packages in a person's face, and with every nuance of thought and feeling, the average face goes through changes that are as subtle as the movement of wind on water. If you get the slightest detail wrong, the tilt of the nose or the clench of the jaw, your portrait suddenly becomes a caricature. So the only way I can draw Teresa is by copying her profile, bit by bit.

I'll draw a scene in which we're paddling a canoe. We'll paddle a canoe up that wilderness river at the top end of Rosena.

With scrupulous care, I draw the prow of the canoe curving down to the waterline, a ripple coming off the hull, and then Teresa's figure in the front seat. After a few minutes I've got her blocked in, sitting in the front of the canoe, graceful and straight-backed, drawing a bow and arrow to aim at some distant target. The canoe is a birch-bark type, and she's dressed like an Indian. I like conceiving of the two of us as Indians, because Indians are pure of heart and they wear fewer clothes. As I study her facial profile she raises her head, glances across the hall, and catches me looking at her. This is potentially embarrassing. But she evidently assumes that our eyes have met only by coincidence, and subtly wiggles her fingers in greeting. I nod, and we both return to our work.

I'll keep drawing her, but I'll have to sneak glimpses. I have some kind of relationship with Teresa, but I'm not sure what it is. It's difficult to evaluate the relationship because we've exchanged only about a dozen words all year. At the beginning of the school year, she moved here from England, and she speaks with a musical English accent that only deepens my suspicion that she's some kind of fairy princess who's flown all the way across the ocean with the sole mission of breaking my heart.

The fact that we've barely spoken all year makes me suspect that she likes me too. In Grade 6, the rules of romance are well understood. If you have no particular affection for someone, you talk openly with each other. But if you have a crush on someone, you never talk to one another – not a word. You look away when you run into each other in the hall, ride your bike in the other direction if you encounter each other in the neigh-bourhood, and leave the table, immediately, if you happen to end up sitting together at lunch time. You finally come to iden-tify each other by a process of elimination.

The only time Teresa and I ever had a conversation was on a Sunday night when we ran into each other at the skating rink. My father is a good skater who plays inter-office hockey and is urging me to play organized hockey with the various teams at Crescentwood community club. But I've never really enjoyed the high seriousness of those Saturday afternoon games, where all the kids suit up like little gladiators, and the spectators scream for blood. Like most of my buddies, I prefer the pick-up hockey games we organize by ourselves, at night, when the adults aren't around, and where we can all pretend to be the legendary Andy Bathgate, Gordie Howe, or the regal Jean Beliveau.

On savagely dark Manitoba nights, when my single-paned bedroom windows are rimed with frost, and Ed Russenholt the TV weatherman is predicting overnight temperatures of 32 degrees below zero, I can't wait to finish Sunday dinner so that I can sling my hockey bag over my shoulder and head for the rink. Usually when I arrive, a gang is already there. Some kids will be wearing pads, and some won't. Some can't even afford skates and will be galloping around in rubber boots. But there's a rough egalitarianism to our games. Left to our own devices, we make difficult decisions on our own, and there's never a fight or even an argument during our dire scrimmages.

On the Sunday night when I had my conversation with Teresa, it was so cold that my mother wanted me to stay home. But I had important work to do – I had to practise my slapshot. For anyone who doesn't pay attention to hockey, I should provide some background. It's 1962, and the Montreal Canadiens are unbeatable. They've won five straight Stanley Cup titles, and there's no longer any doubt that they are the greatest team in history. Beliveau is the captain, the slight graceful Dickie Moore is the league's top stickman, and Rocket Richard chases the puck so intently that when William Faulkner attended his first hockey game a few years ago, he described Richard's fierce dark eyes as reminiscent of the "passionate glittering fatal quality of snakes."

Among them is Bernard "Boom Boom" Geoffrion, a hockey idol who has devised a whole new way of shooting the puck. Traditionally, there have been only two ways to shoot the puck – a wrist shot or a backhand shot. When Bernie Geoffrion was twelve years old, playing hockey at a local rink in Montreal, he missed an easy goal one day and took a frustrated golf swing at the puck, sending it sailing over the boards. He was so impressed by the speed and loft of the unintentional shot that he started secretly practising it. He worked on it for years, and when he signed on with the Montreal Canadiens in 1951, he brought a new and fearsome weapon with him – the slapshot. It changed the game of hockey forever.

Sports writers wax poetic about the slapshot's blistering 100-mph speed and the terrible roar it makes when it strikes the boards. But for me, the slapshot is a thing of beauty. A slapped puck floats the length of the rink in slow motion, as if suspended from the laws of gravity, and enters the goal with such vehemence that the net billows like a flag. Word on the street has it that you can pull off a cheater slapshot if you slice open a soda straw and tape it along the bottom edge of your stick. And I've tried that, tried everything in fact, but the magic of Boom Boom's slapshot still eludes me. For that reason, dangerous wind chills or not, I go to the rink every Sunday night to practise.

That Sunday evening, as I got within sight of the rink, I saw that the big mercury vapour lights above the hockey rink were turned off and the clubhouse was dark. Normally you saw little shadows racing back and forth, and heard the warlike boom of the puck striking the boards. But tonight, all I heard was the whisper of the night wind, and a distant, bell-like sound that was like a child singing. Singing?

I paused at the edge of the wide-open field and listened. Yes, it was certainly a voice. So I trudged closer and saw that it was Teresa. She was cutting loops and figure-eights, and singing to herself as she whirled. I knew the song, and liked it. I'd heard it a few times on Bob Burns' *Top 10 Countdown*. It was called "I Told Every Little Star." The way Teresa sang it, in a proper English accent, the song sounded inadvertently comical, like Julie Andrews singing Brenda Lee.

When Teresa became aware of my presence, she waved. I approached the rink and asked her if any of the guys had been here, playing hockey. She said they'd been here, but the manager never arrived to turn on the lights so they went home. We talked about school a bit, and I laced on my skates and took to the rink, thumping the boards with the puck while Teresa cavorted at the far end of the rink. When I got out of breath I rested for a moment and observed the scene. A winter moon illuminated the ice. Teresa was practising her jumps and twirls. And as she went spinning through the air, scintillae of light flew away from her fingertips.

I returned to my work, shooting the puck. I felt that there was something deeply intimate and weighty about the two of us inhabiting this pool of ice and darkness. This was what I imagined marriage might be like, two people occupying the same silent place, joined by mystic understanding.

Since then, I've felt that Teresa and I have a secret relationship. And my appreciation of her deepens as I draw the line of her back, and the clench of her slender arm as she draws back the bowstring. If I were a sculptor, I'd carve her in white marble or stamp her image on a coin. But I'll do the best with what I have – this sheet of general-purpose mimeograph paper embossed with tiny flecks of mashed bark.

In my drawing, it's a hazy summer evening on Rosena Lake. Ripples of pastel water curve away from the canoe as it slides through the lily pads. The sun is down; the sky is piled with burning clouds. I'm in the stern of the canoe, paddling. At least the guy in the stern of the canoe started out being me. Then he developed a hawk nose, ponytail, and big shoulders. I seem to have put on some weight and acquired a tan. Teresa is wearing a buckskin skirt with a big knife at her waist, and a rawhide sort of brassiere with fringes along the front. She has a quiver of arrows slung over her bare shoulder, and a blue jay feather fluttering from her ponytail. She's holding the wooden longbow at full draw, aiming at something just ahead of the canoe.

Maybe a dog would be a good addition to the picture – a stalwart dog like Eubie, the dog that guarded my parents on their honeymoon. My brown pencil is poised just above the mid-point of the canoe, preparing to sketch in the dog's head, when it occurs to me that Sister George has re-entered the room and is standing behind my desk, looking over my shoulder.

"My goodness," she mutters. "What's this?"

I look over at Kenny's desk. Is Kenny in trouble again?

She seizes the pencil from my hand, leans down, and begins drawing on my picture. "Give the girl some clothes, for heaven's sake!" Using the soft brown pencil she covers Teresa's upper body with brown cross-hatching that looks like fur. Wielding the pencil furiously, she scribbles in a pair of long sleeves and then a long skirt down below Teresa's knees. She hands me back the pencil, mutters in disgust, and moves on.

Kenny looks at me, smirks.

Folding my arms, I lean back in my desk. She's wrecked my picture.

This is what I mean. Last year I was a contented kid. But now I'm angry. I don't want to be here. This classroom is like a jail. One day, I swear to God, I'm going to escape this place. I'm going to climb the wall and head for the wilderness.

It'll be my salvation.

∾

It took twelve years before I made the break.

My twenty-fourth birthday found me enrolled in the University of Manitoba, in a master's program in English literature, and lacking only two more courses for my degree – Old English (*Beowulf*) and Practical Criticism (with an emphasis on semiotics). My plan was to finish those courses in summer school.

When I was a kid, I never imagined that I'd be spending my adulthood in seminar rooms with form-fit plastic chairs and acoustic tile on the ceiling. I never imagined that I'd be spending my evenings hunched over a desk, trying to decipher the turgid prose of Jacques Derrida and Edmund Spenser. I imagined that I'd have some kind of exciting job like bush pilot or forest ranger. I wasn't quite sure what forest rangers did all day, but I thought the duties probably involved having a green truck, a pet timber wolf, and a pretty girlfriend in a checkered blouse. Silly as they might sound, those were my expectations. Everyone has expectations. Mine didn't work out for a variety of reasons, the most important one being that I got sick.

After getting home from my camping trip to Rosena, my lower back became so painful that I could barely walk. My parents took me to the hospital in Kenora, where the doctors looked me over, shrugged, and sent me to Misericordia Hospital in Winnipeg, where I spent three weeks getting X-rayed, probed, and paraded in front of different medical teams. They cut open my chest and chiselled some bone out of my clavicle, sent it to the lab, and found nothing. They conducted every blood test in the book, and checked my heart for viral fever. They stuck periscopes up different bodily openings and had a look. Finally they gave up and sent me to a larger hospital in downtown Winnipeg, where I spent another three weeks going through the same tests and various new ones.

One of them was a bone marrow biopsy, a procedure so crude that it's best compared to the medieval technique of brain trepanning. They wheel you into a room and freeze the skin of your lower back with a horse needle. Assorted broad-shouldered assistants circle the table, murmuring calm reassurance and getting ready to hold you down. Then a doctor uses a power drill to punch a hole into the flat bone of your lower back. Once he's drilled into the inner pelvis, he draws out the marrow with a plastic tube. The vacuum tube makes a festive gurgling noise, and the aching sensation of the marrow drawing out of your body gives you a sudden surge of panic, as if your vital juices were being drained by an enormous spider.

After taping a padded bandage onto my lower back, they sent me back to my room to await results. The results came back the next day and showed the same thing as the other tests – nothing. Medical people with clipboards came to my room and conducted long interviews. Doctors are a bit like cops. They distrust each other's investigative skills and want you to retell your story from the beginning. Eventually too, just like cops, they begin to suspect that you're making it all up. One day an orderly took me to the office of a young psychiatrist. He asked me questions designed to determine whether I was crazy. ("The nurses say that you refuse to take your afternoon nap. Do you resent authority?") After talking to me for a while, the psychiatrist confessed that he had no patience for hospitals, either, and sympathized with anyone who rebelled. "I don't know why they sent you here. But I guess we've got an hour to kill. Do you want to go get a bite to eat?"

The psychiatrist turned out to be a good guy. Like me, he was an aspiring adventurer who hadn't had any adventures, and we ended up swapping tales of our single camping trip. Hospitals, being pressurized environments, tend to reduce people to their essence. For every petty despot, there's some decent soul who is spending his or her whole life trying to help people. Patients are in such distress that the smallest act of generosity can burn itself into long-term memory. I know, for example, that I'll never forget the anonymous nurse who materialized at my bedside in the middle of the night, when a sudden assault of pain snatched me out of the world of dreams and flung me gasping and wide-awake into my hospital bed at three o'clock in the morning. In the dark, while the night-sounds of the hospital and the far-off city murmured around us, she rubbed my bare feet with her warm hands and told me stories about her dog, her dad, and her cottage at the lake. Then there was George, a campy middle-aged homosexual nurse, a man with perfect hair and hands like a jazz piano player, who could whip off a bandage or slip in an IV needle with such deftness that you never felt a thing. I first met George when I was getting ready to go into the O.R. for the shoulder bone biopsy, lying alone on a stretcher with a tube in my arm.

There's a kind of fatal gloom to the décor and lighting of the surgical wing, and as I lay there, I pondered all the things I was going to miss about life. I was going to miss the fact that I was never going to have a girlfriend. I was going to miss riding through Europe in a train with her, or canoeing the Oiseau River in northern Ontario, and sleeping together while the rain pattered on our cozy tent. I was going to miss a lot of things. And I couldn't figure out any way to get them back, because I'd never had them in the first place. Worst of all, there was no one I could summon for help. I had always been raised to believe that in times of crisis, you could go to an adult, who would chuckle and explain that you were mistaken, and there was actually nothing to worry about. But this was the real thing, and no human being could save me from it, not the doctors, not the nurses, not even my father, who knew everything, and was afraid of nothing, and approached all problems with the calm, sauntering purposefulness of Gary Cooper in *High Noon*. This was a bogeyman I had to face alone.

I was therefore searching for a perspective of some kind, a little psychic amulet that I could clutch when it was time to go into the operating room, when a great hulking furry-browed gorilla of a man with a voice like Judy Garland sashayed into the room and spotted me lying there. "How are you doing, chum?" he asked, patting me on the shoulder. He checked my IV line and glanced down at my face. "Are you doing all right?"

What kind of a question was that? Being a homo, he must surely know that I was not doing all right. Like him, and like everyone else in this hospital, I was definitely not doing all right. But he was one of those people who have mastered the knack of taking the tragedy of life and flipping it over into repartee and humour. You could tell by the bounce in his walk. He adjusted my intravenous line and winked at me. "You're going to be fine," he said, with the authority of an old campaigner. He said it with a confidence based on inside knowledge. He promised me I'd be fine, and I believed him. And still do.

The operation, of course, turned out to be no worse than getting a tooth pulled. Every time we go into a hospital we think we're going to die, and we never die. Life goes on and on. It's like one of those films they make in Sweden. The results came back from the lab and showed the usual non-results. This was getting to be a real mystery. Or at least that was the way I preferred to think of it, as a gumshoe investigation, rather than the comic tale of a physical reject. Every night my family would troop into my room, brothers and sisters, cousins, and of course my mother, who would have camped at the foot of the bed if I had let her. But I didn't encourage long visits. They created the impression that I was a mere boy, a wheelchair-bound poster child, rather than some gallant young Hemingway type who'd taken a few slugs in the shins while holding off the fascists. So I usually feigned grumpiness and exhaustion until they left, then spent my evenings talking to my buddies on the payphone. One evening, after another round of tests had produced another round of non-results, my father came to visit and said he'd decided to take me to the Mayo Clinic to see if they could sort it out. It must have been expensive to fly me down to the United States and book me into a first-class American hospital, but my dad didn't seem bothered by it. And I wasn't bothered by it either. I saw it as an opportunity to go for a ride in an airplane. As soon as my dad left, I went down to the payphone and called my pal Kenny to tell him the good news.

"We're flying down to the States!"

"So they don't know what's wrong with you?" Kenny asked.

"Nope, they're stumped."

For some reason Kenny thought this was rich, and between coughing gales of laughter, kept asking me if it was really true that they didn't know what was wrong with me. He acted like this was one of our Johnny Horton Appreciation Nights in his living room, and I'd just told him the funniest story he'd ever heard.

I regarded myself as a fairly seasoned traveller. I'd been to Niagara Falls, for example, and on different occasions I'd taken automobile trips to Swift Current, Saskatchewan, and Fargo, North Dakota. But I didn't ride airplanes every day. In fact I'd never been on one before. So in preparation for the trip I dressed in a suit, necktie, and private eye–style trench coat. At the Winnipeg airport, we boarded a sleek and ultra-modern Trans-Canada Airlines four-engine Vickers Viscount turbo-prop and took off for Minneapolis. The Viscount was a first-rate ship (we seasoned aviators like to use nautical terminology). Her turbine engines were smoother than the radial engines on the old DC-3s she replaced, and in a recent big international air race from London to Christchurch, she had beaten her nearest competitor by nine hours. TCA ran a pilot school in Winnipeg, and Viscounts were always flying over our house. One day my brother Danny and I noticed a Viscount flying over the house with a dead engine, and its propeller spinning lazily. After spotting it, howling in alarm, jumping up and down, we sprinted into the house and grabbed my dad, who knows about these things, and he told us that it was only a training exercise. The pilot was probably practising landings with a dead engine. I'd always been an airplane-fetishist and had a home-built plastic Mustang, a Zero, a Catalina flying boat, and even a scale-model Viscount hung on threads from my bedroom ceiling. The Viscount flew proudly among those warplanes for several months until it became soaked with lighter fluid one day and crashed, full of screaming passengers, into my backyard.

After a month at the Mayo Clinic, they diagnosed me with an obscure condition called anklyosing spondilitis. Its genesis is complicated, but in essence it's triggered when your body gets invaded by a very smart little bacterium. We already have billions of bacteria inside our bodies, and most of them do good work. So when a new bacterium enters our body, our immune system reviews its documents to see if it's a friend or foe. Enemy bacteria are always trying to figure out ways to slip past the guards. In my case, a bacterium called HLA-B27 entered my body wearing the disguise of a human cartilage cell. A patrolling antibody arrested the suspect and, after a bit of confusion, decided to err on the side of caution and destroy it. The antibody dispatched a description of the suspect to the central immune system, and it relayed the information to the other patrols. Antibodies are well intentioned, but they aren't noted for their ability to think outside the box. They just follow orders. Other antibodies soon discovered other cells that resembled HLA-B27 and destroyed them too. Trouble is, they weren't enemy bacteria, they were cartilage cells. This destruction of natural cartilage caused distress and inflammation to my spine, which in turn triggered a more aggressive response from my immune system. After two months in Winnipeg hospitals and a month at the Mayo Clinic, the whole lunatic feedback cycle began to settle down, and I could walk again.

My doctors told me that my prognosis was hard to predict. They told me that I should avoid heavy lifting and overexertion. They said I might totally recover, and on the other hand, I might have recurring episodes and wind up with a stiff back. With most victims (the syndrome occurs in only one of ten thousand people) the prognosis is somewhere in between. I hoped that I'd be one of the lucky ones.

When I got back to Winnipeg, I reviewed my options. It seemed that I wouldn't be able to seek a career as a trapper, lumberjack, or some other type of outdoorsman, so I decided to become a pilot. I figured that it couldn't be a physically arduous job. My new buddy, Chris, had the same ambition, and while we walked the streets of River Heights, we played a game where you had to identify the name and model of airplanes flying overhead by listening to their engines.

Chris was a little older than I was, and by the time he was sixteen he was taking flying lessons. After he soloed, he took me out flying with him. As most people do, he was learning to fly on the Cessna 150, a little trainer that aviation schools rent out to students. On spring evenings, instead of studying for our Grade 11 final exams, we'd go out to the Winnipeg Airport and practise stalls and spins. You weren't allowed to practise over a built-up area, so we'd fly west and level out at 4,500 feet over the great checkerboard of fields beyond the city. Practising stalls and spins is a required part of every pilot's training, and it sounds more dangerous than it really is.* To incite a spin, you first have to incite a stall. Most non-pilots think that when an airplane

---

* Although some planes have a scary plaque riveted to the instrument panel – *Do Not Intentionally Spin This Aircraft.*

"stalls" the motor cuts out. But in aviation, the term "stall" refers to a wing that has lost its lift. To stall an airplane, you pull the stick back and commence a steep climb. It's like ascending to the top of the arc on a playground swing. The plane pauses, shudders, and then tips over and nosedives. As it's falling, it begins to corkscrew. With your stomach hovering up in your throat somewhere, you shut off the throttle, push the stick forward, and apply hard opposite rudder, a kind of kicking motion that draws the plane out of the spin. Chris let me try all these manoeuvres too: stalling the plane, spinning it, landing it. It was illegal, but he was my buddy.

As soon as I turned eighteen, I paid $25 and went to have my medical at the CNR station. To loosen up, I gobbled a fistful of aspirins ahead of time, but the doctor was a wise old fellow who sensed that something was amiss. He made me jump up and down and touch my toes until he ascertained that I seemed to have some kind of stiffness in my lowest three or four vertebrae. The stiffness was, of course, working its way up my spine. But I was involved in the full zest of teenage denial and believed that the doctor should just sign his name on that sheet of paper, and I could go off and become a Class One commercial pilot. He flunked me, of course. And the last I heard of Chris, he was an Air Force major, flying Starfighters in Germany.

Once again, I considered my future. In high school, the only course I'd ever excelled at was English. I'd always been an avid reader, and my schoolteachers had sometimes complimented me on my creative writing – stories written in scrupulous longhand, bound in Duo-Tang folders, and illustrated with coloured pencil (*Curse of the Rabid Wolverine*). I wasn't producing these stories out of some long-term ambition to become a writer. I knew that most writers were rich American expatriates who lived in places like Cuba and Paris. I was writing them because it offered the same creative satisfaction that you might get from puttering away on an intricately detailed model airplane. For as long as you focused on the project, you were free. It was just like flying, except you didn't need a pilot's licence.

I therefore began writing stories, and after graduating from high school and starting university, I decided to specialize in English literature. I thought I might eventually become a university professor. I didn't know much about professin' work, but I imagined that a professor's duties involved wearing comfortable old tweed jackets, reading great novelists and poets, and showing a willingness to become the confidant of numerous flaxen-haired young coeds in black turtleneck sweaters.

Over the next few years I discovered that I was misinformed. The leftist intelligentsia had formed a sort of unofficial politburo that set the tone on campuses across North America. Under the new regime, nobody studied great poets any more. They studied great theories. Poems about nightingales and graveyards were written by DWEMs (dead white European males) and were therefore passé. To become an English professor under the new order, you had to know your "semiotics" – structuralism, deconstructionism, or one of the many other *isms*, most of which regarded classical literature as a sort of appalling remnant of colonialism. Instead of sitting in my study carrel pondering *Tintern Abbey*, I pondered passages like this:

> Saussure focused on linguistic signs, whilst Peirce dealt more explicitly with signs in any medium, and noted that the relationship between signifiers and their signifieds varies in arbitrariness – from the radical

arbitrariness of symbolic signs, via the perceived simi-
larity of signifier to signified in iconic signs, to the
minimal arbitrariness of indexical signs.

I hung in, thinking that once I got my Ph.D., I could get a
job teaching on Vancouver Island or some place where they
hadn't yet heard about the Death of Literature. I'd buy a rambling old house by the sea, acquire a Jeep and a dog, and settle
into a rustic literary life. During my four-month-long summer
vacations, I'd do some writing and perhaps build a boat with
my own hands. But as I advanced into graduate school, I also
began to notice that everyone avoided one question – would
there actually be jobs available when we graduated? My
professors acted as though the subject of employment was
beneath them. And if I couldn't ask them, who could I ask?
Some of my fellow students might have been studying semiotics
because it was just so darned fascinating. But I wanted to get
something out of my degree, and I was worried that there might
be nothing more than a brown envelope and a diploma waiting
for me when I finally graduated. University enrolments were
dropping, and some of my seminar groups had only a handful
of students. One seminar consisted of exactly one student – me –
and the professor who ran the class made it clear that she'd lose
a third of her income if I dropped out. I had three more years of
this ahead, plus a thesis. And by the time I hit the job market, I
feared that my doctorate in semiotics would qualify me to drive
a cab anywhere in North America.

So that bright green summer morning in June, as I cruised
down the road towards the University of Manitoba, I suddenly
experienced such an intense attack of ambivalence that I

pulled over to the side of the road and sat there with the turn signal blinking.

What should I do? Should I quit school and try something else? Or should I keep a stiff upper lip and finish what I started?

The logical half of my brain suggested that I should carry on, or live forever with the knowledge that I was a craven quitter. I'd signed up for graduate school, and it was my duty to finish it. Apprenticeships in any field are designed to weed out the weaklings. And nothing is easy.

The other half of my brain – the half that always got me in trouble – argued that it wasn't a matter of being a quitter. I'd given university a good shot, and it wasn't working out. The longer I stayed, the worse it was going to be when I finally bailed out.

I felt that I was sitting at a major fork in the road. Each choice seemed equally plausible and unacceptable. At times like this, people tend to fumble around for some tried and true formulaic way of making decisions. And as I sat there, pondering my future, I recalled a tiny bit of allegorical wisdom from my old hardcover wilderness survival book, *I Live in the Woods*. The author, Paul Provencher, had spent his whole life working as a timber cruiser in northern Quebec. He never explained what a timber cruiser does all day. (I guess we're supposed to know that.) But he spent a lot of time explaining how to avoid getting lost in the woods.

People get lost because they get caught up in the details. When you're down in the underbrush, climbing over deadfalls and detouring around thickets, you quickly lose your sense of grand direction. You can't see the forest for the trees. According to him, you have to ignore the immediate environment while you're travelling, and concentrate on following a line, which you maintain by keeping your eye on distant landmarks. You pick a tall, odd-looking tree that's a mile away, for example, and move towards that. At the same time, you maintain a sense of the path behind you. You stop, once in a while, and look back on the distant landmarks you've passed. When you lose sight of where you're going, you have to look back at where you've been.

∾

When I was a boy, I thought I sprang up out of these scruffy Winnipeg sidewalks like a prairie weed. But now that I was in university, studying literature and history, I was beginning to understand that everyone in this country came from somewhere else.

I'd learned that the MacDonalds came from the Scottish Highlands, and that in the old days, the English regarded all Highlanders as illiterate savages who stood in the way of British sovereignty. I'd read about the ethnic cleansing of the Highlands and the royal edict that resulted in "every MacDonald under the age of seventy" being dragged from his bed and put to the sword at Glencoe. And I'd seen the 1747 Act of Proscription, in which the English parliament banned the teaching of Gaelic, the wearing of tartan, and the playing of bagpipes. I'd read that the Scots were gradually harassed and bullied off their lands by wealthy men who wanted to convert their small plots into large sheep ranches. In 1773, a group of 179 of those landless farmers sailed to Nova Scotia aboard a ship called the *Hector*. They were my ancestors.

According to old newspaper clippings and other historical records, the MacDonalds carried on doing what they knew best, working the land. One newspaper obituary, for example, describes my great-grandfather, John MacDonald (who passed away on December 25, 1907), as a man of "sterling and upright character" who spent his entire life farming the same plot of land. His son, my grandfather, drifted down to Halifax and moved west in search of work. He wound up migrating to what Churchill called "the breadbasket of the empire," the western prairies, and found a job in Winnipeg selling farm equipment for John Deere. He must have been good at it, because I've seen photos of his big house on the river, and pictures of his son, my dad, going off to school at the University of Toronto, and then later in his naval officer's uniform, going off to war.

When I got to know my grandfather he was already an elderly man, but a strong and independent one. Every Sunday when he came over for dinner, my brother and I would run to the window and watch him arrive. He stood six foot three and until he was ninety-three moved with the measured saunter of someone athletic enough to shoot his age in golf. He always looked somewhat intimidating in his dark business suit and necktie. Spotting us at the window, he never smiled. His face was like the face of those stone-faced men you see in the framed portraits stacked in dusty piles upstairs in country antique stores. While my mother prepared dinner, my brother and I would sit in the living room and try to talk to him. Those were our marching orders – go and talk to your grandfather. One of the fingers on his right hand was missing. No matter how many times we asked him about his missing finger, he always said the alligator ate it. He wore a Freemason's pin on his lapel, and during dinner, he would often launch into a speech my brother and I had memorized word for word: his personal indictment of the cowardly French under Duplessis. Nobody ever argued with him, not even my dad, who was a lefty and knew his history.

He was, in other words, not one of those twinkly-eyed and kindly old grandfathers you saw on Sunday nights on the Walt Disney show. But he had emotions, buried somewhere under that dark suit. Every year at Easter, he would pull his curtains and take his phone off the hook and remain incommunicado for several days, listening to *Messiah* and weeping. He disliked cities and always mourned the fact that he'd left the Nova Scotia farm and spent his life working in a city. He sometimes told us stories about his childhood, growing up on the family homestead, and he told us that when we grew up, we should go and find a place in the country, a little house on a river, with trees and birds all around, a place where you could get up every morning and feel God's earth under your feet.

I'd already decided that's what I wanted to do. But his sermons on that subject made me realize there was a continuity of purpose stretching back through the generations. Casting my eye back over a century of family history, I could see that the MacDonald men had always tried to stay connected to the land. The idea of being a farmer didn't appeal to me. But when my grandfather talked about being part of the land, I don't think he was talking about sitting on a tractor driving back and forth all day, chewing on a straw and thinking about hog prices. He was talking, I believe, about being in touch with unbroken earth – wild earth like the plot of woods down at the end of the field where the creek made its turn, and the blackbirds teetered among the bulrushes, flashing their red wings and singing like rusty gate hinges. My dad's favourite poet was Gerard Manley Hopkins, which surprised me, since Hopkins was a Jesuit and my dad never had much time for the church. But some of Hopkins's work summed up nicely what he and my grandfather probably felt about Nature:

What would the world be, once bereft
Of wet and wildness? Let them be left,
O let them be left, wildness and wet;
Long live the weeds and the wilderness yet.

When my grandfather died, he left me a bit of money, which I used to buy a delivery van. I fixed it up with shag carpeting and a fridge and a bed, and whenever I had a bit of time and a few hundred dollars, I went off exploring. I wanted to find my own little piece of wild earth. Several of my friends wanted to do the same thing too. So we hit the road and did the research. On various trips, we drove from Alaska to Florida and back again. We explored California, investigated the offshore islands of the Carolinas, and drove down into Mexico. We combed the Midwest, and we combed Texas. We even combed Wheeling, West Virginia, home of WWVA, the hillbilly radio station that drifted like a spectral fog all through the night skies of the eastern seaboard and once, long ago, convinced a Nova Scotia farm boy named Hank Snow to buy his first guitar.

We had many adventures, but it seemed that we'd arrived late. The music had stopped, and every chair in the United States was taken. You couldn't drive from Boston to Miami and find a single piece of ocean-front real estate that wasn't grabbed up, developed, or fenced off in anticipation of an exciting new condominium project. (That we couldn't afford to buy an exciting new condominium didn't seem relevant. The point was that we didn't want one.) The more I travelled, the more I realized how lucky we were to live in Canada, where the wilderness started an hour's drive outside any major city and sprawled all the way up to the Arctic.

Despite the superiority of American myth-making, it eventually occurred to me that the best country in North America was in fact our own, so I began spending more time exploring the Canadian backwoods. I thought it was a good place to investigate the big mystery that everybody knows is out there. I didn't know what the Big Mystery was, but all those travels, images, and memories felt like pieces of a puzzle, and I was intrigued by the idea that they might eventually add up to something one day – if not an "answer," then perhaps a code to live by, or an insight of some kind into the principles that make the world tick.

In Canada, the challenges are approximately the opposite of what you encounter in the States. In the United States, it's all been explored, and everything is spoken for. In Canada, it's all wide open, and there's so much wilderness you don't know where to begin. I felt the deepest connection to the myriad lakes and sprawling wilderness of the Shield country. It was the great blank space on the Canadian map, the desolate realm studied by painters like Tom Thomson, and mined for symbolism by writers like Hugh MacLennan. ("This anomalous land, this sprawling waste of timber and rock and water . . . this tract of primordial silences and winds and erosions and shifting colours . . .") It was the landscape that first captured my heart when I was a kid, and it was where I always imagined myself building a cabin one day.

But where would I begin? The Shield country is big – very big. It covers about half of Canada, which is an area of land about the size of the Indian subcontinent. If you were looking down at it from outer space, you'd see different zones of vegetation covering it. The southern edge of the Shield is clad with the so-called Great Lakes forest, which is mostly hardwoods, mixed with spruce and pine. A little farther north, the hardwood forests transition into boreal forest, which is dominated by jackpine and black spruce. In the boreal forest, soil is thin to nonexistent and the ground is covered by duff – a thin carpet of matted pine needles and moss. In many places there's not even much duff, just bare rock, weathered granite that has been sanded by so many glaciers that it resembles bleached skull, covered with a ragged scalp of moss and thumbtack trees.

Farther north the boreal forest yields to the taiga zone, a featureless monoculture of bog and stunted spruce. The treeline at the top fringe of the taiga isn't so much a line as a ragged edge, beyond which the bent little spruce trees can't stagger any farther into the north wind. The barrenlands aren't really barren. The landscape explodes to life with berries and flowers in the summer. The rivers swarm with fish and the hills are alive with caribou. It's hard to believe that this is the same geographical region as the heavily wooded Shield country of the south, but what all these habitats have in common is water – lots of water. Impervious granite makes for poor drainage, so everywhere you go on the Shield, north, south, east, or west, you'll see shimmering water. Water is often called an element but it's actually a compound, and it changes constantly. The way it moves, the way it smells, the way it vaults through granite predicaments and tumbles through a rapid: these are filled with enough nuance and subtlety to keep the observer entranced, as if watching a fire. Calm water, too, never stops changing. If you glide over glassy water on a hot day in summer, the slightest zephyr will alter its colour from pastel blue to olive black. And the slow-moving, tea-coloured water of the muskeg zone couldn't be more different from the cold water of Great Bear Lake, which is so transparent you can see the pebbled bottom at fifty feet. But although the water is infinitely various, wherever you go in the Shield it's also the same, in the sense that it's the Shield's defining feature. It's what brings people to its lakes every summer, to fish, to swim, to canoe, or just to sit on the decks of their cottages and stare at the water, as if observing an enigma.

Canada possesses only .05 per cent of the world's population, but our country contains about 30 per cent of the planet's fresh water, and the bulk of it resides in wilderness lakes, most of which don't even have names.* There's so much water that overland transportation is difficult, and highway construction is such an arduous undertaking that roads tend to be nasty and short. In the olden days, the principal means of travel was that unique Canadian invention, the canoe. Nowadays, the main method of getting around is the float-equipped airplane. The DeHavilland Beaver, the Twin Otter, and the Noorduyn Norseman were all designed in Canada specifically for travel on the Shield. And although Canadians tend to regard float planes as mundane transportation, foreign visitors are amazed when they drive through Kenora or Red Lake and see airplanes cruising along on top of what amounts to boxed-in aluminum canoes.

I couldn't afford to explore the Shield by airplane, so I drove the roads. The Trans-Canada Highway heading over the top of Lake Superior is, in places, as spectacular as the more famous Highway One along the coast of Big Sur, and has the added advantage of being deserted, because most trucks go around the

---

* Some lakes are named in honour of Canadian aviators who died in the wars. I met one family that camps out at a wilderness lake in the summer, in honour of their uncle, a Lancaster crewman killed at the age of eighteen.

south side of Lake Superior, through the States, which is a faster but less interesting route. The north shore is A.Y. Jackson country. He spent his formative years painting in rural Quebec, but eventually fell in love with the rugged northern Ontario wilderness. Like the other members of the Group of Seven, he became a lobbyist for the notion that the Canadian landscape is a worthwhile subject for serious art. That might seem like a self-evident proposal today, but his rough, uncultivated landscapes were haughtily dismissed by art critics of the day. I'd read a bit about him, and he seemed the most charismatic of that bunch, except for perhaps Tom Thomson, his pal and room-mate, whose legend, it should be allowed, has been burnished by the fact that he died mysteriously. Like Thomson, Jackson was a loner, an affable but solitary man who'd survived the inferno of the trench campaigns of the Great War and used the tonic of clean air and God's own wilderness to cure his heart. He liked roughing it, sleeping on the ground, and he undertook many explorations here, riding north in an Algoma Central boxcar with his legs hanging out the door, his backpack full of painting supplies on his knees, and the spectacular cliffs rolling past.

I went to visit a friend in Thunder Bay, who took me to a high precipice overlooking Lake Superior. You walk through the woods and come to a clearing where the flat rock just ahead of you drops into nothingness. The wind is so strong that you fall to your knees and crawl the last few yards to the edge, lest vertigo or an errant gust nudge you off. If you threw a penny, it would fall straight down, winking in the sun and drifting in the wind, falling forever. You can see for countless miles across the wrinkled lake, and it's so far down to the water that the tiny flecks of black ash far below are soaring ravens. In northern

Manitoba, in the midst of another road trip, I met a fellow who took me down beneath the Shield, rather than high above it. We donned boots and hard hats, climbed into a rude elevator cage, and descended into a nickel mine. It was a primitive mine, with makeshift equipment, no lights except for our headlamps, and a minimal crew of miners on duty. But still, the shaft went thousands of feet down into the earth, deep enough that when we fumbled our way along the wet, utterly dark tunnel at the bottom of the mine, the rough walls felt warm.

My long-term hope was to get past the reach of roads and rails, and spend the entire summer working in the wilderness.

∾

One spring day at the university I spotted a note on the bulletin board in front of the Canada Manpower Centre. It was only a hand-lettered file card, but it changed my life.

> Remote wilderness fly-in lodge in northern Ontario
> requires fishing guides. Must be skilled in boating and
> the outdoors, and enjoy working with people. Inquire
> within re. Bending Lake Lodge.

It sounded too good to be true. I went inside and scheduled an interview. A few days later I returned with my university chum Fariborz Tajidod, who'd grown up in Iran and had only a basic grasp of English, but shared an interest in nature and the outdoors. The lodge owner, a steely-eyed ex-military pilot named John Hansen, conducted the interview and seemed amused by our apparent willingness to tell him anything we thought he wanted to hear. "We have lots of white water on our river system," he warned us. "Would you be afraid of shooting rapids?"

Fariborz, who with his doe-eyed and slightly apprehensive manner resembled the young Dustin Hoffman, assured John Hansen that he'd seen many rapids and wasn't afraid of them. "In Tehran, my uncle shot a rapid in his garden."

After our final exams, Fariborz and I drove three hundred miles to Ignace, Ontario, where we reported to the local float-plane base to arrange for our ride into Bending Lake Lodge. Our pilot looked like he'd slept in his clothes. His plane, a beat-up old Beaver, had sooty exhaust pipes and dented sheet-metal floors congealed with half a century's worth of fuel oil, powdered milk, and moose blood. We climbed aboard and strapped ourselves into our seats and the engine exploded to life, trembling with a rough and guttural idle that sounded more like a tractor than a lighter-than-air flying machine. But soon enough we were roaring down the lake and lifting off, ascending a bumpy staircase of thermals into the extraordinary spring sunshine.

Down below the plane the country rolled off to the horizon, a patchy, rumpled mould culture of forest, rock, and hammered lakes glinting in the sun. What an adventure! I pressed my nose against the dirty window and drank it all in. Fariborz was sitting up front with the pilot, and at one point he leaned over and asked the pilot what would happen if the engine failed. The pilot gave him a grim look, reached over, and shut off the engine, and the plane nose-dived like a falling piano. After making his point, the pilot restarted the motor and we carried on. Eventually we arrived at Bending Lake Lodge: a rustic village of buildings on the south end of an otherwise uninhabited lake.

We were assigned bunkhouses and put to work. The guide contingent consisted of a few white university boys like us, and a dozen Ojibway men, most of whom had many years of guiding experience. It was early in May, and the fishing season wouldn't open for another few weeks, so the boss's priority was to whip the camp into shape and get the new rookies trained as guides. All day long we chopped firewood, repaired docks and levelled cabins, and went out to learn the river system with our Indian instructors. My teacher was Stewie, a thin young Ojibway man with Beatle boots, a pompadour hairdo, and a bad complexion. Stewie's routine was to pretend to see the cheerful side of any misfortune. Even if it was a cold and miserable morning, he always came hunching through the sleet with the same absurd greeting. "Hey dere, boys! Nice morning dis morning!"

The Turtle River system sprawled off for many miles in several directions, and white-water rapids formed links between the lakes. Stewie took me to fishing spots in the different lakes and paused long enough at each spot to demonstrate to our mutual satisfaction that he could whip my ass anytime when it came to jigging lake trout with a spinning rod. (He could out-fish almost anyone in camp.) He showed me how to run down the rapids and how to get back upstream again – slewing and bounding the boat through the powerful waves, dodging boulders, climbing the muscular chutes of green water, and quickly killing the motor to prevent the boat from capsizing if it suddenly was overcome by the force of a wave and sent caterwauling backwards. Like a kung fu master, he'd stand up on the high, slippery rocks and watch me trying to reproduce his performance, waving and pointing to hazards I couldn't see. When I swerved the boat sideways and filled it with water, he'd clutch his head in theatrical dismay, and when I did it right, he'd clap and grin, shouting inaudible praise across the roaring water.

Learning the rapids was nerve-racking work. Most of the rookie guides and a few of the less experienced Indian guides had close calls. One university student from Winnipeg reared his boat like a horse and flipped it back on himself in Number Six Upstream. He was pulled unconscious from the water and medivacced out to the hospital, where he eventually recovered and decided he didn't want to be a guide after all. Another guide, named Sidney, an Indian but an inexperienced one, swamped his boat and almost drowned. I was sure that my turn was coming up next, and when it came to practising the more difficult rapids, such as the fearsome Number Two Downstream, I was sometimes so apprehensive that I'd go into the bush and retch before climbing into the boat. But gradually I got the hang of it, and by the time the guests arrived on the May 24 long weekend, I was confident enough of my boat-handling skills that the familiar bounce and kick of the rapids felt more like an amusement ride than a toboggan run to hell.

Every night there was a card game in the Swingin' Teepee, the big bunkhouse where the Indians lived, and we white boys gradually got to be friends with the veteran guides, some of whom were walking encyclopaedias of knowledge about fish, animals, weather, and the bush. There was lots of wildlife around – moose were a normal sight along the river, and we had lots of problems with bears interrupting our shore lunches. The Indian guides knew these wild animals in a way that wasn't abstract but specific – based on personal experience: spending long months at a stretch in trappers' cabins with no company but a few squirrels living in the eaves, a car radio hooked up to a

12-volt battery, and the brooding silent forest right outside their door. A scientist might have known the Latin names of the local trees and wild animals, but old guides like Junior Robinson knew practical stuff, such as how a bear of a certain age, size, and gender would likely react if you tried to shoo it away. They weren't reluctant to share the information either, as long as you didn't mind a joke or pun included with the lesson. Spending days on the river with old-timers like Junior was like taking university classes in forest lore. And because the information was applicable to immediate problems at hand – like trying to preserve a campfire in the midst of a sudden downpour* – it was like studying French in France.

I guided two summers at Bending Lake Lodge, then managed to get a job doing the same thing up in the Northwest Territories, on Great Slave Lake, where we had to sleep with blankets on our windows because it never got dark, and the great high rocky cliffs along the lake were constructed of the oldest rock on the planet. Great Slave Lake is tremendously deep and cold. The camp was, and still is, one of the most prestigious sport-fishing lodges in the world, with crisp white buildings arranged with military orderliness on the remote east arm of the lake. Except for a few white guys, the guides were mainly Dene, and the lodge's guests were wealthy Americans, whom we took in pursuit of lake trout, which in the north grow to an enormous size. In frigid water, a lake trout grows only half a pound a year, and a fifty-pound trout is conceivably almost a century old. They look it too, ancient brutes with hooked jaws, battered heads, and the blank, stone gaze of a pagan idol. Great Slave is

---

* Throw a large rotten stump on the fire.

one of the largest lakes in the world, and we had to cross enormous passages of open water, not a pleasant experience in an open sixteen-foot boat. The water is only a few degrees above freezing, and when the wind started blowing, pushing fifteen-foot-high swells, it was like crossing the north Atlantic.

Sometimes we took the camp Norseman and flew side trips out to the barrenlands, to Artillery Lake, where the trout were black, or Lac Du Gras, a spooky place where the fish had enlarged heads and serpentine bodies, and were so desperate for food they'd almost chase the lure up onto shore. We went to the Thelon River, which is an arctic oasis surrounded by tundra, through which every autumn the tens of thousands of caribou of the Qaminurjuag and Beverly herds pour, and where the English eccentric John Hornby built a log cabin in 1926, determined to become this river's white lord. Like Mr. Kurtz, he was a charismatic loner, and he brought along disciples: two English schoolboys named Edgar Christian and Harold Adlar. Hornby planned to kill enough caribou to get them all through the winter, but the caribou never came. Apparently they usually come, but sometimes they don't. Hornby and the boys spent six months starving to death. Edgar Christian's journal was found with their skeletons the following year, and all three are buried behind the decrepit cabin, their graves marked by three rotted wooden crosses.

Sometimes, while my guests wandered the riverbank and fished, I'd sit on a glassy-smooth hump of granite next to a thundering rapid, soak up the sun, and wonder what I could learn from this primitive landscape. Like most English majors, I was reading a lot of contemporary poets, trying to decide which ones I most wanted to imitate. I favoured the California bunch, particularly Robinson Jeffers, who wrote of ancient tragedies like the Christ and Icarus legends. As a boy he built home-made wings and tried them out by jumping off a roof, and as a grown-up he often wrote of dangerous things – hawks, eagles, and other fierce-eyed flying creatures, symbols of the poetic impulse. He moved to Carmel, California, and on a hill above the ocean he built a stone house and an observation tower, from which he contemplated "the great blue eye of the Pacific," imagining that, like all great bodies of water, it was expressing an eternal truth, and that he needed to learn the ocean's own alien language before he could comprehend it.

These ancient rivers and lakes seemed to emit the same eternal message. But you'd have to be pretty naïve to think that you could decipher the code by bombing into a remote location like this and spending a few hours lounging by the rapids in your sunglasses. I suspected that you needed to slow down and pay attention to the water. You needed to spend some time here alone, like Siddhartha. I liked to kid myself that I was exploring the edges, but remote camps like Great Slave Lodge were just divots of civilization dug up and transplanted to the wilderness. We could drink canned beer as we explored this river, play with million-year-old fish species on ultra-light graphite spinning rods, and know all the time that there was a great dinner waiting for us back at the lodge. It was so comfortable that sometimes it seemed that we weren't in the wilderness at all. We were just looking at it, as if through protective eyewear.

Once I was back at school, cracking the books, I had to confess that my summer in the wilderness hadn't changed me much. How could it? I'd spent the whole summer surrounded by all the comforts of home. I fancied myself to be a woodsman, but the truth was, I'd never even spent a night alone in the forest.

It was just play-acting. And I was getting too old for that kind of thing. If I quit school, I had to roll up my sleeves and get serious about an alternative education. If I stayed in school, it was time to grit my teeth and make a long-term commitment to my Ph.D. program. Either way, I was tired of halfway measures. It was time to make a decision. For a few minutes I sat there. Then I shifted the van into gear and voted with my foot.

∽

For the next few days I gathered supplies – tent, lanterns, sleeping bag, tools, books, fishing rod, gun, boots, rain gear, rope, cooking utensils, and all the hundreds of other things you need to simplify your life. Hunting through the classified ads I found an old square-stern canvas-covered canoe with a 3-horse motor for $200.

Several days later, I pulled out of Winnipeg and headed east on the Trans-Canada Highway, with the wind humming in the guy ropes and the warm June air pouring in the window. Thirty miles east of Winnipeg, the highway climbs out of the old floor of Lake Agassiz and ascends a gentle gravel beach ridge into the great eastern forest. Scrubby poplar bush gradually turned to jackpine forest, and a few miles farther on, the first rocky outcrop appeared in the ditch. I stopped the van and took a look at it, squatted down and scraped away the scalp of dirt. This stub of granite marked the edge of the Shield.

An hour later, I stopped for coffee in a log-and-stone roadside restaurant, where bass and shovel-jawed pike hung from the walls. I ate lunch and browsed my maps, formulating a plan.

In my boyhood days, you couldn't drive any farther north than Rosena Lake. It was the end of civilization. But nowadays the map showed a crooked blue road that led farther north to the village of Minaki. When I was a boy, you could reach Minaki only by train. I liked the idea of driving there, going to the end of the road where you couldn't drive any more, then putting the canoe in the water and heading up the river. I liked the idea of studying the larger world by getting to know one specific place. As it says in the Bible, God is in the details.

Just before the town of Kenora, I took a left turn and headed up the rough gravel road to Laclu. I drove past the road into our family cottage, past the old wooden church and the dump where we used to hunt gophers when we were kids. It was eerie to be driving past these places, my old childhood haunts. Almost by accident, I was picking up where I'd left off. The road was in rough shape, and it took almost two hours before I finally bounced across the CNR tracks and into Minaki, a small community with lots of abandoned cars, dismantled snowmobiles, and crooked little unpainted plywood houses. Above the harbour was a train station, an antique and weathered-looking old building with geraniums in its window boxes, a chalkboard with train schedules on the wall, and a big block-lettered MINAKI sign hanging above the platform.

It was too late to launch the canoe, so I decided to sleep in the van. My best bet was probably to find a public parking lot. After checking out a few places down by the water, and rejecting them because they looked like private property, I drove over the hill and cruised down a long undulant driveway bordered by golf fairways. At the end of the driveway, backlit by a flaming sunset, stood a high castle of log and stone that I deduced to be

Minaki Lodge. My older sister Wendy had worked here as a waitress, years ago, and always described it as the most adventurous summer of her life.

After parking the van next to the golf course, I walked across the fairway to get a closer look at the lodge. The delicious aroma of prime rib and roasting potatoes wafted on the air, and violin music issued from the broad verandas. Walking up the flagstone steps and through the front door, I entered the Grand Rotunda, an immense hall appointed with stuffed elk heads and hanging tapestries. In the bookstore, I browsed through some guidebooks, some maps, and a short history of the lodge. According to the book, during the 1920s both the CPR and the CNR were involved in constructing some of the finest resort hotels in Canada. The president of the CNR, Sir Henry Thornton, got the idea of attracting business by offering plush cross-country railway tours of Canada, with overnight stopovers at grand resorts in each natural region. To showcase the Rockies, he built Jasper Park Lodge. In Nova Scotia, he built Pictou Lodge, and in the Shield country, he decreed the construction of this place.

His crews stripped the topsoil off a farm in Manitoba and shipped three thousand boxcars of earth to Minaki. They blasted away the granite and used the soil to upholster a rolling nine-hole golf course. They built a beautiful hotel that put the CPR to shame, and when it was finished, Sir Henry dubbed it the Minaki Inn. On June 11, 1925, one day before the lawn party marking the grand opening, a summer student employee accidentally set fire to a gallon of linseed oil and burned the place to the ground. Nice move, son.

Sir Henry started over again. This time, he brought in the Scottish stonemasons and Norwegian log builders who'd just finished Jasper Park Lodge. The fire was a cruel setback, but it also provided a unique opportunity for client, architect, and contractors to work out the wrinkles they'd encountered in putting up the first building. The new Minaki Lodge was completed in 1927 and was a masterpiece. Critics of the day described it as "the finest log structure in the world," and I could see why. As I stood reading the little history book, the evening sun poured down through the stained-glass windows and illuminated the high ceiling, which was a sixty-foot-high vault of interlaced blond logs hung with immense iron chandeliers.

Nowadays, Minaki Lodge was ailing. The CNR no longer owned it, and it was limping along from one private owner to another. The clerk in the bookstore said that the construction of the new highway had helped. But judging from the number of muffler pipes I'd seen littering the gravel road on the way, you wouldn't want to be coming here in an expensive car. "We're so far away from everything," he said. "If we had a big city like Toronto within a couple of hours, we'd be the most famous resort in Canada."

Walking down the hill, I checked out the water. You can't really say you've visited a place until you go down and look at the water. There's never anything much to look at, just waves splashing on the shore and a few seagulls flying by, but the water nevertheless seems to be where a resort's ineffable spirit resides. The water is why we're here. The lodge seemed to have a large fishing operation, maybe thirty Lund fishing boats tethered with military precision along the big dock. It was getting late, and the workday was over. But as I was standing there, one last fishing boat glided towards the dock. After manoeuvring his boat into its stall, the tanned young fishing guide snapped a lariat around a dock ring and stepped out. His Kodiak boots were well-scuffed, the collar of his denim jacket was flipped up, and a leather-sheathed knife dangled from his belt. I hadn't driven a boat since last summer and was immediately filled with nostalgia for the life of a guide – no worries, no ambitions. Just fooling around all summer like Tom Sawyer.

Climbing out, he dragged a monstrous fish onto the dock. His guests, a man and his wife, were clumsily trying to stuff film into their camera. Their hands were trembling with excitement. The fish was about four feet long and had gleaming wet skin that transmitted flashes of blue and silver iridescence, and gaping jaws that opened and closed dumbly as the guide hefted it for a photograph. The woman, who'd evidently caught it, stood beside him and smiled bravely while her husband snapped a picture. It was a muskellunge, a fish so mythic and elusive that I'd never even seen one before, although I'd been coming to this country for half my life.

Night was falling quickly, and I renewed my search for a campsite. Finally I pulled into a place called Murray's Camp, which looked like a fishing lodge, albeit one more humble than Minaki Lodge. According to my map, this was the end of the road. There wasn't another road, fence, or hydro line between here and Russia, so I felt like this was the perfect place to launch my exploration, a jumping-off place on the edge of the world.

I went looking for Murray. The river was invisible in the darkness but its scent drifted up through the trees. Bugs whirled around a high mercury vapour lamp. Under the light's glow a dapper old gentleman was walking across the lawn. He was sauntering along with a drinking man's wobbly-kneed walk, each tottery leg deployed as if by remote control. I hailed him and introduced myself.

He shook my hand and said his name was Don Campbell. He said that he owned the place and didn't know anyone named Murray. He said he had no idea how Murray's Camp had got its name, and that no, nobody had ever asked him about it before. He didn't seem surprised that I'd driven into his parking lot with everything I owned. He was Max Yasgur and I was just another hippie. "Just park it back in the trees where it'll be out of the way," he instructed in a Chicago drawl. "If you want to leave it for a while, that's okay. Just give me a couple of bucks whenever."

Moving the van to a quiet corner of the parking lot, I cleared out some space in the back for my sleeping bag. My faithful truck had done a good job today. In fact everything went more smoothly than I expected – no flat tires, no mechanical problems, and no mental breakdowns from my parents. Most of their seven kids were on their way to becoming doctors, lawyers, and prominent professionals of one sort or another, so one black sheep in the mix wasn't a bad average. Anyway, when your twenty-four-year-old son tells you that he wants to quit university, buy a tent, and go searching for the Lost Secret of the Canadian Shield, what else can you do but wish him good luck.

Before I got into my sleeping bag, I gobbled a couple of aspirins to numb the nagging pain in my back. It had been a long day of carrying, packing, loading, and driving, and my vertebrae weren't pleased. For most of my adolescent years, the stiffening of my lower back had been gradual enough that I was able to dismiss it with painkillers and healthy doses of denial. But lately, both tactics had been less effective. When I was working up at Great Slave, some of my guests had made comments ("What's the matter, did you hurt yourself?"). And it was becoming obvious, even to me, that things were getting worse. Oddly enough, this made me want more out of life, rather than less. Illness and the constant background ticking of Time's stopwatch make you greedy. I admired people like Walden Robert Cassotto, who grew up a poor kid in the Bronx, knowing from the age of eight that he had a defective heart that would kill him early. He drove himself to become one of the great singers of his era, Bobby Darin, before he died at the age of thirty-seven. Ditto for the doomed Jim Morrison, who wanted the world and wanted it now.

Tennessee Williams once proposed that there are two planes in life, the realistic and the fantastic. I wanted to find the fantastic plane and stay there. But as I lay in the darkness, listening to the wind, listening to the whisper of the pines, listening to the far-off laughter of someone telling a story in the fish house, I knew that it was entirely possible that I'd just committed the biggest blunder of my life.

∿

In northwestern Ontario, the first white-throated sparrow starts whistling at three o'clock in the morning. It's still utter darkness, but the birds can feel the planet turning. By four o'clock, the eastern sky is growing pale, and by four-thirty, it's another brand-new day.

When I woke up the sun was shining through the windows, and the interior of the van was as hot as an oven. I climbed out of the side door, pulled on a T-shirt and some blue jeans, and peed against the tire, keeping an eye peeled for tourists. It's a great life, being a vagabond, but the open road is skimpy on washrooms.

I boiled some tea on the Coleman stove, made a breakfast of porridge and granola, and started unloading the truck. Using my brain instead of my temperamental back, I managed to get the freighter canoe off the roof, and some kindly American tourists helped me carry it down to the water. The cedar canoe was old and heavy, but once we slid it into the water, it floated like a leaf. With my jeans rolled up, I waded in the cold water and loaded the canoe with camping equipment and supplies. The motor was a museum piece, a 3-horse Evinrude with a built-in gas tank and a toy propeller. But it worked fine, according to the owner.

I locked the van and left the keys on the tire. Goodbye, Minaki, I'll be back when I get back. I pushed the canoe away from shore and primed the Evinrude. On the fourth or fifth pull it erupted into a cranky idle, snarling and coughing out those big clouds of aromatic blue smoke that Canadians always associate with the great outdoors.

I steered the canoe away from shore and opened the throttle. With the motor bawling, I cruised down the channel, and past the stone fountains and opulent gardens of Minaki Lodge. During the next twenty-five years I would see it fall, rise again, fall once more, rise again more glorious than ever, and then finally, as the century ended, crumble once again, like an operatic hero experiencing multiple deaths. Its lawns would run rampant and its beautiful golf course would grow hip-high with thistle. Its verandas would rot and birds would fly among its broken stained-glass windows. But this morning, it looked like an enormous, flower-bedecked symbol of beauty and possibility.

Past the lodge, the river flowed beneath the steel girders of the CN railway bridge. The current was strong, and for a full ten minutes I had to work my way up through its whorls. Finally, the bridge glided overhead and I was moving forward again on the wide-open river.

As I cruised along, I studied the map on my knee. I reflected that several centuries ago this waterway, the Winnipeg River, formed the western leg of what used to be Canada's main highway. Surveying the passing scenery, I wondered how many explorers and voyageurs had cruised along this same channel. Surrounded by primal forest, I found it hard not to think that I was travelling into the past. Rivers like this one formed an unbroken chain from western Canada to the St. Lawrence, which served as the original doorway into the country. Jacques Cartier was one of the first guys to enter the St. Lawrence, back in 1534. Like many European sailors he hoped that Canada's rivers might provide a short cut to the Far East, where he could fill the ship with cinnamon, pepper, and other spices, which were prized in Europe as food flavourings, preservative agents, and aphrodisiacs.

As Cartier cruised down the St. Lawrence, he realized there was no passage to India here, just a "land that God gave Cain," a rocky wilderness full of biting insects and hostile natives. Cartier overwintered in Stadacona (the current site of Quebec City), almost died of scurvy and was almost murdered by Indians, and might have gone back to Europe a complete failure, if he hadn't found his own version of buried treasure – *Castor canadensis*, the beaver. Because of the bitter winters that prevail across the north, Canadian beavers wear the thickest and glossiest pelts of any fur bearers in the world, and back in Europe those furs were worth a lot of money.

When Cartier returned with fresh beaver pelts from Canada, it was big news for the European fashion industry. At the time, there was no greater fashion statement in France than a wide-brimmed hat. Hats in general were *haute couture*, ordered with much ceremony and consultation, and each hat was designed for each particular gentleman, characterizing and even caricaturing his personality. The best hats were made from beaver, not from the actual fur, but from the felt, which produced a lightweight, attractive *chapeau* that was handsome, warm, durable, and waterproof.

Based on the intelligence gathered by Cartier, Samuel de Champlain went over to the St. Lawrence River himself in 1603. Champlain rambled around the Shield country, persuaded the Indian tribes to hunt beavers for him, and gave them steel traps, kettles, axes, guns, blankets, and various other coveted items in return. The beaver industry moved into higher gear in 1670, when the British caught wind of the fur trade and established the Hudson's Bay Company, which laid claim to the Hudson Bay watershed – that is, all the lands draining into Hudson's Bay, which happened to be most of Canada. Backed up by a Royal charter, the HBC became our country's first government.

Over the next century, the HBC made so much money from beaver that it became the most powerful corporation in the world. Its employees were mainly Indians like the Cree and the Ojibway, who like hunter-gatherer peoples all through history avidly participated in the industry that eventually destroyed them. Instead of living off the land, the natives became self-employed fur trappers. They may have known it was the devil's bargain, but they sold out for the same reason that anyone sells out – money. A dozen pelts bought a brass kettle, which boiled water a lot more quickly than a birch-bark tub filled with hot stones, or a gun, which could kill a deer from across a river. Soon enough, the Indians depended on the fur trade, and the fur trade depended on the Indians. The link between them was the "Made Beaver" (MB), or finished beaver pelt, which was Canada's first dollar.*

The London-based HBC conducted a centralized business from fortified trading posts. This created an opportunity for their old rivals, the French, who detoured around the HBC monopoly by going deep into the backcountry and buying directly from the Indians. French fur traders became "runners of the woods": *coureurs de bois* who learned native survival skills, slept in native villages, and took native wives. If the symbol of the British fur trade was the log palisade and snapping flag, the symbol of the French fur trade was the birch-bark canoe and fringed buckskin jacket. Even today, you can see the cultural difference written into Canada's maps. Rather than selecting European names for the country's lakes and rivers (Thompson, Mackenzie, Nelson, Churchill, etc.), the French retained the aboriginal names, which not only are more lyrical (Wapegeesi, Pekagoning, Kinmoapiku) but teach you something about the river itself. This river, for example, is named after *Gitchi Weenipake*, its destination.†

As the nattering Evinrude pushed me ever farther from civilization, I took off my shirt and enjoyed the warm sun. I pulled out a cup and took a drink from the river. From looking at the map I could see that the river system branched out in four directions from Minaki. Each branch was fifteen or twenty miles long and

---

* Along the hem of a Hudson's Bay point blanket or coat, black stripes or "points" indicate its value in MB dollars.

† Weenipake means "sea," and "Gitchi" means "great," as in *Gitchi Manitou* – Great Spirit.

consisted of countless islands, bays, and channels. My plan was to establish a camp and use it as a base for explorations. I didn't have a specific methodology in mind. But I reasoned that in exploring a subject, you can either go wide or go deep. My plan was to go deep: pick one piece of wilderness real estate and get to know it intimately. I'd brought along a box full of natural history guidebooks, and I planned to sketch any species I couldn't identify.

Half an hour after leaving Minaki, I experienced the first sign of trouble. The little Evinrude issued a loud *bang*, hacked and sputtered for a second, then quit. I checked the gas tank. It was half full. Removing the cowling, I examined the innards. Except for waves of heat pouring off the cylinder head, everything seemed normal. The bolts were all bolted on and the wires were all fastened to their usual wire-places. Despite my years of guiding, I had little experience fixing outboard motors. I yanked the cord a couple of times, but there was no resistance. I believe that a motor is supposed to have a certain quality called compression, and this one didn't seem to have any. I was no expert, but it seemed that the engine was definitely broken.

It was a long way to shore. For some reason I had been travelling down the middle of the river. The canoe was badly overloaded, and now that it had swung stern-first into the wind, waves were splashing over the lip of the transom. In a few more minutes, I'd be swamped. I didn't have a life jacket, of course, because real men don't wear them. I wouldn't freeze to death in this water, but it was a long way to shore, and I'm not the world's best swimmer. So moving gingerly, I dug around beneath my now-wet supplies and located the paddle.

The big freighter canoe handled like a waterlogged tree, and it took half an hour of hard paddling to reach the nearest landfall –

three islands, tethered like ships alongside the heavily wooded mainland. The first two islands were scruffy and nondescript, covered with tangled second-growth balsam and poplar. They looked like woodtick farms. But the third island was a beauty, a high, blunt-nosed hump of weathered granite, covered with massive pines. On the lee side of the island, a little bay afforded some shelter from the wind. Minaki was only five or six miles away, but that seemed like a good distance, close enough that I could sneak into town and buy supplies, if needed, and far enough that I could still feel like I was confronting the savage wilderness.

I dragged the canoe onto the beach, climbed the terraced granite, and explored the island. Mostly it was weathered rock, covered with moss, lichen, and carpeted pine needles. When I stopped on a high ledge, the only sound was the faint creak of the huge pines stirring in the wind. I unfolded the federal hydrographic chart and found out that this spot was called Tower Island. The map indicated that it was Crown land, which meant that it belonged to the citizenry – in other words, me.

I explored the island and found a patch of flat ground among some big pines, just the right size for my nine-by-twelve prospector tent. I set up the tent, ate some lunch, and sat on the ledge of mossy rock, gazing out at the blue water. So now what? Ah yes – that's always the big question. Back in the city there's never any shortage of things to do. Always lots of homework, errands to run, people to call. My former roommate Paul, when he wasn't ushering women through the turnstile on his bedroom door, was studying Transcendental Meditation, and when he got home from TM class, he was usually all wide-eyed with meditative elation. He would open a tin of mushroom soup, spoon it into his mouth in big gelatinous gobs, and talk about nirvana.

His guru explained that our minds are like restless toddlers. They hate inactivity, and they're always daydreaming about sex or trying to remember the words to some inane Top 40 song. The idea is, you have to force yourself to focus on the present, focus on your breathing. You have to gaze at a distant cloud and rid your mind of all restless chatter. You have to imagine you're a flower. You're neither in the past or the future. You're just sitting here in the sun, a living thing. No less than the trees and the stars, you have a right to be here.

I meditated for a while, sitting motionless, breathing in and breathing out. I could feel the breeze on the left side of my face. I could feel the sun on the nape of my neck. I could feel myself breathing in, breathing out. I could sense that time itself was slowing down. I spent a long time avoiding all thought, until my brain ached like a bicep in the middle of an isometric curl. Finally I looked at my watch. I had meditated for a total of ten minutes.

Now what.

I did some exploring. I crept through the woods and discovered many spiderwebs. At the far end of the island, I found an old cabin that looked like it might have once belonged to a mad trapper. The roof had fallen in, the floor was covered with animal droppings, and the door was peppered with bullet holes. It seemed unlikely that the owner would be returning any time soon, so I salvaged a tin cup and a rusty frying pan and walked back to my campsite, which hadn't changed in my absence. The wind gushed through the trees overhead. The sun sparkled on the water, but there were few signs of life. Most coffee-table books about the Canadian wilderness promote the impression that there's a never-ending pageant of wildlife residing in the wilderness – moose standing belly-deep in the lily pads, and bears and beavers and eagles peering from behind every tree. On this island, I seemed to be the only living thing.

In the evening, the sun finally descended behind a bank of low cloud, and the river turned calm. I listened to the silence, a silence so absolute that I could hear the faint spatter of a duck's wings half a mile away. Then, just as dusk descended, a rumbling, keening dynamo-like hum rose in the woods – mosquitoes.

Soon a hostile swarm gathered around me. I hurried into the tent and zipped up the door. Until now, I'd entertained a vague notion that I might paddle back to Minaki and drop off the broken Evinrude at the repair shop – if they had one – and maybe clean myself up a bit and go for a beer at Minaki Lodge. After all, I was here to conduct research. After drinking lots of beer and maybe even smoking a few cigarettes, I could walk over to Murray's Camp and sleep in the van. I was accustomed to the van, and it wasn't as lonely as this place. But now that I was inside the tent, with half a million mosquitoes clustering on the netting of the door and darkness falling on the river, I realized I was stuck here. It was going to be my first night alone in the woods.

For several hours I read a book by the garish light of a pressurized gas lantern. The lantern's pneumatic hissing drowned out the ominous rumble of the mosquitoes. But finally, at midnight, the lantern began to run out of gas, and I wondered if I should refill it or go to sleep. Closing my book, I watched the lantern gasp, flicker, and slowly die. Then the darkness of the night settled all around.

With fingers laced across my chest I lay flat on my back, listening to the sounds of the night – ducks quacking, frogs croaking along the shoreline, and rodents scurrying through the undergrowth. In the interests of taking a positive slant on the situation, I tried to play a sort of nature quiz. What kind of animal is making that odd noise? Is that darned non-stop croaking sound a duck or a frog? It's way too loud to be a frog, but if it's a duck, why didn't I notice any ducks when it was daytime? Is that persistent chewing noise a termite in a nearby tree? Do we have termites here? Or is it a rodent of some kind, a virus-riddled rodent, trying to gnaw a hole in the side of my tent?

Sometimes there was a sound I couldn't identify, like a stick snapping, or the clink of a rock, and my heart would jump. Is that a bear? Or something worse? When I was a kid, sleeping in the woods, I wasn't afraid of animals so much as Frankenstein monsters. Now that I was older, I knew that every little snapped twig didn't necessarily mean that I was about to be attacked by a member of the undead. But oddly enough, this knowledge didn't make the noises any less alarming.

Lying there, I thought of my friend Mark, who rides a Norton motorcycle, works the door at a tough bar, and studies eastern mysticism – Gurdjieff, Krishnamurti, and the Sufi philosophers. If Mark were here, he'd probably say that my nervousness wasn't just a vestige of the days when we were hunted by sabre-toothed tigers. He'd say that here in the Western world, we carry around this self-image that's constructed of our background and upbringing, personal ethics, sexual attachments, scientific beliefs, religious upbringing, and so on.

When someone sneezes, we say, "God bless you." We still adhere to the old folkloric belief that our bodies are evil, and that the loss of our identities, for even a millisecond, allows our fallen animal selves to seize control. Mark would say that going into the wilderness alone is frightening because we don't want to lose our identity. But there's no choice; that's the price of admission. You have to say goodbye to safety. You have to turn away from the known world, sink into this impenetrable darkness, and open yourself to the fear.

I tried to accept it. I tried to accept that in comparison to this land I was nothing, a glitch, a footnote, a two-legged accident whose passing would make no more impression on this island than the death of a day-old gnat. I tried to accept the truth, but the more I accepted it the more desolate I felt. For the next few hours I drifted in and out of sleep, dozing off for a few minutes, then coming awake with a spurt of raw terror. Each time, I was certain that something was about to attack me. But the sounds of the night were always the same, the same quacking ducks and croaking frogs.

Sometime very late in the night, I heard a far-off boom, like distant boxcars. And for the next hour I lay awake and listened to the approaching storm. Gradually the wind strengthened, moving through the high trees with a sound like rushing water. Then a flash of raw light illuminated the tent and thunder crashed overhead. Rain drummed on the canvas, and it occurred to me that these huge pines all around the tent, which seemed so benign in daylight, were dangerous now. It was unlikely that a three-hundred-year-old tree would pick this particular night to blow over. But even a heavy limb, torn off by the wind, could make a jagged and lethal missile if it fell through the tent.

Finally the thunderstorm passed, and a driving rain settled in. When daylight came it was drizzling. One corner of the tent floor had flooded, and water was dripping from the ceiling onto my sleeping bag. I climbed into sodden jeans and hiked barefoot through the jagged woods, looking for a decent place to answer the call of nature. This was one aspect of wilderness living that I could do without. Squatting down among the cobwebs and dripping limbs, I reflected on the sorry state of the human animal, reduced to the basics. If it weren't raining so hard, I'd fetch my tools, cut down some poles, and build a proper biffy. But right now, it was taking all my willpower just to consider spending the day here, let alone the rest of the summer.

I went down to the shoreline, where the canoe was pulled up. It was filled with water and blown leaves. I emptied out the water, hauled it onto shore, overturned it, and stowed the paddles. I noticed a small ragged hole in the underside. During the storm, wave action must have rubbed it against a rock. Now I was stranded here, or at least stranded until I could somehow patch it.

It rained all day and all night, and the next day it rained more. I passed the time reading books and eating crackers and cheese. For three days it poured rain. It seemed impossible that the sky could deliver so much rain. But then again, I could remember times in the city when it rained for ten days straight, and I barely noticed it. It was just a wet spell. In the city, you don't notice the weather as much. You can always get your umbrella and walk down to the corner, and have a coffee, read the newspaper. You can go home and take a hot bath. You can call up some friends and go to a movie. Here, life was boiled down to its miserable essence – avoiding swamp monsters, staying alert, breathing in oxygen, exhaling carbon dioxide, stuffing food in your mouth. It could rain for weeks, or even months, and it would make no impression on this island whatsoever. I could spend my entire summer here, in this tent. I could catch a cold, die, and get eaten by insects, and this island would look exactly the same. Nothing had happened here for ten thousand years.

.   The next day I did catch a cold, or at least a flu-like malady that I probably got from drinking river water. Along with intestinal distress, I spiked a high fever and spent several days lying in my sleeping bag drifting in and out of dreams that featured giant spiders climbing on my head. I slept most of the day and lay awake most of the night, and it was right in the middle of one of these endless nights that the vermin arrived.

It was some indeterminate hour between midnight and dawn, and the wind was gusting through the trees. The tent was swaying, and I noticed a large moth climbing the canvas wall above my bed. I lifted my hand to brush it away and it fell, with a sharp squeak, onto my face. It wasn't a moth. It was a mouse. With a surge of disgust I slapped it away and yelled, scrambling for the light. With the flashlight in one hand and a shoe in the other, I explored the tent, intending to kill the mouse. But it was gone. I lit the lamp, searched the tent, and found a little hole, which I stuffed with a sock.

I left the light on for a while. But it's impossible to sleep with a gas lantern hissing over your head. So I finally turned it off. The tent was no sooner plunged into darkness when tiny feet skittered across the sleeping bag. The damn mouse was back. There was no time to light the lamp, so I fumbled for the flashlight and yelled, and in the flashlight's faint glow I saw the mouse bolting for cover. But then I saw another flash of movement, and another, and realized that the tent was full of them. They had smelled the food. And they were coming in.

I had no particular fear of mice. But this was like a scene from Edgar Allan Poe. I yelled and threw a shoe at them, but they only darted from one end of the tent to the other. Finally I realized there was no stopping them. My tent was leaking and Nature was pouring in. I grabbed my clothes, stuffed them into the knapsack, and did the best to save myself. I plunged out into the darkness and blowing rain. The night was wild, and the great trees howled and cracked in the wind, swaying like the booms of a dying ship. With the flashlight in my hands, barefoot, I hobbled down across the bare rock to the shoreline. I paused momentarily, to deal with a wave of nausea. My stomach was heaving and I was weak enough to faint. I knelt down and propped one hand against a fallen tree. The tree's bark was damp and ragged under my hand. With a calm scientific part of my brain I took notice of everything that was happening around me, as if the main thing was to keep an accurate record, no matter what happened.

I wondered if I should launch the canoe, fight my way back to Minaki, and sleep in the van. But then I remembered the canoe had a hole in the bottom, which I'd never be able to plug properly in the dark. I could try stuffing the hole with something, but if the plug failed, I'd never make it to shore.

I fumbled through my knapsack and pulled out some dry clothes. I climbed into my rain pants and my waterproof jacket, flipped up the hood, zipped it to my chin, and climbed under the canoe. This is how the voyageurs used to spend their nights. The moss was soft, and although the rain rattled on the hull, it was reasonably dry. I curled up and bunched the knapsack under my head for a pillow. I couldn't imagine doing this in winter. How did the Indians ever survive here, five hundred years ago? Obviously, they were tough. And it wasn't just physical toughness. They needed to be emotionally tough to endure the cruelty of Nature. As far as Nature was concerned, people didn't matter and neither did mice. We could all survive the storm or not survive the storm. Nature didn't care. Nature was managing this island on the four-billion-year plan.

Huddled under the canoe, I hoped only to stay reasonably warm and remain alert for any rodents that might eat my face. But I must have fallen asleep, because one minute it was dark, and the next minute it was light. Mosquitoes were buzzing around my ears. I was stiff from lying on the ground, and it took a few moments to climb out from under the canoe. Mist drifted on the surface of the river, and the trees dripped water. But through the trees I could see the sunrise burning through the shaggy clouds. The rain had stopped.

I gimped up to the campsite and opened the tent. The mice were gone. They were deer mice, and they come out only at night, like vampires. The tent didn't look too bad. Perhaps in the darkness they'd seemed more numerous than they really were. One box of crackers was torn open and crumbs were scattered on the floor. But everything else was just as I'd left it – the sock stuffed in the hole and the sleeping bag thrown open. I cleaned out the tent, emptied the cooler, and spread my wet boots, clothes, and sleeping bag outside to dry off in the sun. I was so dehydrated from being sick that I drank an entire cardboard box of apple juice, and stood there quietly for several minutes, hoping it would stay down. Some of my books were wet, so I put them in the sun too. Finally there was nothing in the tent but the mattress. I stripped off my wet clothes, lay on the mattress, and covered myself with a sheet. Compared to the rocky ground it was as soft as a cloud, and I immediately fell asleep.

I woke up at mid-morning. Outside, wet rocks glistened in the heat and birds chattered in the forest. The river was calm and pale blue. I wondered if I should take advantage of the bright sun by patching the canoe, breaking camp, and paddling back to Minaki. I'd load the van and keep going, maybe head down the highway to the Lake of the Woods and get a motel room for a day or two. I needed to rest up. I needed to lie in bed on a stack of pillows and watch a movie. I needed to get out of here.

But then I'd probably go back to Winnipeg. And with no job, and no courses lined up for the summer, I'd be worse off than when I left. The Cheyenne Indians had a good concept – the dog soldier. A dog soldier always carries his integrity on his belt, in the form of a wooden peg and a ten-foot length of rawhide. When pursued by his foes, the dog soldier drives his stake into the earth, draws his belt knife, and stands there tethered, making his last stand.

As I stood there, thinking about it, I decided I'd be stubborn, like a dog soldier. I was pretty good at being stubborn. I'd been stubborn about deciding to explore this country, even though my aching joints made me ill-equipped for the job. And I'd been stubborn about writing unpublished stories, even though my professors and various others had kindly suggested that it was a waste of time. Even my refusal to finish my M.A. degree in English was arguably a kind of stubbornness. Being stubborn is not particularly exciting. As personality traits go, it's like a Stone Age implement. It's crude and simple, but it was all I had.

I therefore erred on the side of stubbornness and decided to stay. I boiled a bucket of water to make some safe drinking water. I used duct tape to patch the hole in the bottom of the canoe. Paddling the canoe down the shoreline to the trapper's cabin, I dismantled one entire wall. After loading the weathered boards into the canoe, I transported them back to my campsite.

The exertion made me dizzy, so I drank more water, spiked with lemon juice and sugar. I took down the tent and used some old boards to build a solid wooden floor. Then I rebuilt the tent. Now it was waterproof, or at least protected from groundwater. With the rest of the boards, I built a wooden skirt around the base of the tent to repel the mice. With some rusty window screen from the derelict cabin, I made heavy-duty patches for the holes they'd already chewed. The canned food I moved outside, stacked on home-built shelves, and all the chewable foods went into my knapsack, which I hung from a tree. I emptied the water out of the toolbox. The sheepskin gun case had also sopped up some water, and my gun, a little .410 that my dad had given me for Christmas many years ago, had gotten a bit rusty. I cleaned it off with cooking oil and pulled an oily rag through the barrel with a length of fish line. Tomorrow I'd salvage more lumber and build some storage boxes.

I was filthy from all this work – not to mention the last week or so without shaving or bathing. So I stripped naked, waded into the lake, and swam out to where the sun was hitting the water. I floated there for a while, looking at the camp. It was my seventh day on the island. I wasn't much of a creator. But as I floated in the water, gazing at my work, I decided it was good.

The next day my appetite returned. I ate some pasta and went for a paddle. About a mile from the camp, I caught a large walleye, which I took back to camp and cooked for dinner. The next day I went back to the trapper's cabin and scrounged some more boards, then went looking for driftwood planks washed up along the shore. I enjoyed cruising along in the canoe, looking for a telltale glint of blanched wood in the brush along the shore. The boards were like found art, rubbed smooth by years of drifting. I used some of them to build a bed. Next to the bed, where the screened window overlooked the water, I built a small desk to work on my novel (a great walloping heap of scribbled, crossed-out, and re-scribbled foolscap). After years of writing regularly, I was addicted to it.

The mice must have been baffled by my fortifications because they didn't get in that night, and I clocked a solid nine hours of sleep. I felt energized and well rested as I made the morning campfire, and wished that I had a girlfriend to share this experience with. Life comes in fits and starts, and I knew things would probably get difficult again very soon. But that didn't prevent me from relishing the beauty of the quiet morning, going for a long swim, and moving on with the plan.

The days settled into a routine. I went to bed at sundown, got up at daybreak. Had porridge, granola, and tinned fruit for breakfast. Worked on the novel, then went outside and made lunch over the fire, usually walleye, beans, and pan-fried spuds. In the heat of the afternoon, with the river as calm as glass and the big thunderheads piling up in the southwest, I'd paddle the canoe through whatever spooky lily-pad bays and marshes I hadn't explored yet, search for birds and aquatic plants and look them up in my handbooks, cast for pike (a hefty one, caught in deep water, made a delicious dinner, baked with onions in tinfoil), and search for driftwood planks for my little island settlement. Like Robinson Crusoe, I was becoming a compulsive renovator of Nature, and used the planks to build a picnic table, and a bench upon which I could sit and watch the sunset.

The village of Minaki was not far away, and it emanated a sort of invisible energy, like radio waves. I can't pretend that it bothered me to have all those people living just down the river. I knew my Utopia, population One, was essentially an exercise in let's pretend. This island was close enough to civilization that I could always paddle back to town if I ran out of Edwards coffee or got bitten by a squirrel. Sometimes, however, I wished that I was camping on the Thelon River or some place like that in the uninhabited Arctic, facing the wilderness alone. It was hard to contemplate the message of this ancient landscape with so many distractions. At least once a day I'd hear whoops, and water-skiers would go howling by. Float planes flew overhead constantly, and one night, while I was paddling across the river, I almost got cut in half by a huge powerboat.

I was paddling home from an evening of bird-watching. I'd finally learned to tell the difference between a juvenile merlin (*Falco columbarius*) and a juvenile sharp-shinned hawk (*Accipiter striatus*), and I'd drawn sketches of both. My heavy binoculars were hanging around my neck and my guidebooks were stuffed in my pockets. I was paddling hard to keep ahead of the mosquitoes. Halfway across the river, I became aware of the far-off whine of a motorboat. It was unusual to hear boats at night, so I listened absent-mindedly as the sound drew closer. Finally I twisted around and looked in the direction of the noise, and saw a nebula of coloured lights.

It seemed to be coming in my direction. It was making a lot of noise and looked big. It kept coming, and at two hundred yards, I realized it was headed straight for me. I had no flashlight, like an idiot, and since I'd quit smoking I didn't even have a lighter. But a quick search of my jacket pockets produced a book of matches. The first match fell apart as I struck it. The second match adhered to my thumb, cooked the skin for a moment, and went out. The third ignited, but as soon as I lifted it up in the air, the flame petered out. Now the boat was only forty or fifty yards away, coming fast, and I had to make a decision. If I stayed broadside, the skipper might spot me, and swerve out of the way. If I turned head-on, the canoe presented a smaller target, but he'd be less likely to see me.

I decided to turn and face the boat. Digging the paddle into the water, I gave the canoe a violent thrust and swung it head-on. The boat thundered past and soaked me with its rooster tail. It kept going and never slowed or wavered until it was out of sight.

Marvelling at my stupidity and good luck, I took a moment to shake the water off my notebooks. Then I heard the distant noise of the boat again, coming back for another pass. I was probably three hundred yards from shore. But I don't think it took more than a few seconds to paddle that big freighter canoe to the safety of the island.

I'd brought enough food to last five or six weeks. I was managing to gather lots of fresh fish, blueberries, and an occasional male ruffed grouse from the nearby woods (shot illegally; the season wasn't open until October), so my pantry was holding out nicely. And now that I'd settled into the easy life of mid-summer camping – writing every morning, exploring in the canoe every afternoon – the days went by fairly smoothly. For more than a month I never spoke to another human being. I discovered that a hermit's life can be quite idyllic, if you don't mind going a little funny in the head.

When working around the campsite, I'd fallen into the habit of conversing with inanimate objects. "Oh sure, coffee pot, why don't you just *tip over?*" Sometimes fishing boats puttered past the island – a couple of tourists usually, squired by some bored-looking young guide from Minaki Lodge or Murray's Camp – and I'd hide behind a tree, peering out from the undergrowth. One day a pair of canoeists stopped by the island, and I was struck dumb. What should I do? I had *company*.

The guy, whose name was Martin, sported army pants, a cotton rope for a belt, and a ragged goatee. The woman, whose name was Lillian, had tanned, muscular arms, ripped cutoffs, and the lush tangled hair sported by Raquel Welch in the movie *One Million Years B.C.* They told me they'd been in the bush for two months, canoeing the English, the Wabigoon, the Turtle, and other remote waterways of northern Ontario. They said Tower Island was the most beautiful camping spot they'd come across. As we knelt around the fire, brewing coffee, I realized two things: that I'd forgotten how to talk, and that their condition was even worse than mine. They had gone feral, like cats.

That evening, as I prepared dinner, a great storm, tall as a dreadnought, grumbled and shot tracers of fire in the distant west. I had used all the plates preparing the fish, and because I was busy cooking, I assumed that my friends would wash the dishes before we sat down to dinner. But they didn't seem concerned. When I activated my rusty vocal cords and announced that dinner was ready, Martin dug into the frying pan with the flipper and dumped a heap of fried fish, kernel corn, and hash browns onto the bare granite. Then they both reclined on the rock and began eating with their fingers.

I had managed to find out a bit about them. (She was the daughter of a prominent architect. His parents were psychiatrists in Toronto.) They were full-blown urbanites, in other words. But they had gotten right down to the bottom of the bucket and broken through to the other side. As we ate, a whip of lightning lashed across the sky. And Martin, who was propped on his elbow, fingering hot fish in his mouth, looked up at the sky, narrowed his eyes, and issued a low growl.

That night we brewed a pot of tea and took turns with his old guitar, serenading Lillian. Martin sang the "Ballad of Stagger Lee" and I sang "Long Black Veil." This wasn't very interesting, least of all for Lillian, so after a few more tunes we put away the guitar and drank our tea. We stared at the fire, listened to the sounds of the night, and exchanged stories of the north woods. I told them I'd always had the feeling that this big, brutal rocky landscape of the Shield was like a Rosetta stone or a rune. I was sure it contained some deep and inexpressible mystery, if only you could figure it out.

Martin said that the summer before, they'd found a sacred artefact: a birch-bark scroll upon which some Ojibway shaman had written down the ancient teachings. He said, "There were eight levels of the Midewiwin Society, and you had to start studying when you were a child. If you lived to be eighty, you might reach the highest level, called the Sky Lodge. The Sky Lodge priests knew the secret of life, and they wrote it on these scrolls, which they hid in special places, usually a high cliff facing the rising sun."

Lillian nodded. She lit a rolled cigarette from a flaming twig. She exhaled a languorous cloud of smoke. "They're like the Dead Sea scrolls."

I asked, "Where did you find this scroll?"

"It was on another river system, not far from here," said Martin. "But I shouldn't say the exact place. Anyway, I climbed up on this cliff to take a picture and saw something hidden behind some rocks. It was like a long wooden cylinder, very old, with a birch-bark scroll inside. I started pulling it out, then I saw the pictographic writing, and I suddenly felt like, 'Holy smoke, maybe I shouldn't be touching this.'"

"So what did you do?"

"Put it back."

"Don't you think you should tell a museum curator or someone?"

"If I meet the right person, I'll tell them."

I took out my notebook. "How do you spell Midewiwin?"

He told me. I jotted it down. "And what did you say the name of that lake was?"

"Nice try," said Martin.

The next day they decided to move on. I helped them break camp. We would have exchanged addresses, but didn't have any, so I gave them the address of my parents, and Martin gave me the address of his. They were stopping in Minaki to replenish their supplies, so I gave them some postcards addressed to my friends and family, just to tell everyone I was alive and well.

Martin climbed into the canoe. "Take it easy," he said.

Lillian was already in the canoe. She waved and pushed away from shore. Just as she was digging her paddle into the water, she paused and pointed over my shoulder. "Look at the bear," she said.

I didn't see it at first. Then I saw the upright black ears and the inquisitive face peering at us from the underbrush. Yes, a bear.

It didn't look like a big bear. A big bear has small ears, and a small bear has big ones. The ears, of course, stay the same size;

it's the bear's head that keeps growing. It was the first time I'd seen a bear this summer, and it always perks you right up, seeing one close by. "Scat!" I shouted, clapping my hands.

The bear lowered its head but didn't move, as if it assumed that perhaps I was shouting at some other bear.

Martin banged his paddle on the gunwale of the canoe. The bear wheeled and disappeared into the bush.

"You told me bears didn't go on islands," said Lillian.

Martin smiled and looked at me. "Lillian doesn't like bears."

"I like them fine," I said. "I just don't want to share a small island with one."

Martin said, "They live here."

"Thank you for that information."

We concluded our goodbyes and they paddled off. I watched them until they were out of sight. I walked up the hill to the tent, keeping an eye peeled for my furry visitor. I was thinking that when it got dark tonight, I would load my little single-shot .410. Not that it would do any good. Light shotguns are designed for two-pound grouse, not bears.

∾

I cooked dinner and waited for the sun to go down. What I knew about bears was a combination of information from old-timers like Junior Robinson, book research, and some first-hand experience with bears in the bush. They were intriguing animals, and I liked them. But I liked them in daylight.

When the first Europeans arrived in North America they encountered three species of bears. The most abundant species was the blond-haired plains grizzly, *Ursus horribilis*, a behemoth that prowled the plains from Mexico to the Arctic. When Lewis and Clark travelled up the Missouri, they encountered these bears almost daily. Grizzlies have a touchy sense of personal space, and they often attacked the explorers on sight. The expedition members carried only primitive muskets, and sometimes had to fire a dozen balls into an attacking bear before it died.

It's very difficult to visualize the Great Plains of that era. Driving across Manitoba or North Dakota today, through a manicured landscape of roads and geometric cereal farms, you have to make a considerable effort to visualize the Serengeti-like wilderness that once existed on the prairies. You have to imagine a rolling ocean of thick green grass spangled with wildflowers. The dominant species of grass was big bluestem, a magnificent species that grew eight feet tall. A prairie covered with bluestem rolled off to the horizon like a purplish-green ocean, changing colour in the gusts of wind. Big bluestem was tall enough to hide a rider on horseback, and herds of buffalo flowed through it like schools of fish.

No one knows how many buffalo roamed the Great Plains. It was certainly tens of millions. In 1870 Phil Sheridan, who was an excitable boy, saw a herd of buffalo he estimated at 100 million. But only ten years later they were all gone. One autumn day in 1883 a large bull ran through the town of Souris, Manitoba, crashing through fences and clotheslines. A local man named A.S. Barton grabbed his gun and his horse and chased the bull. Here was a chance to bag the last one! Barton lost the bull when it swam the Souris River, and although the *Plain Dealer* notified the public, the bull was never seen again. With the passing of the buffalo the grizzlies also disappeared. Modern-day farmers occasionally dig up a skull, but grizzlies no longer survive on the plains. A few grizzlies still eke out a living on the northern barrens, but most have retreated into the dense forests and mountains of British Columbia.

The second species, polar bears, live in the Arctic and spend most of their lives either hunting on the ice or hanging out on the coast, waiting for the ice to return. They have a Velcro-like coating on their feet, which provides traction on the ice. Polar bears are actually black, but their translucent pelts make them appear white. Each hair is like a hollow fibre-optic cable that pipes sunlight down to their skin. Bears are highly individual animals, and trying to predict a bear's behaviour is like trying to predict a person's behaviour. Some polar bears befriend dogs, their ancient enemy, and spend hours romping with them. Some bears are playful, some are mischievous, and some are grumpy. A good-natured bear will run when it sees a grumpy bear coming. All polar bears retreat when they see a full-grown male coming. A male polar bear is the largest carnivore on earth.

Females spend six months of the year asleep. While they're hibernating, they give birth to two or sometimes three cubs in a snow cave. Moses Alyak, an old hunter from Rankin Inlet, once told me that the third cub usually dies of starvation. There's only so much milk to go around, and its siblings are usually bigger and more assertive. Moses says that if the third cub survives, it will grow up to be embittered and dangerous from the treatment it received when it was young. It sounds a bit like Dr. Spock, but Moses knows what he's talking about. Most modern-day Inuit live in large settlements with schools, hospitals, food stores, and satellite television, but Moses still spends most of his time living out on the land. He's hunted whales with harpoons, slept in igloos during howling arctic blizzards, and on three separate occasions been assaulted by polar bears.

During a four-day layover in Rankin Inlet, weathered in by fog, I heard stories about Moses and thought he sounded like someone worth meeting. I spent several days trying to find him, but it's tricky asking directions in an Inuit community. Everyone is happy to help out. In fact it's considered rude not to give advice. Some people knew for sure that Moses was south of town, at Corbett Inlet, while others were certain that he was out west, or down north. The search finally led to a fishing camp on the Melanine River. Whenever you find someone in this country there always seems to be water nearby. The sun had finally come out and the river looked like spilled sunlight: wide and shallow and ribbed with boulders. The Inuit clan were camped out on a gravel bar alongside the water. Honda dirt bikes were parked among the cabins and wall tents, and rows of fresh-caught char were draped over clotheslines like red stockings.

I was talking to a young woman who spoke fluent English when an elderly man pulled up on a Honda dirt bike. "This is Moses," she said. I gathered that she was either a granddaughter or someone who felt protective of him, because she didn't seem very happy to introduce me to him. She suggested that I was taking advantage of him and asked me to pay him something. "How much?" I asked. She talked to Moses. Moses didn't seem as distrustful as she was, but agreed that he could use some money for gas, perhaps five dollars. I gave him twenty, and we sat on the riverbank and talked, drinking tea and eating whale blubber, while the young woman sat on a plastic crate across from us, translating.

Moses' face was long and narrow, rugged and dignified looking. He wore a wool cap to cover the terrible scars of a bear mauling. He said he grew up with his grandparents in hunting camps. There was no town then, and life was not difficult. There were many animals and they lived in the same way that his people had lived since the beginning. His grandfather taught him to hunt and to use every piece of the animal. It wasn't a matter of practicality; it was a matter of respect. If you take away an animal's life, you must use every part of it. He said this duty was very private. It was between you and the animal. One time he killed a caribou without realizing it had a fawn, and for days afterward he apologized to the spirit of the caribou and asked it to forgive him.

His grandfather was a great hunter and fought Nanuq the old way, with a spear. In the dark of the winter night the dogs would bark and the people would know that Nanuq was coming. If they stayed inside their snow huts, Nanuq would break through the roof, so the hunters would dress quickly and go outside to engage him. Moses said that when Nanuq attacks a man, he first tries to push him down. He won't bite a man until the man is on the ground. So it's important to stay on your feet, to fend him off and back away from him like a man fighting another man. Nanuq is left-handed or right-handed, like a person, and you have to watch him to see which paw he is going to hit you with. Just before he strikes, he will twist his head slightly to one side, and that tells you which paw he favours. You strike him with the spear in the opposite side. While Moses recounted these lessons, he periodically stood up and played the different roles. First he would be the hunter, feinting with the spear, then he would play Nanuq, and it was almost as if he would turn into a bear. He would rear up on his hind legs and hunch over, facing his invisible adversary. Then he would sway back and forth, and twist his head to one side as he cocked a paw. Sitting down again, he would explain that these lessons helped him to survive three attacks.

Moses' ten-year-old grandson Kook must have sensed that he was missing out on something, because he came along and joined us, sitting next to his grandfather. Kook was a good-looking youngster, a silent boy with large brown eyes. Moses said the first time he was attacked, it was his own fault. It was snowing and he was wearing white, and Nanuq charged him, thinking he was another bear. Nanuq struck him once, realized he was a man, and broke off the attack. The second time he was at Whale Cove. He went up on the hill to look across the sea, and when he came back he saw two bear cubs at the cabin, getting into the char. Kook was up on the roof, waving at him, shouting. The mother bear came out of the cabin, saw Moses, and ran up the hill and tried to push him down. He backed away from her, trying to keep his feet. She struck him with her claws, tearing his arm open. He said he didn't want the bear to kill him because he didn't want Kook to have to see that. After hitting him, the mother bear assembled her cubs and left. Moses said he didn't blame her for injuring him. She saw him as an interloper and was trying to keep him away from her cubs.

On July 9 the year before, he and Kook and some other people went to camp out at the place where he grew up, Corbett Inlet. They went up to see the camp, and while they were gone the tide came up and the boat drifted away. His gun was in the boat. A woman named Margaret said she'd swim out and get the boat, but he said, You'll get hypothermia. They went into a tent, made tea, and he called Baker Lake on the radio and told them they'd lost their boat. Then Moses, Kook, and Margaret went outside. As soon as he stepped out of the tent he saw movement and froze. Right next to the tent – right between the tent and the guy ropes – there he was, Nanuq.

The bear started bounding towards him. Moses ran, hoping to draw the bear away from the others. He grabbed for the knife on his belt but the knife was inside the tent. Nanuq chased him and caught him with both arms, hugging him. He yelled for Margaret and Kook to run away. The bear started biting his neck, trying to bite the cervical vertebrae. Moses put his hands over his neck and felt the bear's canine teeth driving through his hands. The bear couldn't get at his neck, so it started biting his head. Moses covered his head with his hands but the bear put one foot on his neck, the other paw on his head, and clawed his hands away, tearing off his scalp. Moses acted it out, becoming the bear again, showing how it pinned his head to the ground and tore away his scalp. He said that in the midst of this, the bear suddenly ran away and he heard someone scream.

Moses lost consciousness for some time. He woke up and crawled fifty yards. The bear came back and attacked him again. Moses felt the bones of his skull breaking as the bear bit his head. He passed out. When he woke up it was quiet, and he could hear Nanuq eating something. He got up and walked to a cabin and found Margaret. He said, "I think I'm the only one who survived." They could hear Nanuq outside somewhere, eating, and Moses said, "I'm sure he's devouring my grandson." Margaret said they should walk over to the other cabin. Moses made the walk, leaning against her, but he fell down many times. When they reached the other cabin, the people splashed water on his wounds. He stayed outside because he was soaked in blood and he didn't want to terrify the children who were cowering inside the cabin. He said he knew that Nanuq would come back, and if he went inside the cabin Nanuq would smell the blood and come into the cabin, so he lay on the ground outside and told the people to block the door.

Suddenly he heard a burst of VHF radio static coming from inside the cabin, then a child's voice. "This is me! This is me! I am scared! I'm in a tent!" It was the voice of Kook. He was still alive. He'd found a hiding place at the other end of the camp and he was calling the RCMP. Soon a helicopter landed outside Kook's tent. A wildlife officer spotted the bear and shot it. The bear was eating an elderly woman named Hattie Amitnak. One of the wildlife officers in the rescue party was Hattie's grandson. Moses took off his hat and showed me the claw marks – deep, wide grooves across the top of his head. He said it was very private, the memory of that day. He said it was terrible to lie there bleeding, listening to the sound of Nanuq eating. He could still hear it. The young woman who was translating this story had been crying for some time now. And while Moses talked about the sound of Nanuq eating, he began weeping too.

When it was time to leave, Moses gave me some *muqtuq* – the blubber from a beluga whale. He cross-hatched the white blubber with a knife to make it easier to chew, which is no easy task even with a small piece. You chew and chew, but it's as resilient as a chunk of inner tube. He said that it sometimes takes a full week to catch a beluga. He and the other hunters comb the ocean all day, then sleep in the boat, anchored in the lee of an island. The whales are plentiful; the problem is getting close enough to get a good shot or throw the harpoon. The whole year is taken up by hunting, and the type of hunting changes every couple of weeks. Goose season segues into whale season. At the end of the summer the caribou arrive. When they migrate in the autumn, it's like a scene from wild Africa, thousands of them pouring through this valley like a visitation from the Old Testament.

The Judeo-Christian ethic proposes a world in which mankind is the Lord of Creation. Down here on the stony arctic seacoast the Inuit know that it's actually the other way around. The pyramid is inverted. The simplest organisms, the algae and phytoplankton, occupy the top. They've survived since the dawn of time and they will endure until the sun exhausts its supply of nitrogen and burns out, approximately 4.5 billion years from now. Beneath them are the protozoa, and beneath the protozoa are the bacteria, about a billion of which inhabit a single litre of seawater. The pyramid becomes narrower and less populated as it descends. Each layer clings by its nails to the one above. Large showy creatures like mammals inhabit the lower apex, and when the climate or environment shifts slightly, they peel away and drop into oblivion. (Woolly camels, mastodons, giant sloths, sabre-toothed cats, and all the rest . . . see you later.) At the very bottom is *Homo sapiens*, a poignant experiment. Moses apologized to the caribou because they're higher in the organization than he is.

Kook wrapped the blubber in some paper towel and I put it in the pouch of my camera bag. I'd borrowed an old pick-up truck from an outfitter in town, and Kook accompanied me to where it was parked. As we walked along, he scanned the faraway hills, looking for something, probably animals. Even though he lived out here, he seemed fixated on this environment, these hills, birds, and distant animals. When they airlifted Moses out to Winnipeg for emergency surgery, Kook went with him. It was mid-summer in the city, green, lush, and hot, and

Kook spent the whole week roaming Winnipeg with his auntie, sightseeing. He'd never been to a city before.

I said, "What was the most interesting thing you saw?"

He considered this for a moment. "Squirrels."

∾

The third species of bear in North America is the black bear, *Ursus americanus.*

Untroubled by pride, the black bear has a long history of working the angles and getting by on leftovers. It came across the land bridge from Asia three million years ago, between ice ages, and arrived on a continent that was already claimed by animals a lot bigger and a lot rougher than it was. Lions, sabre-toothed cats, scimitar-toothed cats (all of them larger than any cats alive today), dire wolves, grizzlies, coastal brown bears, and the biggest bear that ever walked the earth – the short-faced bear or "cave bear" (*Arctodus simus*), a wrecking machine that stood almost twenty feet high.

Faced with this kind of competition, the little black bear kept a low profile. It became an adept climber and learned to scoot up nearby trees when an enemy came along. Pursuing a jack-of-all-trades lifestyle, it took whatever opportunities came its way. Rotted carcasses, birds' eggs, insects, frogs – they all went down the hatch. Sometimes a black bear would run down and kill a young bison or camel, but it wasn't a predator. At the end of the last ice age, the glaciers melted, and the shift in climate was hostile to the mammoths, giant bison, woolly camels, and other huge prey animals. Like one of those Bloody Mondays that occasionally visit the stock market, a mass die-off swept the continent. Nature didn't terminate the black bear, though, because it never really had a job in the first place. If it couldn't eat baby mastodon, it would eat grass. There's something a bit buffoonish about an animal that's willing to do anything for a living. But the same quality that makes the black bear a clownish hustler also, on occasion, makes it dangerous.

Most scientists agree that grizzlies are more dangerous than black bears. But a human is more likely to survive an attack from a grizzly, even though grizzlies are much larger and more ferocious than black bears. When a grizzly charges, it's usually trying to make a point. Grizzlies move around inside an invisible defensive perimeter that's about two hundred yards in diameter. When a human inadvertently wanders into that personal space, the bear either flees or charges. What it does is determined by its age, size, temperament, and so on. But it will almost always do one or the other. The safest response to an aggressive grizzly is passivity. You're supposed to back away, lower your eyes, and demonstrate that you mean no harm. In most cases, the grizzly will make a "bluff charge," then leave the area. If the bear presses the attack, you're supposed to assume the fetal position and take your licking. If you don't fight back, you're less likely to get a severe mauling.

Black bears, on the other hand, almost never approach in such a flat-out aggressive manner. In the same way that a street mugger will often strike up a conversation first or ask for a cigarette, a black bear will take a few moments to measure you up. When you are approached by a black bear, the best response is rude pugnacity. Open your jacket and enlarge your profile like those fringed lizards from Australia. Throw stones, make threatening gestures, yell angrily, and emphasize the point that you're not someone to be trifled with. Black bears are old hands at estimating risk versus gain. And if you convince the bear that you're willing to fight, it'll usually shrug its shoulders and move on.

Still, they're opportunists, always looking for quality protein. In May and June, deer fawns and moose calves lie unattended while their mothers go off and graze. And during those weeks, they're easy pickings. The average moose calf stands a 50 per cent chance of being killed by a black bear before it's six months old. And a black bear stalking its way along a creek on a May afternoon is not looking for nuts and berries. It's looking for meat. It's walking softly and sniffing the wind. If it runs into a boy with a fishing rod, it might very well look at the kid and think, Well, he's not a moose calf, but maybe he'll do.

About forty-five people have been killed by black bears since anyone started keeping records, and the incidents show a pattern. People tend to think that only "sick or starving" animals will attack a human. But killer bears are usually large, healthy males. One spring afternoon in Algonquin Park, four Boy Scouts went fishing along a waterway called Stone Creek. Fifteen-year-old George Halfkenny walked down a trail with his fishing rod, unaware that a 275-pound black bear was following him. The bear rushed him, killed him, dragged him away, and was eating him when the victim's brother, twelve-year-old Mark Halfkenny, came along looking for him. The bear killed Mark, too, and was burying the body under some brush, to secure it from ravens and other freeloaders, when sixteen-year-old Billy Rhindress came along, looking for his friends. The bear killed Billy too. When Billy's older brother came down the trail, the bear crouched in the woods and let him pass. When wildlife officers shot the bear two days later, they found that it was an adult male in good health.

A few years after the Boy Scouts were killed in Algonquin, a middle-aged couple from Toronto went camping in the same area. A black bear observed them from the undergrowth as they unloaded their canoe and set up their tent. Their groceries were sitting in full view on the picnic table. But the bear didn't want their groceries. It wanted them. After a few minutes, the bear sprang from the bush and attacked the woman. When the man broke a paddle over its back, the bear attacked him too. It stayed at the campsite for five days, eating regularly, until the Ontario Provincial Police showed up and killed it.

The newspapers rounded up the usual biologists, who issued the usual statements, that is, that this was "bizarre and highly abnormal behaviour" and the bear was probably sick, starving, or provoked. Some suggested that the campers had done something wrong, by leaving their groceries out in the open. Biologists tend to believe that their job is to defend wildlife, and like dog owners, they sometimes have a hard time admitting that their charges might have bitten someone. But like the man-eater that killed the Boy Scouts along Stone Creek, this bear turned out to be a large male in good health.

This would come as no surprise to Dr. Stephen Herrero, a noted bear expert from the University of Alberta. Like other biologists, Dr. Herrero sees himself as a defender of wildlife. But he's also a defender of seeing the nose on the front of your face, and he insists that predatory attacks on human beings fall within the range of normal black bear behaviour. After all, if a bear will tackle a moose, why wouldn't it tackle a person? Do we really think that humans somehow enjoy special status from the other members of the animal kingdom? All predators tend to focus on traditional prey animals. But that's a practical choice, not an aesthetic one. If a red and white spoon looks enough like a meal, darting through the water, a northern pike will snap at it. And if human beings behave like a potential meal, they run the risk of being snapped at by a meat-eating predator. Of course it's important to balance this against the odds. There are many thousands of human-bear interactions in the bush country every summer, and seldom is anyone injured. The message that emerges from Dr. Herrero's work is that black bears are complex, adaptable animals capable of a whole range of feeding strategies. If you spend enough time in the woods, you may eventually run into the wrong bear in the wrong place. And if that happens, you have a problem.

Usually the culprit bear is a large and self-confident animal that lives in a backcountry wilderness or national park. Bears that live in such pristine wilderness areas have not been hunted, and they haven't learned to be afraid of people. If such a bear meets a person, it may show initial wariness, followed by curiosity. On occasion, anglers and campers have taken films of this sort of black bear following them in the woods. The footage shows the alert, calculating expression of an animal weighing an opportunity. There's none of the snarling and bloody-eyed ferocity depicted by illustrators in outdoor magazines. After all, the bear isn't angry. What's to be angry at? It's just interested in a meal. The bear looks like a cautiously hopeful dog following a kid with a cheeseburger.

Unlike polar bears and grizzly bears, female black bears are not usually aggressive about defending their cubs. Biologists have found that they can inspect black bear cubs and the mother will usually retreat and watch from a distance. It's the males that are dangerous. This has less to do with feminist theory than with the fact that male bears have different nutritional needs than females. Sow bears are smaller, and they're homebodies. They establish a territory and stay within it. The Ontario Ministry of Natural Resources sometimes deals with nuisance bears by catching them in a trap made from a steel culvert, mounted on a trailer. Once trapped, the bear is trucked to a new territory. The conservation officer releases the bear by backing the trap into a lake before opening the door. The bear has to swim a bit before getting to shore, thus allowing the officer time to scramble back into the truck.

Female bears, being homebodies, need to be dropped off at least eighty miles away, or they come straight back home. Once, a three-legged female with cubs was taken 120 miles away from Thunder Bay, and she returned home within a week. When released, female bears swivel their heads for a moment, and then strike off. Biologists suspect that bears find their way around by homing in on familiar smells – the odour of a river, distant pulp mill, or highway. If the transplantation is going to work, the bear has to be taken far enough away that she can't smell her home.

Males, on the other hand, are transients. If you trailer a male thirty miles away from where he was caught, he says thanks for the lift. He's driven by the urge to meet as many females as possible, and he travels incessantly, getting into a lot of territorial squabbles with other males in the process. It's in his interest to "bulk up," which he can do best on a high-protein diet. So the curious bear following a person through the woods is often torn between two opposite urges. Should I try to exploit this opportunity? Or should I play it safe and move on? Usually, his genetic predisposition towards prudence carries the day, and if a prospective victim behaves aggressively, the bear moves on.

Mating season happens in mid-summer, and the males run themselves ragged, looking for sex. By the end of August the party is over, and it's time for all bears to get back to work. The pregnant females must be in prime condition before they hibernate. They're eating for two (or three) now, and they need lots of body fat. Their adolescent cubs – having been kicked out of the house during mating season – also face a tough autumn. Without a home territory, they wander around, looking lanky and lost, getting beaten up by other bears, hit by cars, and shot by homeowners. Big dominant males face the worse odds of all. Like full-grown males of many species, male bears are viewed by Nature as nothing more than delivery vehicles for spermatozoa. A successful boar is a boar that manages to live for a couple of years in his prime. Once the mating season is over, he has to gain up to thirty pounds a week before he goes into hibernation. So late summer is when bears of all ages and sizes become truly serious about food, roaming twenty-four hours a day.

There's lots of informed opinion about the best ways to co-exist with black bears in the wilderness. But all the authoritative books, Ph.D. studies, and back-porch homilies in the world aren't much help when you introduce food into the picture.

And these were my worrisome thoughts as darkness descended on my campsite.

∾

After I fastened the flimsy tent door against the mosquitoes, I lit the gas lantern and kept myself busy with a few chores.

My nonchalance was an act. Just as some airline passengers are convinced that the plane will remain airborne only if they stay awake, I operated on the theory that the bear would steer clear of my camp as long as I remained busy. I knew, of course, that the bear was probably miles away by now. But I wasn't so much apprehensive about the bear, as apprehensive about being apprehensive.

At least the food was outside the tent. My larder consisted of some cabinets I'd built along the back wall of the tent. Most of the food was canned, but bears can smell food through a can, and they're quite happy to rip open tins of Libby's beans with their teeth. The cabinet also contained jars of wild rice, dried apricots, granola, and sugar, all of which rate high on a bear's list of favourite foods. If it came back tonight, it would probably hit the cabinets first, which would give me enough time to get out the front door. But what if it pushed against the food cabinets and knocked the tent down?

As I lay in the darkness, thinking over the possibilities, the bear's possible visit began to play out like a bad home movie – the collapsing tent, the dark confusion, the bear, frightened by the kicking motion, biting down on an ankle. I'd slipped the shotgun under the bed. But it's not like in the movies. You don't immediately gain the upper hand just because you display a gun. And this was just a little .410, a Nancy Reagan gun. Bears are durable animals. To kill one, you need to know its anatomy. You need a moment or two to line up a clear shot. You need to be a cool and steady hand, like Atticus Finch. Would the gun be of any use inside a darkened tent in the middle of the night? Not likely.

I began to feel, once again, like the author of my own folly. Probably the only workable use for the gun was to bring it to bed and, at the first sound of a cracking twig, shoot myself between the eyes. Thankfully, that didn't prove necessary because I finally drifted off, and when I opened my eyes it was morning. As the sun grew stronger and filtered through the mosquito netting, I realized that I'd wasted all that time worrying about nothing. Unzipping the door, I walked down to the waterline and threw my sleeping bag on the moss. I took a nap in the sun-dappled morning shade. When I woke up a few hours later, I saw the bear swimming across the river towards me.

Bears don't see as well as people, and it wasn't until the animal was fairly close that it spotted me. It veered away, swam down the shoreline, and vaulted up into the undergrowth. Now that it was daytime, I didn't feel as vulnerable as I had during the night, and I went up to the tent to make sure there wasn't any food left in the open.

About an hour later, I was sitting outside at the picnic table under the big pines, working on my novel, when a flicker of movement caught my eye. The bear was a good distance away, peering from behind a tree like a drug dealer checking the street for cops. I clapped my hands and yelled at it, and it took off. Then an hour later it showed up again, a little closer this time, walking along the outer perimeter of the clearing and swinging its head back and forth. You can determine a bear's gender by the shape of its head. Females have narrow heads and longish noses. Males have broad foreheads and blunter snouts. This one looked like a male. I went into the tent and got the gun, loaded it, cocked the hammer, and walked towards the bear. When he began moving away, I shot him in the rump with a load of bird-shot. It was a quiet afternoon, and the gun boomed like a cherry bomb. He was fifty yards away – just the right distance for the No. 6 pellets to give him a scare rather than an injury – and the detonation of the gun probably had as much effect as the birdshot slapping his rear end.

He ran like a scalded cat. But only five minutes later he was back, shaking his fur and woofing as if in embarrassment. All afternoon, he loitered in the nearby woods. And as time passed, he paid less attention to the noise, the threats, and the warning shots I fired into the foliage over his head. Among my stack of reference books I had a government guidebook called *Safety in Bear Country*. The book recommended a number of bear deterrents, including, as last resort, the "three slug method," a strategy by which you fire a warning shot in the form of a 12-gauge firecracker shell when the bear is three hundred feet away, a non-lethal plastic 12-gauge slug aimed right at his body when he's two hundred feet away, and a lethal lead slug if he's closer than one hundred feet. I didn't have access to such refined munitions, and this bear seemed well past the point of being frightened off by gunfire anyway.

Late in the afternoon, I was kneeling by the campfire cooking fettuccini when I heard a noise and saw him coming. With his head lowered, he advanced towards me, hissing, swinging his head back and forth, and folding his ears back in the universal body language of warning. He wasn't a large bear, perhaps a two-year-old. He might have weighed 150 pounds, about my size. But wild animals are about four times stronger than humans, and with a bear you can probably double that again. No doubt the smell of the bubbling fettuccini was giving him whisky courage, and he'd decided that I was nothing he couldn't handle. When he got within three or four yards, hissing like a punctured tire and waving his head, moving closer, moving closer, I picked up a jagged chunk of granite the size of a grapefruit and threw it at him. It caromed off his forehead. He didn't even blink. When he got within two yards I stood up, took a step back, and ceded him the pasta.

I stepped back a ways and watched him snuffle up my dinner. After a few minutes I went up to the tent and put together an emergency overnight kit – my jacket, sleeping bag, gun, fishing rod, and manuscript. When I came out of the tent the bear was still face-first in the pasta kettle, with cream sauce all over his forehead. Our little dispute had clearly been settled to his satisfaction, and when I walked past he didn't even look up. He was so engrossed in his meal that he might just as well have been a Shetland pony face-deep in a bucket of oats. I went down to the shore and loaded the canoe. If this was a Shakespearean drama, it would be the perfect nadir for the hapless protagonist. *Exit, pursued by a bear.* Launching the canoe, I paddled around to the front of the island and viewed the scene from the water.

The sun was getting low, and it was hard to see the bear among the shadows. The tent began shaking, and his rear end emerged. He was working on the pantry, no surprise. The tent quivered, then the shelving fell onto the rocks with a mighty crash.

I drifted in the canoe, thinking it over. I felt like I was judging a court case, and acting as both prosecutor and defence attorney. If the bear drove me off the island, I had nowhere else to live. And with nowhere to live, I'd probably have to go back to the city.

I could probably devise a way of killing him. It wasn't against the law. The Ministry of Natural Resources was trying to get out of the nuisance bear business. It was too expensive, live-trapping bears and giving them one-hundred-mile rides all over Ontario. So their new policy was destroy the bear if you must, but dispose of the carcass properly. And please stop phoning us.

Eventually, the bear would have to swim back to the mainland. I could paddle up to him while he was swimming. One shot right behind the ear would kill him instantly. Then I'd float him out into the middle of the river, tie a few rocks to his neck, and say goodbye. Maybe I'd slice open his paunch, so he wouldn't pop up a few days later, all tangled up in yellow rope like some bloated Hells Angel. Then I could repair the camp and start over. There was still some fine summer weather left.

On the other hand, you could put forth the argument that this wasn't wholly a dispute between the bear and me. It was more like a dispute between me and Nature. The whole point of going to the wilderness and descending to rock bottom was to accept that you didn't run things. And no matter how attached I was to this island, the bear probably had a more legitimate claim on it than I did.

So after floating quietly for a few minutes, I slipped the paddle into the water and decided to move on.

~

Minaki's great black railway bridge was silhouetted against a smoky sunset as I paddled into town. Motorboats occasionally sped past me, so I stayed close to shore. As I paddled through the narrows leading to Murray's Camp, I noticed a strange sight.

It was a little cottage that looked like a witch's hut. It seemed, however, to be *floating*. I altered my course slightly to get a closer look. The owner was out on the deck watering his flowers. He waved, and I paddled over to say hello.

His name was Dave. He was a good-looking young guy, bare-chested and tanned, with blond hair tied back in a pony-tail. I didn't recognize him at first. But when he told me he worked as a fishing guide, I realized that I'd seen him at the lodge when I first arrived. He was the guide with the big muskie. He said that he recognized me too. While he'd been out fishing, he'd seen my freighter canoe and my camp, and said he admired me for going "hard core" in the bush. He said that he'd done the same thing when he first moved here. He'd lived in a big tent in the bush, but a bear wrecked it. Then he built a yurt, but a bear wrecked it too. He'd shot the bear, but regretted doing it, because it was "such a waste of a cool animal."

This houseboat was his latest solution. It floated on a pair of twenty-eight-foot-long steel pontoons. The building itself was a charming little shack with curved windows and flowerboxes everywhere. It was clad in rough cedar shakes that overlapped like giant feathers. He showed me the inside, which was decorated like a Victorian curiosity shop, full of antique furniture, glass lanterns, and animal skulls. The sleeping loft was supported by buttresses made from bent tree limbs. The walls were decorated with photographs of Indian renegades. Red Cloud. Poundmaker. Almighty Voice. (What names they had!) The driftwood shelves were stacked with books about aboriginal mysticism – books like *Seven Arrows*, *Black Elk Speaks*, and *Hanta Yo*. Sometimes it seemed like every interesting young white guy I met wanted to be an Indian.

Outside, we walked around the deck and he explained how he'd built the houseboat. As we stood there a raven flew up and, to my surprise, landed on his shoulder. "His name is Gonzo," Dave explained, patting the bird's feathers. "I adopted him when he was a chick, now he's my buddy."

From close up, a raven is larger than you might expect. It preened Dave's hair with its heavy chiselled bill, then squawked, demanding food. Dave told me it lived on a perch at the back of the houseboat and flew after him when he was out in his motorboat, following along overhead like a B-52 bomber. He said that he'd always been fascinated by wild things. He grew up in a tract-house neighbourhood in the south end of Winnipeg. When he was a teenager, he came to Minaki for a weekend and felt like he'd come home. "I'm never going back to the city," he said. He nodded towards the fading sunset and the river, which was glowing like a sheet of rose-coloured glass in the dusk. "How could I ever find a better home than this?"

I climbed into the canoe and paddled over to Murray's Camp. My van had a dead battery and a film of dust on the windows. Unlocking the doors, I dumped my stuff inside, then headed off on foot in the falling dark, looking for a place to eat. Walking up the railway tracks, I crossed a lush fairway towards Minaki Lodge, which was silhouetted against the sunset like a medieval castle. Inside the lodge, I strolled through the main rotunda, admiring the varnished log walls, the big stone fireplace, and the magnificent cathedral ceiling. Downstairs, I found a staff lounge where a group of young men sat at the bar, drinking beer. Because of their tousled hair and dark suntans I guessed that they were fishing guides. At their belts, they wore the guide's trademark long-bladed knife scabbard, minus the knife. (Sign above the cash register – CHECK KNIVES WITH BARTENDER.) In the centre of the room there was a small dance floor, and some girls were twirling and jiving to the thunderous fuzz-tone guitar of "Smoke on the Water."

The music was so loud you could barely talk, but I ordered a cheeseburger and a beer. Soon I was talking to the guide next to me, who told me he'd been in fine arts at the University of Manitoba, but had decided to become a full-time fishing guide instead. I asked him where he lived, and he told me he rented a cabin with a bunch of other guys. "It's a rather modest little abode," he said, with a grim chuckle. "Why don't you come on down and see us sometime? It's called The Swamp."

We talked for a while, but I didn't want to get carried away and spend what little money I had, so I drained my glass and told him I was going to call it a night.

He said, "You're paddling all the way back to Tower Island?"

"How did you know I was staying on Tower?"

"Hey . . . this is Minaki. There are no secrets here. If you're in the Witness Protection Program, you picked the wrong place to hide out."

I slept in the van that night, and the next morning went back to the island to clean up the mess. As I expected, the campsite looked like a bomb had hit it, with shelving, punctured cans, and broken glass flung everywhere. The tent was knocked down and the sidewall was torn open. When I flipped the tent over, I saw that the bear had ripped open an even larger hole on the other wall. I've seen a number of tents destroyed by bears, and for some reason they never use the same hole going out as the one they used going in. It's a matter of principle. They always have to cut two big holes. There was no way of repairing it, so I stuffed the tent into a big garbage bag.

For the next couple of hours I cleaned up the mess, gathering every last piece of broken glass in garbage bags. Then I dismantled and burned my driftwood-plank furniture. It saddened me to watch everything go up in smoke, but it felt good, too, to return the island to its natural state.

By late afternoon, the campsite was so clean that I reckoned an RCMP forensic investigation team would have a hard time determining whether anyone had actually lived here. I needed a souvenir, so I picked up a pine cone and put it in my shirt pocket. Loading the wrecked tent, garbage bags, and defunct little Evinrude 3-horse into the canoe, I pushed away from the shore and paused, for a moment, to look back at the island that had been my idyllic home.

∾

When she was twenty-one years old, Lisa earned $20,000 a week working as a model in New York and Paris. She slept with rock stars, cruised the Mediterranean, and got engaged to the heir to an American breakfast cereal fortune.

One morning she woke up and found her boyfriend dead of an overdose. She wasn't entitled to a cent of his money, so she went back to modelling. But her hard living was starting to show and she wasn't as much in demand. Her next boyfriend was a Saudi playboy who gave her hepatitis C. In an effort to wean herself off the sporting life, she started smuggling Rolex watches between Orly airport and LaGuardia. She got caught and would have gone to jail if it hadn't been for Ray, a grizzle-haired ex-hippie with a pirate moustache who was one of the best organized-crime lawyers in New York.

Ray got her off, and they began dating. He loved her unpredictable brain. She had such a smart mouth, she could entertain an entire dinner party. They eventually got married and moved to Livingstone, Montana, where they built one of those phony *Architectural Digest* log homes and tried to figure out ways to spend Ray's money. Ray took up fly-fishing and dragged Lisa all over North America in pursuit of Alaskan salmon, Bahamian bonefish, and Ontario muskies. When Lisa ended up in my boat, she confessed that she missed those nights in Manhattan, sleeping late, taking long lunches, and going shopping. But she knew that Ray was her last chance at a straight life, and if the price of being together was spending a week, every few months, lounging around in a fishing boat and working on her tan, she figured she could put up with it.

In her sunglasses and blue bikini Lisa was sprawled like a lynx in the front of my boat, smoking a joint and reading a paperback edition of *Dune*. In the other seat, her friend Mickey was tinkering with the ghetto blaster. Mickey, whose bare shoulders were as brown as varnished wood, was tougher, older, and slightly less forthcoming about her personal life. I knew only that she was from Aspen, had been married a number of times, and had lots of money. (One night at the bar in Minaki Lodge, she showed up wearing a necklace that spelled out "Rich Bitch" in diamonds.) Their respective husbands, Ray and Steve, were off somewhere looking for muskies with my partner, Glen.

Lisa, Mickey, and I were ten miles north of Minaki, drifting on the flat calm waters of Big Sand Lake, trying to catch some walleyes. But the fish weren't biting. We'd caught half a dozen earlier in the morning, but nothing for hours, and the day was getting quieter, and hotter – quite unusual weather for the first week of September. At noon, we reeled in our lines and headed off to meet the other boat for lunch. Mickey and Lisa had been feigning indignation about the slow fishing ("Jake, if we don't start catching fish, we're not going to take our tops off"). And when I started the engine and ran the boat across the immense flat, steamy lake, I think they were just as happy to be quitting.

At Skinny Island, Glen's boat was already pulled up on shore and the men were unloading it. I approached the shore and nudged the prow of my own boat onto a granite ledge. The women got out and I unloaded the boat, including the bleached and very dead walleyes we'd caught earlier in the morning. The other guys had spent most of the morning fly-fishing for muskies. After getting the update on their morning (no muskies, Ray cannonballed out of the boat in his underwear, they saw a wolf), Glen and I got busy making shore lunch. We'd been guiding together for four days now, and I liked working with him. He was a better guide than I was, but he treated our part-nership as a democracy.

Using the wooden paddle as a work surface, I cut and parried the fish, removed the bones, peeled off the skins and built a pile of fresh fillets, and kept an eye on the guests, making sure that they didn't do anything to hurt themselves. Steve and Ray had fished all over the world, but I kept an eye on them out of habit. It was a normal part of the job. It was like being in charge of a group of youngsters at a lawn party. You never knew when one of them was going to get a bright idea, like sawing at a can of beans with a bowie knife or tossing a tin of gasoline on the fire.

I'd been guiding almost every day for the last month. And that was a good thing, because I was flat broke. Early one sunny morning, not long after the bear banished me from Tower Island, Dave knocked on the door of my van. He knew that I had some guiding experience, and asked if I wanted to come out of retirement. I quickly got dressed and accompanied him to Minaki Lodge, where we gassed up a couple of boats and fitted them out with paddles, life cushions, minnow buckets, and all the other stuff you need to spend a day on the water. I was a bit uneasy, having never guided on this river, but Dave said it wasn't going to be a problem because we had an elderly foursome who wanted to stay together. "Just follow my bubbles."

We had a good day on the water, and I learned some new parts of the river system. Every day, we went to new places, and I began to build up my knowledge of the river and all its attached lakes. The following week I picked up a few days of guiding out of Holst Point, then Murray's Camp, then Minaki Lodge. Soon, I was making money.

Minaki was a road-accessible fishing area, so the tourists weren't quite as wealthy as the ones who patronized fly-in resorts like Great Slave. Some had saved up for years to come fishing in Canada. Even when they flew here, it sometimes took them a day and a half to make the flight connections, rent the car in Winnipeg, and drive to Minaki. It was as hard as travelling overseas, when you added up the hours and the expense. And frankly, I sometimes wondered why they went to so much trouble, just to catch a few little walleyes.

One night in the bar, I ran into a marketing executive from Ontario Tourism. He said that he'd polled twenty-seven thousand American anglers, and it seemed that they weren't just here for the fishing. The survey asked the visitors to name their "top ten" reasons for coming to Canada. It turned out that "catching a big fish" was actually the least important reason, and "catching lots of fish" ranked second-last. The most popular reason was something like "experiencing the beauty of Nature."

Most of them, in other words, were trying to connect with God. All the equipment – the tackle boxes and fishing rods and polarized sunglasses and so forth – were just accoutrements. They needed to have an excuse for being here, and fishing was their cover story. Serious fishermen like Ray and Steve probably would have scoffed at such talk. But they wouldn't have scoffed because they disagreed. They'd have scoffed because as a fishing guide, I was supposed to play along with the game. You couldn't find God by following an agenda. You had to go about your day and hope that you'd catch a glimpse by accident. It was like looking up at the night sky. In order to see those faint constellations, you can't look straight at them. You have to look a few degrees off to one side.

So I knew that even Lisa and Mickey, with their foul mouths and flinty hearts, were keeping their eyes open for some subtle glimpse of beauty that would make their trip worthwhile. And no matter how much they smoked weed and played loud music and nattered on about their self-indulgent lives, I knew they were hoping for a moment of spiritual connection. As their guide, it was my job to help them find it.

When I finished cleaning the fish, I walked up to the fire pit, where Glen was preparing the spuds. He was down on one knee, wielding his razor-sharp filleting knife with a blur of dexterity that reduced eight ultra-large Idaho red potatoes into a bowlful of dice-sized cubes in a few moments. As the fire kicked in, Glen set the huge frying pan on the rolling orange flames, laid out a pound of bacon, and with his other hand, broke eggs and stirred them in a plastic bowl. I prepped the fillets and opened cans of corn and beans. Meanwhile Ray, Steve, Mickey, and Lisa stood around us, watching. Ray had spent most of his life in a courtroom, trying to swing jurors around to his point of view, and he never stopped talking. His specialty was jokes and one-liners. I don't know where he got them from, but he had an inventory of literally thousands of jokes, which he would launch into, unbidden, whenever there was a lull in the conversation. But when Glen and I started cooking shore lunch, even Ray lapsed into silence.

Maybe hunger and anticipation had something to do with it. There was nothing that worked up an appetite like being outside all morning. But shore lunch was also a spiritual ceremony. It took all the elements of angling – the excitement of the quest, the beauty of nature, the sacredness of wild things – and wrapped them all into this ceremony: the meal. Glen and I had done this job so often that it was like a dance routine – batter the fish, start the fire, wash the fillets in the lake, skin the onions, unpack the lunchbox. Don't let them see the tin of Spam in the bottom of the box. (Every guide carries a tin of Spam in his lunchbox, like a trooper's last bullet.) Remove the cans of beans and corn, and nestle them against a rock alongside the fire. Don't forget to open the cans. Sitting in a fire for a few minutes, an unopened can of beans becomes a grenade.

We brewed coffee in a gallon can full of lake water, and laid a green twig across the top of the can to keep it from boiling over. I poured two cups of olive oil into the big frying pan, and tossed a wooden match into the oil – a floating thermostat that would allow us to concentrate on other tasks for a few moments. (When the match ignited, the oil would be ready.) I cracked an egg into a bowl of tinned milk and stirred it up with a fork, filled a paper bag with flour, dipped the fillets into the milk, and dropped them into the bag. Now the fillets were ready to go. I put them where they wouldn't get stepped on. They were tender enough already.

Squatting by the fire, we worked silently, blinking our eyes in the stinging white smoke. It would be pleasant to wear T-shirts and shorts, but most guides dress in the standard bush professionals' outfit of long pants, leather gloves, and Kodiak workboots. With all this boiling oil sloshing around, you don't want to deep-fry your ankles. Shore lunch is one of those undertakings that sounds good as a concept but threatens to fall apart as soon as you begin. Myriad small details conspire to ruin the whole undertaking. Did you forget the spatula? Forget the matches? The week before, I was working with a guide who accidentally ignited a whole clump of wooden matches in his pocket. He jumped up and whacked his head against a coffee pot, spilling hot coffee down his back. He grabbed the kettle and poured coffee into his pocket, extinguishing the fire but scalding his thigh. He was a good fishing guide but was riding an unlucky streak. A few days before that, he'd been making lunch on a deserted rocky point at the top end of Big Sand Lake when his guests noticed an unoccupied boat drifting way out on the lake. "Hey, look at that!" he chuckled. "Some idiot lost his boat!"

There's no such thing as a minor glitch when you're fifteen miles from help. And if you screw up, it's not the weather's fault. It's not the motor's fault. It's your fault, and you have to spend the rest of the day with guests who'd rather be with someone else.

∾

Before partnering up with Glen, I worked with some of the other local guides.

George Kelly was a muskie specialist. He was an old-timer with fierce squinty eyes and a rural drawl. (He was an Ojibway, but he'd spent so much time with Americans he talked like them.) He had a collection of several hundred hats and wore a different one every day. He liked baseball caps with golf tees on them, or clownish antlers, or messages (*Instant Asshole – Just Add Liquor*). When George was young, his American guests would take him down to Chicago to attend the big fishing shows, and he would entertain the audience by walking around with eight hundred pounds of flour on his back. He was in his sixties now, but still strong enough to walk a one-mile portage carrying a Mercury 20-horse motor in each hand like a pair of attaché cases.

The rumour was that George knew the location, size, and individual feeding preferences of every large muskie on the river system. He would never divulge his secrets, but he seemed to have some odd methods for catching them. I'd heard that he would pull into a bay and run his boat in crazy circles, revving the motor and whacking his paddle on the water to get the fish's attention. (So much for whispering while you fish.) When anyone asked him about his methods, he would just laugh and wag a finger. "Don't get rowdy!"

As George specialized in muskies, Jimmy Anderson specialized in walleyes. Jimmy weighed about two-fifty and, like George, was a masterful native guide who seemed to know forbidden secrets. Jimmy was so good at catching walleyes that all the other guides would just shrug their shoulders and eliminate him from the argument. He didn't count because he was on another level. I'd watched Jimmy fish, and his method was simple. He would toss a rubber-tailed jig overboard, tighten the line, and right away he'd have a fish.

He'd chuckle, wind in the fish, release it, toss the jig overboard, and do it all over again. He would catch about a hundred fish a day and chuckle every time he did it. You could copy his technique but it didn't make any difference – because he didn't have a technique. It didn't matter whether he twitched the lure, jiggled the lure, or let it sit still. He would even trade rods with you. It didn't matter. He would catch one fish after another, and you'd catch nothing. I wanted to find a scientist who could explain this.

Guiding was so effortless for Jimmy that he had lots of spare time to entertain himself. He and his brother Robert devised nicknames for everyone in Minaki, and the monikers were clever enough that they tended to stick. Jimmy and Robert put a lot of thought into the process, arguing with each other in whispery voices, so a newcomer might not receive his nickname for quite some time. Robert was the younger of the two, and with his great belly and tiny baseball hat he resembled a Samoan prince on a fact-finding tour. He stood around the marina, not saying much, jingling change in his pockets and studying everyone. It was demanding work, and Robert took his work seriously. Whenever he got a chance, he'd slip in a few innocent questions, adopting the mildly uninterested tone of a secret policeman. ("So, uh . . . are they living together, those two?") One day I caught a ride into Kenora with them. Sitting jammed between them in their pick-up truck, I found myself being squeezed, both for space and information. It was quite chatty and pleasant, but they still ended up with all the gossip I knew.

I enjoyed guiding with Jimmy because he knew so much about fishing. But all bets were off if you were working for a different lodge. One hot and dead-calm day, I pulled up near Jimmy, and my guest shouted to his guests, "Are you catching anything?"

The tourists in the other boat smiled. "Oh, we're doing all right."

My guest grumbled, "We haven't caught a thing."

"Do you want a couple of walleyes?" Jimmy asked.

This was a demeaning offer, but my guest was happy because at least now we'd have shore lunch. Jimmy reached into his live well, took out a walleye the size of a French loaf, and threw it. It was a perfect spiral pass, and the walleye drilled into the water a few feet away from my boat. The next fish went over our heads, and the next one went off to one side. He threw half a dozen large fish, each one splattering into the water and disappearing with a flick of its tail. Then he issued a regal wave and drove away.

A lot of corporate groups came to Minaki Lodge for their annual convention. These kinds of outings produced mammoth shore lunches, with sometimes forty people gathered on an island. The guides crouched like galley slaves at a long fire and worked perhaps a dozen frying pans at once. Holding empty plates, the guests lined up like bums at a soup kitchen. Most of the guides were fairly deft comedians, and the banter was incessant and merciless. George Kelly had a son named Johnny who, because of his jet-black ducktail, gravel voice, and habit of playing the guitar for spare change, had been nicknamed Johnny No-Cash by the Anderson brothers. Johnny was a wry storyteller, and while he worked at the fire he sometimes delivered one of his comic monologues, like "Johnny's Trip to Kenora."*

By the time the first meals were doled out, the guests would be lining up for a second portion. And by the time the second

---

* "So the judge he says to me he says, 'So do you know why you're here, Kelly? You're here for drinking.' So I says, 'Okay, let's get started.' Everybody in the courtroom starts laughing, eh? So he says, 'Order! Order in the court!' So I says, 'I'll have a rye and Coke, your majesty.'" Etc.

portion was doled out, some of the guests would be expressing deep satisfaction with their lives, rubbing their bellies, lighting cigars, wandering around, and suggesting that maybe it was time to clean up these dishes and get back out on the water. (The sweaty guides, of course, hadn't eaten yet.) One day a fat businessman cleaned off his plate, patted his stomach, and glanced fondly at his buddies. "Well, boys, where are the poor people today?" Squatting by the fire, Johnny No-Cash declared, "They're cooking your lunch."

∞

Towards the end of our week with Lisa and Mickey and Ray and Steve, the wind turned around to the north. The heat had engendered an algal bloom on the lake, and big lime-green waves pounded and thumped against the shore.

On the last day of the party, it was cold and rainy, with squall lines sweeping down the channel like towers of biblical punishment and the peaty smell of the green waves heavy on the wind. As the day progressed the weather worsened. Most tourists would probably have quit at noon. But our party seemed to regard the storm as a sort of survival game, so Glen and I took a short cut across Big Sand Lake, running downwind and side by side through the four-foot waves. Our boats surged like broncos through the rollers and the women yipped with delight. By the time we got back to the Lodge at the end of the day, we were all soaked and frozen.

Glen and I went up to the staff lounge and warmed up while the other guides came in, looking tousle-haired and wild. We sat there eating toast and chili and watching the storm slather the windows. We could see the boats surging as if in slow motion through the whitecaps beneath the bridge. And then a freight train appeared, its orange diesel and black tanker cars rolling slowly across the river. The bridge was the eternal symbol of Minaki, a monstrosity braced with heavy black girders. Sometimes when a train rumbled over it, it was fun to shift the outboard motor into neutral and spin through the turbulent current beneath the girders, looking up through the steelwork at the train's underbelly. Today, I was happy to be watching it from here.

Neither Glen nor I knew it yet, but years from now, on a dark winter midnight, he'd be crossing that bridge on his snowmobile and run into everyone's standard Minaki nightmare, an oncoming freight. He abandoned the machine and tried to get away from the train but didn't make it. The morning after his death I would go looking for some memento of him, searching the snowy girders where he died for a piece of tail light or some scrap of clothing that I could take home to remember my old friend.

Death comes as a surprise to everyone, and a good thing too. Glen and I might not have felt so comfortable, sitting in that log-walled lounge and looking at that rainy bridge, if we'd known it was where his life would end.

After we finished our chili and went down to the shed to clean our fish, Ray came into the shed to give us our tips. Our hands were bloody, so Ray laid the money on the intestine-splattered metal table, slapping down fifties like he was paying for a car. Every time he laid down a few bills he paused and grinned, to tease us, then snapped off a few more. By the time he was finished, there was $600 on the table. He punched our shoulders. "Thanks, boys. You did a great job."

I hadn't made a fortune over the last month, but I'd done all right. In wages and tips, I'd made about $2,500, which would go a long way towards launching my next phase. I didn't know exactly what the next phase was going to be, but I knew it was going to cost money.

ᘯ

The leaves were turning yellow, and the nights were turning cold.

During my long afternoons of guiding, I'd entertained a fantasy about staying in Minaki for the winter, perhaps renting a cottage on the lakefront and fortifying it against the winter. At night, while the north wind scratched and snuffled at the door, I'd sit by my fireplace and work on my novel. By day, I could find some bookish local job (Faulkner was a postmaster) and perhaps learn more about the history of the area, the fur trade, and the traditions of the Indians. I was still trying to establish some kind of working relationship with this country, but I didn't want to put a deadline on it. These projects took time, and they worked best when you went about it indirectly. It was like going fishing. Sooner or later something would happen, as long as you kept your line in the water. But you needed to carry on with your life in the meantime.

Wherever I ended up living, it seemed that I would never escape the universal dilemma of backwoods living – finding a toilet. Like most Canadian bush country hamlets, Minaki is built on bare rock, so houses like The Swamp tended to have no plumbing. The Swamp was nestled in a patch of forest under the bridge. The furnace in the living room had been leaking for so long that the floors and walls were soaked with fuel oil. If you went over there to play cards, you couldn't get the smell of fuel oil out of your cranium for days. But the worst room in The Swamp was the bathroom, with its toilet that consisted of nothing more than a large shit-filled plastic pail with a garbage bag for a liner. The air inside the bathroom was so foul you had to hyperventilate beforehand, as if preparing to duck into a room that was on fire.

One of the guys who lived at The Swamp was a carpenter from Toronto named Tony. He was a broken-nosed ex-hockey player, a thug, but a pleasant guy. He and his wife and kids had discovered Minaki several years before and fallen in love with the place, the lakes, the pristine forests, and had decided to move here. They were tired of the traffic, the lineups, the cost of living, and so here he was, trying to establish himself as a small contractor before he sent for the family.

His bedroom was the only civilized room in The Swamp. He made his bed and hung up his clothes. His wife was always sending him packages of fresh underwear and photographs of the kids. But Tony wasn't having much luck. His construction jobs were always in a state of disaster. He had to drive for hours just to buy lumber. And everything was always going wrong in such cruelly expensive ways that he'd often work a twelve-hour day and come home broker than when he had left in the morning. One night we all played poker and Tony got as drunk as a fifteen-year-old. He wound up crawling into the bathroom and vomiting in the bucket, and when he woke up in the morning discovered that his upper plate was missing.

This wasn't good news. He couldn't afford to lose his dentures. He searched under the bed, under the furniture, and finally summoned the nerve to search in the toilet bucket with a stick, which, as it turned out, was where he'd lost them. I don't know how he cleaned off those teeth; perhaps with bleach? I never had the chance to ask him, because he packed up his van that same afternoon and headed back to Toronto. He was a hard worker, and it was a shame that Minaki lost him. But he was just another of the thousands of people who try to start a new life in the woods and finally give up. There's a common idea that the Big City is the ultimate proving ground for talented and resourceful people. According to people like Frank Sinatra, if you can make it in New York, New York, you can make it anywhere. But it's probably the other way around. If Frank had lived in Minaki, he likely would have ended up selling minnows.

So I lived in the van, took sponge baths, and used public washrooms. I thought about renting a cottage. But the local people told me that winterized cottages were few and far between. And I had certain social aspirations. There was a standard of housing that I wouldn't go beneath. I wanted the kind of place that Jack London or Jack Kerouac might have rented. It could be lacking in class, but it had to lack class in a certain kind of way. Log cabins with rusty woodstoves and squirrels in the walls were okay, but house trailers fitted out with wall-to-wall shag and motel furniture were unacceptable. If I couldn't find a place with a good view of the forest and the lake, I'd go back to the city, which right now didn't seem like such a bad idea. I hadn't written a single paragraph since my departure from Tower Island, and nowadays, the idea of having running hot water and a plug-in typewriter seemed as exotic as any tent camp in the wilderness.

I was sitting in the coffee shop at Holst Point one day, mulling this over, when I looked out the window and saw something out on the river. It was Dave, moving his houseboat. He was pushing it along with his motorboat, and his raven was sitting on the peak of the roof, bobbing its head, squawking, supervising. He was no doubt moving it to some quiet anchorage where it would be safe for the winter. Then it occurred to me, the solution.

ᘒ

Over the next few weeks I made several trips to Winnipeg and purchased several loads of second-hand building supplies – empty forty-five-gallon drums, used planks, second-hand plywood, used windows, and assorted loads of hardware, chimney pipe, insulation, vapour barrier, and roll roofing. I unloaded the whole mountain of stuff on the beach at Murray's Camp, observed by the ever tolerant and solemnly intoxicated Mr. Campbell.

I had no idea what I was doing. But I reasoned that building a home was no different than building an extra-large version of a birdhouse. I felt a bit guilty about copying Dave's idea and believed that I had an ethical obligation to take his original concept and make it better. Late at night, I drew fanciful designs – round windows, ornate swimming ladders, hanging flower baskets, oaken-slab doors with massive iron hinges, and a circular stair leading to a high balcony. I imagined myself sitting up on the balcony in my driftwood easy chair, drinking tea, and surveying the glittering water. I would emulate Sir Henry Thornton and build my very own floating Xanadu:

> In Xanadu did Kubla Khan
> A stately pleasure-dome decree:

Where Alph, the sacred river, ran

Through caverns measureless to man

Down to a sunless sea.

The first step was to decree the foundation, a large square area upon which I could nail up the walls. I considered using a second-hand construction barge for a foundation. But a few phone calls satisfied me that I couldn't afford a barge, not even a second-hand barge, not even a sunken one. In British Columbia they used gigantic cedar logs for flotation, and in Yellowknife they used long sections of heavy-duty petroleum pipe. I didn't have access to either, so I'd decided to use steel barrels.

There were no instruction manuals for this sort of project, so I hauled a bunch of empty barrels into the shallow water off the beach and tried to get them to float in obedient rows while I assembled and hammered together a deck on top of them. This was like herding sixteen toddlers. I'd no sooner get one drum attached when another would bolt from its desk in row number three and wander off. I was working in knee-deep water with my jeans rolled up, and the water was so cold that I could chase drums for only five minutes or so before I had to retreat to the beach to thaw my shins. I didn't know even the basic principles of construction. How did carpenters build a foundation? I crawled underneath one of Don Campbell's rental cabins (observed, with some concern, by the people inside it) and saw that it consisted of two rows of boards – one row of fat boards running one way, and another row of skinnier boards running crosswise on top of them. Every ten feet or so, there was a support post holding up the whole works. Hmm. I could see that there was some logic here. I thought you called the long, fat planks "joyces," but since I was working alone, I didn't worry about terminology. Memorizing the pattern, I lined up eight barrels on shore and built a long set of joyces on top of them. Then I pried and pushed the whole arrangement into the shallow water where, to my delight, it floated.

I then ran a row of long planks across the pontoons, nailed them in place, and began laying down a plywood floor. Once I'd nailed down the plywood, I realized the seams had no support underneath. This was a problem. I foresaw the day when my foot would slip into one of these plywood seams and I'd be caught by the ankle, howling. So I took the floor apart and started over, repositioning the joyces so they corresponded to the sheets of plywood. Then I started building the walls, nailing the two-by-fours in upright rows. The walls were very exciting because they commanded so much space and looked so much like walls. But in no time I ran into the same problem – the seams of plywood didn't match the two-by-four uprights behind them. So again, I tore down and reassembled the walls. It was beginning to occur to me why carpenters always seemed so fussy about measuring things.

Don Campbell seemed interested in my rickety edifice, and now that the tourist season was winding down he occasionally walked down to the beach and offered suggestions. Although he lived alone, he was a bit of a dandy in his own shopworn way, and with his clean-shaven saddlebag jowls and lavish silvery ducktail he looked like he was putting his best foot forward on behalf of the town's elderly widows. "Do you want a bump?" he'd ask, producing a flask of Golden Wedding. I'd unscrew the cap and take a bump, and grimace as the high-octane whisky burned its way into my chest. He'd take the bottle back and study the project. "All right, what's playing today?"

There's something about a floating structure that brings out the Tom Sawyer in people. It seems that everyone has dreamed at one time or another of either writing a novel or living on the water. After watching me work for a while, Don Campbell would often climb onto the deck and offer his expertise. As a carpenter, he felt offended by anything that wasn't fastened with about a dozen spiral nails. Seizing a hammer, he would slash vigorously at the wall until it gleamed with battered nail heads, then he'd give it a satisfied wiggle. "Okay," he'd announce. "That's not going anywhere." His spiral nails made it almost impossible to take anything apart. But he taught me to measure twice before I cut.

The storms of September had settled into the calm, sunny days of October. The water, blue as a flag, was tagged with yellow leaves. It was pleasant to get up in the early morning and see frost sparkling in the grass when I walked up the road for coffee. But my house was going slowly. I'd seen construction projects in which they built a house in a week. I was such an inexperienced carpenter that it took several days to complete the most minor task. At this rate, I wouldn't get the place finished before winter.

One day while I was trying to install a window, I saw a tough-looking Indian guy coming down the road. He was in his early twenties, slanty-eyed and shaven-headed, with a wide-shouldered physique and torn, dirty clothes. He went up to the office and asked Don Campbell if he had any work, but Don told him he was shutting down the camp and didn't need any more help this season. So the young guy came down and watched me work for a while, then climbed onto the deck, unbidden, and began to help out.

I was a little uneasy, because I didn't want to get browbeaten into giving him money. But he was a good worker and didn't ask for anything. His name was Noah Hunter. At one point, I was taking apart a wall with the nail-puller, and thanks to Don Campbell's beloved spiral nails, the wall was fighting me every inch of the way. Noah asked me if he could take a shot at it. I said sure, and handed him the nail-puller. He said he didn't need it. He took a running leap and hit the wall with both feet. There was a frightful bang and the sheet of plywood flew off. I withdrew the nails and fixed the wall in a couple of minutes. After that, we didn't waste time pulling nails or taking boards apart. Noah did the dismantling with his feet. It made me realize that for some people in this world, doors are only a convenience. If you were an executive at Columbia Pictures, and you were trying to duck a meeting with Noah, he'd just come through the wall.

Finally Noah announced it was five o'clock. ("Time to shut her down.") I told him I felt bad about him working for free and offered to give him a few bucks. He said no thanks, a deal was a deal. He said he just wanted to keep busy until he found a job. That evening, in the bar, an off-duty OPP constable approached me and asked if Noah had been causing trouble. I said no, quite the opposite. He said that just the same, be careful, because Noah had just gotten out of the penitentiary, was "extremely dangerous," and that I should call them immediately if he ever showed up with liquor on his breath.

The next day, Noah showed up for work again. He wasn't much interested in fine carpentry, but if there was heavy work to be done, he was your man. He liked manhandling big logs. When he went into the bush to get some firewood (it was getting colder, and we kept a fire in a barrel to warm our hands), he'd disappear for ten minutes. Then I'd see a mountainous tangle of logs coming out of the bush, with Noah's two legs wobbling along beneath. He'd somehow picked up the habit of punctuality in prison and kept an eye on his wristwatch. At twelve o'clock on the nose he'd announce that it was time to "shut her down for lunch." We'd go to Holst Point, and I would buy him two milkshakes and a double order of cheeseburgers and fries. He was an eating machine. You didn't want to get your fingers anywhere near his moving parts. I'd seen enough Jimmy Cagney movies to know better than to ask him why he'd gone to prison. But he said that the penitentiary was "not a bad place." The food was good and the inmates, most of whom were Indians like himself, got along. He'd finished some high school courses, lifted weights, and studied karate. He'd gone to sweat lodge ceremonies and purified himself, learned more about his native heritage. I'd heard that the guards were tough. But Noah shrugged. "Naw . . . they're pretty good guys. This one guard? I borrowed him a smoke? The next day he gave me half a pack."

Meanwhile the houseboat was taking shape. I'd toned down its original fanciful design and had settled on something simpler – your basic wooden box. It's easier to draw turrets, balconies, and widow's walks than to build them. But when it came to building the roof, I was stumped, as was Noah. The typical roof has a ridge down the middle. How do you make the ridge? We didn't know. We considered using a row of support posts. But it seemed like a crude solution. Nobody else's roof had support posts. We pondered the problem, sketched various designs in my notebook, and at one point even considered building a flat roof. Aside from the likelihood that it would spring a leak, I wasn't keen on living in a place that looked like a shipping container.

We called it a day, and Noah asked me if he could borrow my van to drive up to the reserve and visit his family. I could hardly say no, after all he'd done for me. But the next day he didn't come back, and I wondered if I'd made a bad decision. He probably didn't have a driver's licence, which meant that my insurance would be void if he crashed. But the code of the wilderness was to keep your cool, no matter what. Even when it was a matter of life and death, it was incumbent upon the victim to laugh it off. One night at Great Slave Lake, for example, I heard the camp Norseman come droning in for a landing; then suddenly there was a *whack*, like a huge canoe paddle smacking the water. Another guide and I jumped into a boat and sped out to the middle of the lake, where the wreckage of the plane was littered on the water. The boss, the pilot, and the passenger were all treading water among the broken pontoons and boxes of floating groceries. "Sorry to make you guys work overtime," the boss remarked. "Don't apologize to them," said the pilot. "They were probably just worried about the beer." It sounds like bad B-movie dialogue, but it was coming from men who had just finished colliding with rock-hard water at ninety miles per hour, had kicked their way out of a sinking plane, and were trying to stay afloat in water that was only a few degrees above freezing. Maybe people felt obliged to keep their cool under these circumstances because they knew their performance was being observed and would be recounted in bars for years afterward. Whatever the reason, it established a certain rule of decorum, and I wasn't about to get all flustered over a missing vehicle.

I spent the day insulating the walls of my roofless house, and when evening arrived, I got in the boat and went over to Dave's houseboat to ask his advice about building a roof. When I cruised up to his houseboat, I couldn't help noticing the sawed-off head of a bull moose propped on the front deck. He explained that he'd called it by bawling like a cow moose into a birch-bark megaphone ("You pinch your nose and say, 'Ann, Ann . . .'") and shot it as it came out of the bush fifty steps away. He said it was an old bull, and he felt sorry for it when he saw its scarred head and worn teeth ("He thought he was going to get laid but he got shot"). Now he had four hundred pounds of meat for the winter. He showed me the hindquarters and sliced off a slab of dark meat. "Just fry it up with onions and mushrooms, like a sirloin." He sliced off another one and wrapped them in tin foil. "Give one to Noah, too. I hear he's a pretty interesting guy, been in prison and everything?"

It was the end of a cold October day, so we adjourned to the rustic, pine-panelled pub at Holst Point Resort to discuss the theory and practice of roof construction. The pub stayed open year-round and functioned as the community watering hole. The old-timers sat along the bar, and no one was allowed to take their stools. Johnny Rheault was a former game warden and had a million stories. Connie Gevoga was a train engineer, and when he rolled through Minaki in the middle of the night, he played "Shave and a Haircut" on the locomotive whistle. Another old-timer, a German fellow named Hans, had served as a lance corporal in the Afrika Korps. He was captured by the British, and like thousands of other German soldiers, was brought to Canada and incarcerated in an isolated northern Ontario bush camp.* After the war, Hans was repatriated to Germany and instantly emigrated back here, established a fishing lodge, and started a family. He was a pleasant fellow, and it was hard to believe that such a gentleman could have once fought for Adolf Hitler. But some of the other old-timers in the pub weren't in a big hurry to let him forget it. As Jack Stevens pointed out one night, "I used to get paid fifty cents a day to shoot you bastards."

Most of the younger crowd, my generation, had rolled back and forth across the country like loose pinballs before finally fetching up in this ragged little town at the end of the road. Norman looked like Popeye and came from Liverpool. Evan was a young squash pro from New York. One morning he turned left instead of right, drove north for a thousand miles, and ended up in the yard of Minaki Lodge, where he couldn't go any farther north without driving his van into the lake. Anita was a beautiful girl from Edmonton who'd unrolled a map of Canada one day, closed her eyes, and dropped her finger on Minaki. She had no idea what kind of place it was, but she was ready to take a chance. So she packed everything into her car and drove a

---

* There were six different isolated POW camps on the Lake of the Woods. The prisoners cut wood during the mornings and took the afternoons off. It was a relatively easy life, and no one tried to escape. They built kayaks, held regattas, went fishing, and got paid for their logging work. In the fall, they even borrowed guns from the guards and went hunting. Compared to prisons in Germany, it was like being in a YMCA camp. Sigfried Hauser, a former submariner who spent the war in a POW camp and now lives in Kenora, told me that he fell in love with Canada and Canadians when he was incarcerated here. "Those were the happiest days of my life," he said. His wife, who was serving us coffee at the time, was not amused.

thousand miles. The day she arrived, she met her future husband.

Dave and I sat at a table, sketching roof designs on a cocktail napkin, and our planning session attracted the notice of some of these local folks. Soon, they gathered at the table to talk about the various ways of building a roof. I hoped that Dave, or someone else in this crowd, would actually volunteer to come out and help me build the accursed roof, but they were gracefully ducking the issue. At one point, as Dave sketched a typical truss assembly, I asked him if we could pre-build the trusses on the ground. He looked perplexed. I repeated the question. "What if we just build the trusses on the ground?"

He lifted the flap on my jacket and peered inside. "What . . . have you got a mouse in your pocket?"

"What are you talking about?"

He took a sip of his beer. "You keep saying 'we.' "

Despite their attempts to avoid getting drawn into my little disaster, Dave and the others showed up at the houseboat the following day. The men brought tools and the women brought coffee and sandwiches. It was an old-time barn-raising party. I didn't even know some of the volunteers. Kelly was a big, powerful guy with Harpo Marx hair and a clownish sense of humour. I found out later that he'd been on his way to a serious career in hockey, but had gotten into trouble because he was like Ferdinand the Bull. He refused to fight. His teammates made a few cracks about him being chicken, so he invited them to come at him in the shower room and find out how chicken he was. The hockey career didn't work out, so he moved to Minaki, where he kept law and order in the bar at Holst Point. ("In two years I've never punched anybody.") Long term, he planned to start a canoe-outfitting business with his wife, Sally.

We got to work. Some people sawed and measured. Some nailed down the plywood. I crawled around on the roof, tacking down the shingles. It was a weird feeling up there, with the houseboat canting and shifting in the cold wind, and I kept glancing behind so I wouldn't back off the edge. By four o'clock the roof was finished and we climbed down. Carl Jung once wrote that when we build a house, we're building ourselves. And indeed, as I climbed down the ladder and gazed at the finished roof, I was filled with a new sense of my inarguable status as a human being. I was no longer one of those scoundrels you read about in the police column of "no fixed address." I had a residence, a residence with a roof. And anytime I wanted to change the view, I needed only to rotate the building.

That night I stayed in the houseboat for the first time. As soon as I blew the lantern out it became fiendishly cold. It was hard to get comfortable on my improvised bed of planks laid across a pair of sawhorses. All night long, the houseboat shifted and bumped against the dock, and when I awoke, there was snow on the doorsill. Winter had arrived. My front yard, an immensity of charcoal-dark water, was corrugated by wind. Moving carefully on the icy front deck, I checked the frozen ropes to make sure they had survived the arrival of winter.

While I was checking the ropes, I heard a honk and Noah came coasting down the hill in my van. The van looked fine, and I could tell by his face that he felt bad about showing up late. He parked and climbed out, leapt across the ice-filled culvert, and waded through the snow. He said he'd gotten a flat tire up at the reserve, and it took two days to find the gear to fix it. He said the van was fine now. He'd filled it up with gas and checked the oil. He said he'd decided to move on. He hadn't been able to find any work in Minaki and didn't expect that things would change. "All these goddamn cops," he said.

"Well, good luck, Noah. I know you'll do all right. You're a good man."

"I'll get a job," he said. "There's no way I'm going back to jail."

I didn't run into him again until years later. It was a hot summer day in Thunder Bay, and the streets were jammed with tourists. Turning left, I heard the chirp of a siren and saw flashing lights behind me. Damn, had I made an illegal turn? I shut off the ignition and watched the officer's striped pant legs approach my window. He asked me to step out of the vehicle.

Because of the officer's bulky uniform and dark glasses, it took me a moment or two to recognize Noah's smile. We stood leaning against the cruiser. He told me he'd gone to Aylmer for the training and was now a Special Constable. He took out his wallet and showed me pictures of his wife and kids. He was posted to the same reserve where he'd grown up and got along with everybody, except the local bad boys, who didn't like him because he was a cop. "They throw rocks at my satellite dish."

∞

Long before Noah found a job, long before George Kelly begat Johnny No-Cash, and long before Jacques Cartier bumbled his way along the rocky shores of the St. Lawrence, the village of Minaki was already established.

When I walked along the town at night, I was intrigued by the obscure but undeniable fact that this was an ancient community; older than London, older than Rome. You could walk along canoe portage trails a few miles out of town and crunch your way across thousand-year-old pottery shards. Just north of here, you could climb a high ridge and find a row of mossy boulders arranged in the shape of a gigantic snake. Why was the snake here? Nobody knew, not even George Kelly. Or if he knew, he wasn't saying. I'd met archaeologists who'd told me that this settlement was probably about ten thousand years old. It started when the Pleistocene era ended and the ice sheet that covered most of the northern hemisphere receded and made way for the rise of human civilization and early settlements like this one.

In most modern libraries, the great bulk of historical litera-ture focuses on the rise of humanity in northern Europe and how Europeans brought civilization to the rest of the world. Recently, of course, it has become unfashionable to discuss history in such a lopsided manner. Political niceties must be observed, and smat-terings of applause must be offered to the various non-white races that occupied this or that region before the men in leotards and funny hats arrived. But these are token gestures, and most Canadians, let's face it, think that if the aboriginals had been so smart, they would have invaded Europe and figured out some clever way to exploit Europeans, rather than standing by while Europeans invaded their land and exploited them. When the going gets tough, and when government policy gets written, Canadian lawmakers don't take the aboriginals seriously. They sit in Parliament and declare Canada to be a nation of "two founding races," neither of which is the founding one.

In Minaki you could walk along the river at night, where the current rumbled through the black granite under the bridge, and feel the palpable presence of another history, the untold one. Whenever I went to Winnipeg to visit friends and family, I sifted through libraries and government catalogues to acquire whatever materials were available about that untold history. I kept them in a box under my bed and sifted through them each morning, reading them as you'd read the morning newspaper, eating my meals with some faintly photocopied, obscure anthropological journal propped up next to my cereal (*Bear Ceremonialism in the Northern Hemisphere*, 1926).

The publications tended to have low-end production values, and I couldn't find one comprehensive text that gave me an overview of the whole epoch, as did, say, *The Decline and Fall of the Roman Empire*. But that made the investigation more interesting. Each new article prompted a new question. Where were the boundaries between the Indian nations? Who are the Muskego Cree? Who is this man-eater they call the Windigo? What's the Bearwalk? The Shaking Tent? If the Chipewyans live in the Northwest Territories, then why in god's name do they speak the same language as the Navajo?

It was only a hobby, obviously. But just as some readers sharpen their wits on the *New York Times* crossword puzzle each morning, I fiddled with these fragments of confusing and sometimes contradictory history. It was like being a detective or a jungle explorer. Each shard of evidence led down into a deeper and more complicated level than the one before. It was like stubbing one's toe, brushing away the earth to find that the protruding rock was in fact a piece of carved stone, which turned out to be part of a statue, which turned out to be part of a lost civilization.

Minaki was part of the southernmost region of the Shield, occupied by the Ojibway, who were traditionally hunter-gatherers, spending most of the year travelling around in small-ish family groups, living on wild rice, blueberries, smoked fish, and wild game. Their shelter was the birch-bark wigwam and their vehicle was the birch-bark canoe. Each member of the group specialized in different tasks, and being weak or young or old or handicapped was not necessarily an insurmountable problem. Some of the most respected bow and arrow makers were lame or blind. In winter, the group hunkered down and stayed warm by banking snow against their wigwams and sleeping in blankets of woven rabbit fur. It sounds like a hard life. But they worked when the weather cooperated and spent their leisure time playing games, preparing long meals, telling stories, and sewing deer-hide clothing – soft, beautifully beaded shirts and moccasins that for the most part can be found today only in museums. In the summer, the scattered family groups gathered in one large tribal assembly on some windswept point or island for the mid-summer Feast of the Midewiwin.

I'd talked to white people, old people here in Minaki, who remembered summer evenings long ago, when they went to bed listening to the far-off pounding of the Midewiwin drum. The drum was built with much ceremony by a Midewiwin priest. The priest was invariably an old man, because it was impossible to progress to the eighth level, or Sky Lodge, in less than six or seven decades of study. He built the drum over a period of four days. It was important to do it in four days because four was a holy number, corresponding to the circular quadrants of nature, the four winds, the four directions, and the four seasons of the year.

The drum was made of four materials. On the first day he built the body, using a hollowed-out tree, which represented "our plant brothers and sisters with whom we must learn to live in a respectful way." On the second day he attached the head, which was made from deerskin, representing the community of wild animals. (The skin of the deer was also believed to impart an agility and grace to the drumbeat.) On the third day he filled the drum half full with water, to symbolize the blood of Mother Earth. And on the fourth day the old priest opened a plug and blew into the drum, symbolizing the breath of life. He then carved a living root into the shape of a loon's head, and with this drumbeater, he "sounded the drum's voice" four times.

The sound was carried by the wind in four directions and summoned the people to the lodge to begin the healing ceremony. As the singing and the drumming drifted across the water on a mid-summer night, one can imagine the local missionary rolling his eyes in dismay, and the early cottagers thinking that it sounded like a wild party. But the building of the drum was a ritual of what the Catholics call "transubstantiation," that is, a process by which a material object (such as bread) is transformed into the body of Christ. To the Ojibway, the sound of the drum drifting across the lake on a quiet summer night was the thumping of the Creator's heart.

The Midewiwin priests recorded these sacred teachings on birch-bark "instruction scrolls," which prescribed the methods for living a healthy, balanced life, and they stored the scrolls in secret places. The author and artist Selwyn Dewdney (whose son Christopher is likewise an author) became one of the first white people to learn about the scrolls when he visited a man named Jim Red Sky on Lake of the Woods. It was 1960, and Jim Red Sky lived in a remote log cabin accessible only by canoe. According to Dewdney, Jim Red Sky was a large husky man with an "air of serenity I had sensed in many of the elders I had interviewed across the country." Inside that old log cabin he and Jim Red Sky talked about the Midewiwin, a religion about which Dewdney knew very little. Eventually, Red Sky produced seven scrolls from beneath his bed. Jim Red Sky was an educated man, and conversant with the Bible. But he maintained "there's that much and more in the Midewiwin."

Red Sky was one of the very last of the great Midewiwin priests, and after he died, he gave the scrolls to Dewdney, who gave them to the Glenbow Museum. Years later, Dewdney produced a definitive and hard-to-get book on the subject called *Sacred Scrolls of the Southern Ojibway.* I acquired Dewdney's book and hunted down other, more antiquarian texts, like *The Ojibway Indians Observed,* by Fred K. Blessing.

As I studied these books, I sometimes thought about the birch-bark scroll that Martin and Lillian had discovered. I liked the idea that it was written in code, and that it was still out there somewhere, hidden in a crevice on some unnamed cliff facing east.

∾

Meanwhile I was slowly becoming a citizen of Minaki.

I never thought I'd wind up living in a small backwoods community without a single bookstore, library, or even magazine stand. But human beings tend to draw together in like-minded groups, and most of my new friends were young urban people on the lam who, like me, were trying to start their lives again from scratch.

I was enjoying building my house, learning all the things they don't teach in school. I'd insulated the walls and ceiling, and built a kitchen, dining area, and cozy sleeping loft. I was heating it with firewood, and it was so warm inside that even on the most savagely cold winter night, I could rise from bed at three a.m., go outside jaybird naked, tiptoe barefoot across the ice, pry another frozen log from the pile, gaze up at the millions of stars, pause for a moment to listen to the abdominal, never-ceasing grumble of the ice, and then pad back inside. I didn't have to rush, because after tossing the log into the stove, I could climb back into my great fluffy Woods Arctic 5 Star eiderdown flannel-lined survival sleeping bag (a gift from my parents, who, I think, were beginning to vicariously participate in my wilderness adventure) and soon enough, as the log began snapping in the heater, I could drift back to sleep, worried not in the least about the house getting cold, but hoping, perhaps, that it wouldn't get too hot.

I was becoming part of the community too. Once a month there was a town hall meeting, a genuine town hall meeting – not the kind of staged event that has become so popular on CBC television – during which issues of the day were debated. On the matter of the village acquiring its own cemetery, for example, some of the young people proposed that the older folks, the pioneers, deserved a dignified resting place. But the old folks themselves begged to differ. As old Jim Hayward put it, "Those old buggers don't need a cemetery. Just sharpen their feet and pound them into the swamp."

After the issues were resolved, a list of jobs was posted on the wall. Everyone volunteered for something, and if you couldn't find a voluntary job you were expected to devise one. Some people shovelled the hockey rink. Others organized the Saturday night dances, which were crowded, bacchanalian, dance-your-ass-off affairs that took place at the community hall.

I volunteered to work as a roving correspondent for the local eight-page newspaper, *The Minaki News*. I printed up a laminated PRESS identification tag and used it when I wanted to interview a government official or cadge a ride on a Ministry helicopter to the scene of the action (*Forest Fire Charges Minaki!*).

I also managed Classic Cinema Night, a regular Sunday event in which everyone would gather at the town hall, buy a bag of home-made popcorn, and sit on plywood chairs in the dark, watching some hoary classic like *Double Jeopardy* or *King Solomon's Mines*. My duties as movie host were simple – making the popcorn, refrigerating the drinks, doing a little bookkeeping, and drawing the promotional posters and putting them up around town. Every two weeks I'd drive to Winnipeg (which I enjoyed doing anyway), pick up the cases of film, and, theoretically, preview the movies to make sure they were complete. The only part I didn't enjoy was the previewing. Who wants to wreck a movie by watching it ahead of time?

So I avoided that part, and ordinarily it wasn't a problem. Once, however, I rented *Psycho* and designed a series of lurid posters and tacked them up all over town. We managed to get a full house for Sunday night, and at the climax of the film, where Tony Perkins pops up in a flower print dress and goes after the police detective with a huge butcher knife, the reel made a sudden flapping sound and the projector ran out of film. Hmm, obviously a major malfunction. I searched the cases, but there was no more film. Apparently some craven swine had rented this film, ruined it, and not told the agency. Everyone left in disgust, and after they were gone, ten-year-old Pokey Savoyard and a few of her wide-eyed little friends followed me around, earnestly explaining that they didn't understand the ending.

Along with my civic duties, I had to make a living. I'd managed to get an occasional shift at Minaki Lodge, working as night watchman, and all night long I was the sole occupant of the spooky chateau. With a flashlight and time clock, I explored its dark basements and deserted dining halls, observed by fanged bears as I walked through the Trophy Room. My sole duty was to make the rounds every hour, so there was lots of time to write or to read a scary novel. (Stephen King's *The Shining* was considered mandatory on-the-job training.) The shift finished at eight a.m., and I'd walk home through the crisp winter morning, past the bay, parts of which stayed open no matter how cold the weather, past the stands of trees laden with hoarfrost from the mist that incessantly poured off the blue river, and arrive at my houseboat just as the winter sun was topping the trees and swathing the white shoreline with mauve shadows. Inside the houseboat the fire had usually gone out, the floor was cold, and the windows were coated with paisley swirls of frost. I'd split a couple of logs, stuff them in the heater, and get them going with broken kindling and newspaper. The main advantage of cheap sheet-metal woodburners (or "Indian heaters" as they were known hereabouts) was that they threw off a ferocious wall of heat, and in no time the houseboat would be warm again.

I'd sleep all day, and come late afternoon I'd wake up, put the kettle on, and do it all over again. The houseboat had no running water, no electrical hook-up, and no heating except the woodburner. It wasn't as primitive as an Ojibway wigwam, but it was pretty basic, and spending the winter in it gave me an appreciation for the hardships the Indians must have weathered hundreds of years ago. My first winter in Minaki was the coldest in sixty years, with two record-breaking blizzards that piled high pagoda-shaped snowdrifts all along the lee side of the house. But my impressions of that winter weren't so much hard as vivid – the sharp, clean bite of the air; the silence of early morning, a silence so vast that you could hear the creaking of a raven's wings; the orange sunrise spilling across the white lake; the green snow-laden spruces along the shore; and when I got home from my night's work, the happy crude, solid appearance of the houseboat, frozen stubbornly into the lake, blanketed under an immense Bavarian roof of snow.

A dainty ellipsis of tracks near my door would tell me if my buddy, a beautiful red fox, had visited while I was gone. If he came when I was at home, he'd announce his presence with sharp *yap* at the door. When I opened the door he'd shy away, but I'd prop it open with a broom and resume my work inside. Eventually, his face would peer in the doorway. He'd scrutinize the interior, ensuring there were no unfamiliar humans with me, then trot inside, giving me a polite look that said, Got anything to eat?

I was wary of feeding him by hand (childhood memories of catching hydrophobia and being chained to a tree), so at first I wore gloves when I fed him. He had perfect manners though, and soon I was feeding him with my bare fingers. As soon as I relinquished the snack he would wheel around and trot out the door. One night he showed up with two comrades – another red fox and a lovely black cross fox with yellow eyes. They seemed shocked by the first fox's behaviour. But then I began giving him biscuits and they saw his logic. Within minutes they were circling me like trout, darting in to grab a biscuit when they could, and my own fox was getting upset, making little throaty noises and hip-checking them to keep them away from his pet human.

A bit of warm weather during the winter had a remarkable effect on everyone's spirits. Could this mean spring was coming? Even in February a bit of a thaw had everyone cheerfully remarking, "Well, the worst of it's behind us now." Never mind that in this part of the country the month of March usually delivered up some of the nastiest weather of the year. A big pickle jar appeared on the counter next to the cash register at the grocery store, and for one dollar you could buy a ticket and write down your estimate of the precise date and time that the river would break up.

The arrival of spring was a mixed blessing. The locals told me that sometimes the ice went out quietly. And sometimes, pushed by strong winds, it tore up everything in its path. Anyone with buildings or docks along the shore stood to lose everything in a violent breakup, so there was always lots of debate about the signs – the perceived "blackness" of the ice, the predictions of the *Farmer's Almanac*, the rumoured arrival of the first crows, and countless other folkloric indicators that were ordinarily wrong.

In April the weather changed rapidly. The arctic air mass was weakening, and when it fell away in mid-April, a huge southerly flow of warm air gushed into the Shield country. Within days, temperatures shot up and the snow turned to slop, then to puddles, then to sheets of liquid sunlight pouring down the paved hill. The first winter I stayed in the houseboat, I kept a log and recorded the weather every day. The tropical air mass rode into town on the twenty-first in the middle of the night, and by nine in the morning it was warm enough to work outside in a T-shirt. The snow around the houseboat was white and crisp, but the sun was radiant. And when I looked at my shadow on the wall of the building, I could see a blurry mirage pouring off the head, like one of those spirit photographs that purportedly capture the image of a soul leaving a body.

Later in the day I went for a walk along the shoreline, wearing shorts and sunglasses, getting sunburned in the glare. The lake ice was still solid, but had turned black and was as bare as concrete. Boulders as large as overstuffed sofas were lined up along the shore, deposited there in years past by the ice. In the channel near the lodge I tiptoed past "air holes" – spooky cavities that revealed the deep water underfoot. The air holes widened by the hour and were surrounded by "candle ice," supple stuff that jingled like pop bottles in the wind.

A week later, in the middle of the night, the south wind began blowing hard. The trees moaned and creaked outside my bedroom window. At six a.m., I was awakened by the boom and snap of cracking lumber. The ice was going out.

I hopped out of bed. In the predawn light, I could see the neighbour's docks shearing off. Great sheets of crumbled ice were pushing the wrecked docks up into the trees. There was no way to protect the houseboat. All I could do was take my manuscripts, books, and personal effects and load them into the van. At the coffee shop the waitress told me that some people were fighting ice in Town Bay, so I went to watch. The wind was blowing harder now, a warm wind that carried the smells of spruce forest and thawing ground, and a dozen boats and barges were going back and forth like lawn mowers in the shattered ice of the bay, chewing at the front edges of the floes.

I went down to the marina and launched my boat – a wooden one I'd acquired the year before. It was a lapstrake cruiser with a mahogany deck and a windshield. I'd bought it at the end of the summer from the marina manager, who told me that nobody wanted wooden boats any more, and that if I gave him a couple of hundred dollars, it would save him the trouble of burning it. I cleaned it up, sanded it down, and after a few coats of white paint and varnish it looked sharp. It came equipped with an old 40-horse Johnson that ran fine. The motor had been covered by snow all winter, but it started right away. Shifting it into gear, I cruised off to save my houseboat.

The river was choked with ice, and it appeared impossible to make it around the peninsula to Murray's Camp. But I sneaked through by taking long circuitous detours, worming the boat through cracks between the floes. When that didn't work, I broke the ice – not by ramming it, but by running the boat up on top and letting the boat's weight crack the ice underneath. When I reached Murray's Camp, I found the houseboat sitting blessedly intact in an expanse of blue water. A protruding spur of granite had protected it. But if the wind had come from a different direction, it would have been destroyed.

For the next few hours, I butted and steered the drifting floes away with my boat, which was a pleasant job, reminiscent of those boyhood days when you carved drainways in the street to hurry winter on its way. By nightfall, the big southerly was still clocking around to the west and losing its strength. When the sun rose the next morning, the air was balmy and quiet. I untied the houseboat and pushed it away from shore, climbed into the little wooden runabout and swung around behind it. Nosing the prow of my boat against the houseboat's rear end, I gave the motor a shot of throttle and the houseboat moved. Soon the building was budging ponderously forward.

How exciting to have a floating house! Saying goodbye to Murray's Camp, I pushed my home past Minaki Lodge, under the train bridge, and slowly headed off down the river. You couldn't see a single fleck of ice anywhere. The sun was strong, the water was flat and blue, and it was the first day of spring.

∾

The longer I lived in Minaki, the more I began to feel the primitive stirrings of something you could almost call a social conscience.

When I first arrived here, unloaded my freighter canoe, and headed down the river, I didn't hesitate to liberate Tower Island for the cause. But lately, it had begun to dawn on me that someone else might want to use it once in a while. After all, it was one of the most beautiful camping spots in the whole area. So I decided to move the houseboat to Virgin Island, where Dave parked his. On the south flank of Virgin Island, a broad shelf of bleached granite sloped into the lake, and I anchored my houseboat down the shoreline a short distance from Dave's. This island didn't have the cathedral pines and hushed magnificence of Tower Island. But it was a sheltered spot, with clear water for swimming, only a few miles from town, and when I stepped outside at night, the only lights I could see were the stars.

Dave and I were still working as guides, and we often carpooled to work. At six-forty-five in the morning, with the sun already high above the mirrored lake, we'd cruise into town in his cedar-strip Peterborough boat, drinking coffee and savouring a few minutes of quiet before launching into the twelve-hour day. Like most young men, I'd had many jobs in my life, most of which could have been performed by a well-trained chimpanzee. Guiding was the hardest job I'd ever had, and the fact that I was

only modestly good at it sharpened my respect for the individuals who did it well. There were several dozen fishing guides
working the river, and if you drew their abilities on a chart, it
might resemble a diagram of the tree of evolution. At the bottom
end of the chart you'd find the most primitive skills – the ability
to, say, talk without using the f-word more than once in each
sentence, and operate a boat without endangering your guests'
lives. You had to be able to catch a few fish, cook a shore lunch
that didn't have too many ants doing the backstroke in the
creamed corn, and find your way around the complexities of
the river system without T-boning a reef. The next limb of the
tree would feature a more evolved package of skills.

The better the guides, the less they rely on expertise. Deep
water is the repository of all the world's secrets, and you can't
get at the information with skills you learned from a fishing
magazine. Like the subconscious, the lake is a realm of dreams,
populated by transient shadows, and after all the techniques of
guiding have been practised, you still need to be a bit of a magi-
cian to conjure up the fish. Writers have to throw a line into the
unconscious and try to come up with an insight, and fishing
guides meet the same challenge every day, facing the blank page
of the river. Right at the narrows in front of Minaki Lodge, the
river system separates off into myriad directions, and when a
guide fires up his boat in the morning, he has to review dozens of
options for pursuing the quest. He has to consider the weather,
water temperature, cloud cover, season, month, and week. He
has to think about where the fish are this morning, not where
they were yesterday morning. If the walleyes were ganged up on
the Rockpile yesterday, he can assume they aren't there today.
And he can't afford to drive seventeen miles to a place where

the fish were biting yesterday. In the end, all the knowledge in the world produces a guide who is merely competent. The best guides have a mystic gift. Whatever it is, they out-fish the merely competent guides by an embarrassing margin, every day.

I had some of my old guests from the year before, and some new ones besides. Along with the usual array of ordinary tourists, my guest list included four gorillas from Detroit who owned a fleet of garbage trucks ("Hey Angie . . . you hear that? The kid wants to know if the mob's involved in the garbage business!"); a handsome middle-aged former Green Beret who spoke fluent Vietnamese, had spent time in many evil places and done many terrible things, and who spent half an hour in heavy waves one day, trying to revive a dying fish; and a television pitchman who'd invented the Vegomatic and the Miracle Knife (*And look! You can even cut your shoe in half!*).

With such an array of guests, I sometimes felt like I was hosting a floating talk show (*Good Morning, Minaki!*), with swivel boat seats instead of couches and pine trees instead of tropical plants in the background. In the depths of winter, this little northern bush town sometimes felt like the ass-end of the earth. But now that summer was blooming, there wasn't another place in North America where I would rather be. Another armada of university girls had arrived to work at the various resorts and tourist lodges in the area, and the local bachelors were making up for a long winter. (As Dave ruefully noted one morning, "It's not so much a problem of persuading them to come out to the houseboat for a drink, it's a problem of persuading them to go home.") There were bonfires, dances, masquerade nights, scavenger hunts, and late-night screaming parties in hot tubs, with overflowing mobs of people knotted into great garter-snake mating tangles of slithery flesh. In early June, Dave and I bought a piglet for five dollars and set him loose on the island. By the end of the summer he weighed eighty pounds. We shot him in the head and eviscerated him, lashed him to the drive shaft of a Datsun truck, and cranked him over a fire all day.

A hundred people showed up for the party. We had a generator powering the amplifiers and a dance floor in the woods. People were doing the pogo and jumping in the lake naked. Someone slashed his hand open with a machete and had to be evacuated to the hospital in Kenora. Someone else fell in the fire, rolled around, got up on his knees, shook off the flames, and rose to his feet without a mark. ("It's a miracle!") We had amplified dance music and live guitar accompaniment by Sal, another city boy who'd come here looking for God, and who sported a long lush rock star hairdo, knee-high boots, cape, and mystical rings. (The Andersons had named him Quest for Fire.) Sal was not an outdoorsman. He'd had a hard time finding his way out to our island and had an even harder time finding his way home. On the theory that he would simply follow the same route he'd taken on the way out, only in reverse, he drove home looking backwards. He was going wide-open when the boat hit the shore, and the impact threw him forty feet into the woods.

The summer was a great frolic. But when autumn came, and all the university kids went back to school, and the summer resorts nailed plywood on their windows, and the river turned bitterly cold, and yellow leaves skittered down onto the black water, I found myself looking forward to some peace and quiet. I looked forward to cutting up a good supply of firewood, rustling up a freezer full of wild game, hanging out with the old-timers, and settling into another winter in this town, my home.

So the years went past. Calendar leaves ripped off and tumbled away on the wind. I hadn't lost interest in searching for the Big Answer. But in the backwoods, everyday life is complicated. Like a fisherman, I dealt with whatever rewards and frustrations came along, and trusted that sooner or later I'd catch a glimpse of the Almighty. The first sign that the game was once again afoot appeared, one bright spring day, with the arrival at Murray's Camp of a freshly waxed, chrome-bedecked Ontario Provincial Police car.

I was working outside. The sun was beating down on the black ice all around the houseboat, and I'd assembled a rickety catwalk of old boards to provide a gangway to the main dock. The ice was rotting on an hourly basis, and because of its crumbly nature it would have been bad to fall through. I had lots of friends who'd put snow machines through the ice, put trucks through the ice, for that matter, and so many people had drowned around here – since I'd arrived, even – that you needed all your fingers to count them. But thinking about safety all the time is kind of boring. So I was casually trying to figure out how to cross the ice without drowning when the police car swung into the driveway.

I assumed the cops were coming to see Barry Gibson, the new owner of Murray's Camp. (Don Campbell had died over the winter.) Barry was a middle-aged commercial artist from Winnipeg who'd shucked off the city life and moved his wife and kids to Minaki. Being an advertising man and somewhat of a bohemian type, Barry didn't seem to mind having riffraff like me tied up to his dock. He regularly hosted Sunday dinners to which I was invited, as long as I contributed my nasal honkings to the after-dinner sing-along. He and his family had converted

Murray's Camp into a mail-order sweater company, based on Ojibway designs drawn and created by local matriarchs like Pearl Chicago, and it wasn't unusual to see police cars pulling into the driveway at all hours, driven by some cop coming to pick up a skein of wool for his wife.

For some reason Minaki boasted a generous supply of cops. They always looked a bit furtive, doing private errands on company time, but you couldn't blame them. They were waiting for all hell to break loose, and there wasn't much to do in the meantime. They drove around, hung out at the coffee shop, and spent a lot of time sprucing up their neat red-brick detachment building. When you drove by, you'd see them checking and re-checking their equipment, cutting the grass, manicuring the multicoloured flower beds, raising, lowering, and saluting the flag, and monkeying about on the broad driveway with Turtle Wax and soft rags, polishing the patrol cars until bullets of sunlight flashed off the chrome. I didn't mind having them around, nor did anyone else. It made this feel like a real town. And on a muddy April day such as this, with sheets of meltwater running down the roads and the slop, garbage, dead birds, dog shit, and general dross of winter thawing everywhere in the bright sun, it was actually quite cheering to see one of their white-stocking police cars tippytoeing through the puddles, bearing missives from Her Majesty the Queen.

The car stopped and Constable Fred Seyn climbed out. I knew most of the constables, and Fred Seyn was the most impos-ing – a towering, broad-shouldered, blocky-headed man who looked like he'd been built in someone's basement. Despite his intimidating appearance, Fred had the pleasant voice and doting manner of a kindergarten teacher, and he presented quite a sight at the community dances, where, with his tiny wife, he lurched about the dance floor, wagged his arms, dripped sweat, and rolled his eyes with such abandon that you wondered if he was going through some kind of brain seizure. (The Andersons called him Fred Insane.) I assumed that Fred was here to buy some knitting wool for his wife, but instead, he came down to the dock and asked me if I was interested in part-time work at the police station. He said they needed a civilian employee of "exemplary character" who could work an occasional midnight shift. The responsibilities entailed answering the phone, minding the office, and keeping an eye on prisoners who were held in the lock-up overnight. The pay was good ($19 per hour) and it was usually about a ten-hour shift, starting in the late evening and ending at eight in the morning.

I told him it sounded interesting.

He said, "Can you work tonight?"

For the next few months I worked one or two shifts a week. The cops on the evening shift worked until one or two in the morning, then went home to bed. Until they came back to work at eight in the morning, I was responsible for their prisoners, who were usually local native people who'd been picked up for minor assaults or liquor offences. I knew most of them and had worked with some of them on fishing parties. But they never seemed the least bit confused when I materialized at the door of their cell. ("Hey, Jakes, gimme some water, eh?") They were in jail because they were Indians. And I wasn't in jail because I was white. They understood the system so completely that it bored them to think about it. After guzzling their water, passing a few pleasantries ("Son of a bitch, I got really jagged up, eh?"), they would hand me the plastic pitcher, curl up on the rubber mattress on the floor of their cell, and go back to sleep. I'd lock the main steel door and return to the waxen silence of the brightly lit office, where I'd sit in front of the typewriter and try to remember how my last sentence was supposed to end.

It was a perfect job for a hobbyist writer. The office was equipped with a toll-free telephone, stacks of neat white paper, and ultra-modern IBM typewriters. After I wrote my requisite five hundred words, I would brew up a pot of coffee and recline in the swivel chair and read a book or, failing that, the office's stack of dog-eared law enforcement magazines, ads for ballistic vests, and so on. The nights were long and empty, and obviously I was supposed to remain vigilant, being the eyes and ears of the sleeping town, etc. (One night while I sat with my feet on the desk, reading *The Art of Fiction*, a house across the road burned to the ground.)

The VHF radio crackled monotonously, keeping me company. Most of the radio traffic was from northern Ontario, but sometimes, through the vagaries of atmospheric skip, the monitor delivered snippets of radio chatter from all over North America. Sometimes so many domestic assaults, stolen autos, corner store holdups, and motor vehicle smash-ups were leaking out of the radio at once, it gave me the odd feeling that this small, clean, brightly lit office functioned as a sort of hell-gate for all the bad news in North America. One night, stepping outside in my stocking feet, I stood on the lawn and pulled the cold air into my lungs, shivered, and imagined the curve of the planet, stretching all the way down into the Gulf of Mexico. High above the radio tower on the roof of the police station were the incomprehensible stars. Living in the bush country, so much of your time is spent in distracted awareness of the stars, the daunting abyss of the night sky, knowing that you're not just living in the Canadian Shield but also the Milky Way.

Pondering that sky, and coming up with the usual inconclusive results, I turned to re-enter the office and discovered that I'd goofed. As a security feature, the door locked automatically, and I'd locked myself out. My first concern was for my prisoners. What if there was a fire? It was just a flimsy aluminum door, and I considered finding a rock and breaking the glass, but that seemed a little drastic, given that this was Minaki, so I set off for the sergeant's house, hobbling on the sharp gravel road in my socks.

Sergeant Tom Cooper lived in one of the trailers in Pig Hollow, about half a mile away. I hated to wake him up, given the fact that he'd gone home only a few hours ago. But when I rang his doorbell he stumbled to the door, all rheumy-eyed and dishevelled, and looked relieved when he found out that it wasn't anything more serious. He drove me back to the office and unlocked the door without a word of criticism. His equanimity seemed based not just on his mild temperament, but also on the fact that getting rousted from bed at three in the morning was a normal part of his life.

Tom Cooper supervised the detachment and spent a lot of his off-duty time fishing. Like most of the cops, he wasn't much of an outdoorsman, and he always looked kind of quaint out there on the river, this hound-faced old-timer sitting by himself in his little tin boat. He was a bachelor, and in the evenings, when he was off duty, he would go for dinner at the Filling Station coffee shop. He was a friendly sort and was pleased if you sat at his table and joined him for dinner. Trouble was, he always insisted on buying. And he'd do it sneakily, winking at the waitress when you weren't looking or slipping her his charge card. So there was a kind of invisible circle inscribed around Tom Cooper's table, within which you couldn't venture or he'd buy your meal. I'd sit across the aisle from him, and the other regulars would sit over on the other side of the aisle, and we'd all eat at a safe distance, talking to him from across the room.

One hot summer afternoon at Grassy Narrows First Nation, someone phoned the OPP dispatcher and complained that a gas-sniffer named Tommy Pahpesay was firing random shots with a .22 rifle. In a city, a middle-aged supervisor like Tom Cooper would never be required to handle a firearms complaint. But in the bush, you have to improvise. So Cooper and his young partner, Kevin Orchard, went to check it out. As he approached Pahpesay's house, Cooper didn't even draw his gun. It wasn't his style. He knocked on the door and shouted hello, and from within the darkened interior of the house Tommy Pahpesay stepped out and shot him between the eyes.

Pahpesay then shot Constable Kevin Orchard and took off into the bush. A few days later, during a massive aerial and ground search, Pahpesay popped out of the woods and shot Constable Bill Olynik, an exceptionally pleasant fellow who lived next door to my parents at Laclu and often came over to help them with their heavy chores. Olynik survived, albeit with serious health difficulties, and so did Kevin Orchard, but Cooper was dead when he hit the ground. When Tommy Pahpesay was captured, he gave no reason for the rampage. They were cops; that was the reason. Along with a thousand other people, I went to Cooper's funeral. And nowadays, the big patrol boat on the Lake of the Woods is named after him.

But that particular summer, Cooper hadn't been murdered yet. And one afternoon, while we sat in his office figuring out whether he needed me to work that evening, Constables Jimmy

Calder and Arvinder Parmar came into the office. They were on their way up to the Whitedog reserve, where they usually worked night patrol. Arvy Parmar was a newcomer to Minaki, and he wasn't someone you wanted to stand beside when you were feeling unhappy with your hair. He was the handsome elder son of a Sikh major in the British Army, and with every aspect of his bearing, from his posture to his pressed slacks, he was rigid and sharp as a sabre.

His partner, Jimmy Calder, was a broad-shouldered Ojibway with a wispy Charlie Chan moustache. He'd once played semi-pro hockey and now worked as a special constable in Whitedog. He and Arvy were a relatively new sight around town, and they billed themselves as a sort of super-hero crime-fighting team – the Brown Rice Indian and the Wild Rice Indian.

While they prepared to leave for the reserve, I asked Jimmy Calder if he disliked being called an Indian. Jimmy said it was one of those words that bothered some people and didn't bother others. You had groups like the Saskatchewan Federation of Indians, the Manitoba Indian Brotherhood, the Indian Land Claims Commission. But some leaders, political figures and so on, thought that the word "Indian" was insulting. They preferred the term "First Nations people." He shrugged and sipped at his coffee. "Me, I just call myself an Ojibway."

I asked him if there were still medicine men up at the reserve. He said there wasn't much knowledge of the old ways any more. When the missionaries took the kids off to residential school, they made them speak English and pray to Jesus. If they spoke their own language they got a licking. "I wish I was working in those days," said Jimmy. "I'd have thrown their asses in jail. You imagine that? Taking a kid away from his family? Then every time he talks, hitting him with a yardstick?"

Jimmy said that the residential schools "pretty much broke the circle." He said that the only one who knew much about the old ways was Roy McDonald, the current chief at Whitedog. "He still does the drum ceremony and some other stuff."

I asked him if he could introduce me to the chief sometime.

Jimmy shrugged. "You could probably come up with us tonight, if you want."

I already knew Roy by sight because we often passed each other on the road. Roy drove a blue truck, and you couldn't miss him because he was the only one on the highway who waved with such gusto. Everybody waved, in these parts, but most wavers only extended a couple of grudging fingers, or perhaps resignedly displayed a palm. Roy's wave was a vigorous polishing motion, rendered with such a pronounced twist of the head and merry smile that you had to wonder if you were perhaps a more entertaining fellow than you realized. I'd always wanted to meet Roy and wondered if he'd be a good one to get access to the scroll that Martin and Lillian had found. Tom Cooper told me he could get by without me for the night shift, so half an hour later, I climbed into the police truck with Constables Calder and Parmar and we headed north to Whitedog.

On the way to the reserve, Jimmy Calder told me about his own upbringing. He was lucky enough and young enough to have missed the residential school program and had decided to go into law enforcement because his hockey coach was a well-respected and tough old OPP sergeant. He told me about his dad, who was a trapper, and his grandfather, who lived in the bush and spoke no English. You didn't have to go back too many generations around here to drop right into the culture of Stone Age hunter-gatherers. In his own culture, Jimmy's grandfather would have had an Ojibway name, which was usually a single word about as long as a freight canoe. But at some point, during the last three hundred years, his family had taken on a Scottish surname, which seemed odd unless you happened to know that at the beginning of the fur trade, the Hudson's Bay Company had used Orkney Islanders as trading post managers. At first, the HBC had employed only well-educated young Englishmen, who had seemed like good prospects during the interview process, but once posted to the northern bush had fallen apart under the corrosive drip of loneliness and lust and warehouse rum. So the HBC administrators looked farther afield and finally settled on the Orkneymen, a ruddy-cheeked and uncomplaining breed of Scot who liked rough weather, were handy with boats and tools, and were willing to work for $12 a year. The Orkneymen had names like Scott and Kent and Fobister and Calder. And the native trappers they traded with often adopted their clothing, tools, and surnames.

The reserve was an hour's drive from Minaki, and the rough turnoff was marked by a large and quite beautiful hand-painted plywood billboard that some local art critic had ventilated with a shotgun. Due to the sudden and violent bouncing of the truck, I could tell exactly where the road passed from the provincial highways jurisdiction to the Department of Indian Affairs. After a few miles of violent washboard, we pulled into the community, which wasn't so much a community as a scattering of several hundred prefabricated houses planted on an open muddy hillside above the Winnipeg River. The houses were painted in the queasy colours that seem standard to any government-sponsored undertaking – latrine green, hospital blue, and antacid pink. The yards of the houses were full of weeds, bulldozed mud, pools of water, and derelict car bodies.

The police detachment was a black and white Atco trailer with a stack of pallets for front steps. On the inside it had a battered metal floor, plywood walls, and a couple of rickety desks. Arvy said they'd take me to meet the chief, but they needed to attend to a few chores first. The constables reviewed their paperwork and answered a couple of phone calls. I moved to the far end of the room and sat on a plywood chair, which promptly collapsed. This was probably the northernmost, road-accessible OPP detachment in this part of Ontario, and I could see that Parmar and Calder hadn't been given much in the way of first-class equipment with which to apply the majesty of the law.

Arvy said they had to respond to a complaint about gas-sniffers. We drove across the reserve, parked the Suburban, and climbed out. It was a picturesque spot, a warm summer evening. The river was bright, and far off in the west, the sunset burned. As we walked down the muddy trail, a million dandelion seeds drifted like embers in the low light. We walked in single file towards a low-slung abandoned building with sheets of fresh plywood nailed to the windows. It looked like an old school or hospital, some kind of government centre. We climbed up and down over humps of dried construction mud and descended into a pit where a small hole had been torn in the wall. "I'd like everyone to see this," Arvy said, as if speaking to no one.

He drew the flashlight from his belt, bent down, and slipped into the hole. We followed him. The interior was utterly dark; it looked to be a long hallway strewn with plaster and torn mattresses. The walls were covered with spray-painted obscenities and splatters of flung stuff which, judging from the smell, was dried excrement. We walked down the hall, and the policemen tilted their flashlight beams into the adjoining rooms. Gradually

I became conscious of breathy noises in the darkness – small children, perhaps six or eight of them, barely making a sound. It was eerie, almost frightening, to see them walking beside me. I thought the cops didn't notice until Jimmy, almost absently, reached down and ruffled a boy's hair. "How are ya doing?"

The policemen spent five minutes prowling through the darkness. Arvy climbed across a heap of trash and went into one room, where he pried and poked through overturned furniture, sniffing here, sniffing there, until he finally found a plastic water jug. He screwed off the cap and held it to his nose. "Here's the gas," he said. He looked at the group of kids. "Is this yours?"

One of them nodded.

"Now it's mine," he said.

Another kid was touching Arvy's gunbelt. "Is that for shooting people?"

"Police don't shoot people," he said, in the rote manner of a grammar teacher. "They help people."

"We're going to clear all you kids out of here," said Jimmy. "Come on, let's go."

They herded the kids down the darkened corridor, towards the ragged hole of daylight. Climbing out the hole into the sweet dusk of the summer air was like emerging from some particularly fetid nailed-off corner of your own imagination. Jimmy dragged a big sheet of construction plywood over to the aperture and reapplied it, using a flat rock to pound in the nails. "Don't be coming back here," Jimmy said, glowering at the kids. "You understand?"

"We'll be checking," said Arvy.

Back at the road Arvy opened the tailgate of the truck, put the jug of gas inside. The prisoner's cage in the back of the truck had sheet metal benches and a rail for attaching manacles. Even after quite some time working at the Minaki jail, I still wasn't accustomed to the brute furnishings of the everyday justice system. The kids clustered at the entrance of the cage. They wanted to be arrested. The cops shooed them away. We climbed into the truck and Arvy started it. "They'll be roaming around all night," he said. "Looking for more gas."

"Where are their parents?"

Jimmy said, "Their parents are drunk."

∾

We drove down the road to the band office.

They took me inside, introduced me to Chief Roy McDonald. They said I was "a writer from Minaki." The chief shook my hand. He had a slight limp, not unlike my own, and he looked me up and down and wondered aloud if maybe we were cousins. The cops stayed for a few minutes, making small talk with the chief, telling him about the gas-sniffers at the complex. He seemed to have a cordial enough relationship with the two officers, if a bit standoffish, and after a while they left.

Roy took me into a rather depressing kitchen, with a rusty sink and a dangerous-looking electric hotplate, and tried rustling a pot of coffee. He couldn't seem to find any filters. He was a round-faced and pleasant-looking fifty-year-old, with crinkly eyes and a bemused smile that was more or less his default expression. He wore a white cotton businessman's shirt, rolled up at the sleeves, and black dress slacks that gave no clue as to the source of his limp. It was more of a hitch than a limp, and I wondered if perhaps he'd only hurt himself. When you have an infirmity, you want everyone else to have one too.

We went into his office, which with its rough floors and makeshift furniture suggested a supervisor's office on a backwoods construction project. The windows were spray-painted red, and I could see where someone had been working on them with a scraper, trying to admit some daylight.

"I apologize about the office," Roy said. "We had a break-in last week, and they wrecked the place pretty good."

There was a leatherette swivel office chair with a big splash of hemorrhagic red in the saggy part of the seat. I sat down and told Roy what had brought me to Whitedog. I told him I was studying the history and the native lore of the bush country, which seemed more plausible than saying I was looking for the meaning of life. "I was hoping to meet someone who could tell me about the old Midewiwin religion."

He said the old traditions had been pretty much destroyed by the churches and the residential schools. "Many of our children were sent out for adoption," he added, with gravity. "It hasn't worked out well, for us." He said those upheavals produced much despair and anger. The Ojibways, being a gentle people, turned the anger against themselves. "We have problems with suicide," he said. "I myself couldn't see the way out, so I started drinking. I destroyed everything around me. I was drunk all the time, drunk, drunk. Then one night in Minaki, I walked in front of the train and it cut off my legs."

He stood up and gimped over to a flip chart alongside his desk. He unscrewed the cap from a felt pen and drew a stick man at the top of the chart. "That's when I hit rock bottom," he said. He drew a line down to the bottom of the chart and tapped it with his pen. "Rock bottom."

He sat down again. "I lay in the hospital, thinking that since I hadn't died, the Creator must have had a reason for saving my life. So I stopped drinking, learned to walk again, and learned to raise my family like a proper man."

I took notes while he spoke. He added that he'd been trying to recover the old ways, doing sweat lodges and other ceremonies. I told him about Martin and Lillian's discovery of the old prayer scroll.

Roy listened carefully to my tale and didn't speak until the end. "What's the name of the lake where they found it?"

"They wouldn't tell me," I said. "But they said they would be happy to give the information to someone like you."

He wrote down a few notes. We were both dutiful note takers. The vandals apparently had cleaned out his office and he had only a large felt marker. Or maybe he had only large felt markers at the best of times. He said that these old birch-bark medicine scrolls were exceedingly rare, and it would be terrible if the wrong people found this one and used it to start a campfire or something.

"That's what I thought."

"What's this man's name?"

I gave him Martin's name, and the names of his parents too, who likely wouldn't be hard to track down, given that they were both Toronto psychiatrists.

Roy wrote down the information. The only sound in the office was the squeaking of his felt pen. "I'd like to try and maybe rescue that scroll," he murmured.

"Can I come?"

෨

One rainy afternoon two weeks later five vehicles rolled down the highway towards Vermilion Bay, Ontario, on a mission to find the long-lost scroll.

At the head of the convoy was Roy McDonald, in his blue truck. Behind Roy was a small Subaru wagon with American plates. It was driven by Jim Calumet, a Chippewa native studies professor from Wisconsin. Jim had heard about the mission and had driven all the way from Eau Claire to join us. Behind the Subaru was a big wine-red Lariat pick-up driven by Stan McKay, a Saulteaux elder who taught native spiritualism classes at Stony Mountain Penitentiary. Behind Stan was a low-slung, rust-encrusted Cordoba driven by Trevor Manywounds. Trevor was one of Stan's successful graduates. He'd done time at Stony and now worked with street kids in Winnipeg. Whenever we climbed a slight hill, Trevor's saurian Chrysler unleashed a great cloud of blue smoke, reeking whiffs of which poured in my wind vent. I was low man on the totem pole, playing the role of "back door" as we say in the convoy business. It seemed a bit cumbersome, employing five vehicles to move five people, but no one had volunteered to ride with anyone else.

Around mid-afternoon we pulled into Vermilion Bay. A statue of a huge sasquatch stood on the edge of town, welcoming visitors with a cannibalistic howl. It wasn't apparent why the town would promote itself with the effigy of a monster, but thematically it seemed to fit with the dark rainy afternoon and the mystery that had brought us here. We stopped at the local motel, booked five rooms, and had a planning session in the coffee shop. Roy had telephoned Martin, who was now in medical school out in Vancouver. Martin had mailed him a rough map, which Roy now unfolded and laid out on the table.

Roy seemed to feel that Stan had the upper hand on spiritual authority, and after showing everyone the map, he encouraged Stan to lead the session. Stan was a broad-shouldered sixty-year-old with a baseball hat that advertised Caterpillar Heavy Equipment. He said that he wanted to check in with the local Ojibway elders, just to make sure they had no objection to our mission. But before we did that, the first task was to take Martin's map and determine whether the scroll was still in place.

According to the map, the place that was nearest to the scroll's hiding spot was a fishing camp called Findlay's East Arm. We climbed in our five vehicles and drove over there to try to rent a boat. The lodge owner was clearly curious about the arrival of five stone-faced strangers in city shoes, but he rented us the boat anyway. With Stan McKay at the helm of the eighteen-foot Lund, we navigated down the lake for several miles, worked our way through a tangle of islands, banged along on rough chop down a long windy channel, and went across a wide bay to the base of a tall granite cliff, where great slabs of broken granite were stacked like the remains of a parking garage.

With the hand-drawn map on his knee, Stan trolled along the base of the cliff, scrutinized the high ledges, doubled back, looked at another spot, then folded the map into his pocket and eased the boat into a narrow spot between two shattered boulders. He pointed to a rust-coloured splotch on the rock, six or eight feet above us. It was a petroglyph, a drawing of a four-legged cat with spiky horns. "Misshypishu," Stan murmured.

Misshypishu is one of the more dangerous creatures in Ojibway mythology. He's a horned panther that lives in the bottom of the lake. Out on the west coast the Haida have a similar creature called Skana, whose ever-changing moods produce the storms and squalls on the north Pacific. Misshypishu, his freshwater relative, often lives at the base of a rapids, cliff, or waterfall, and although he doesn't confront people directly, his shadow, according to legend, can sometimes be glimpsed if you find a good set of rapids, gaze down through the crystalline, sunlight-columned upper layers of water, and focus patiently on the depths far below. According to Stewie, my guiding instructor at Bending Lake, you won't see his leg or his head; he's too big. But sometimes you might see the shadow of his huge shoulders as he clambers along the bottom.

Stan asked us to stay in the boat because he didn't want to disturb the site. The mossy rocks looked a bit greasy from the rain, but he climbed out and picked his way up the boulders, moving easily for an older man. He looked behind various rocks, then stiffened as he peered into a crevice. He stood there motionless for a moment, then climbed down again, backwards. He took care placing his feet and half-slid the last part down to the boat. "There's definitely something in there," he said.

We drove the boat back to Findlay's lodge and went off to find the local elders. This turned out to be easier said than done. When we arrived at the local reserve, we discovered that the band office was closed, and there was no sign indicating when it would open again. This was the end of August – the *manomin giizis*, or wild rice moon – and apparently everyone was off harvesting rice. Still, Stan was adamant that we look for someone in authority, so we convoyed up and down a series of gravel roads, looking for encampments of rice pickers. Finally we ran out of daylight and went back to the motel. I was tired from a long day of driving, and it felt good to have a hot shower and flop down in front of the TV.

In the morning we continued with our search for the local elders. It had stopped raining. The morning turned hot and sunny, and a great pall of dust poured off Stan's truck as he forged on ahead of us. We talked to some local Ojibways, and they suggested we talk to a couple of old-timers named Israel and Harriet. We located Israel first, at the end of yet another long gravel road, at an impromptu rice-picking camp of perhaps a dozen wall tents erected next to a river. Israel looked to be in his eighties, a bent and gnarled-looking old fellow with a weathered baseball hat, large bug-eye sunglasses, and a bony face that was as shiny and hard as an axe handle. He didn't seem surprised that we'd shown up to visit him. He didn't seem unsurprised either.

There were sacks of manomin, or rice, stacked in a row next to the canoes, and in his usual folksy way, Roy, our spokesman, made a lot of small talk with the local people. He talked to the old people about the weather, talked to the middle-aged people about the fluctuating price levels of green rice, and asked some nearby kids how each had contributed to the harvesting of so many large and praiseworthy sacks of manomin. A bonfire smoked in the middle of their camp, and the kids dutifully fed it sticks while Roy interviewed them. Roy didn't talk to old Israel, however, who was ignoring us. He was off by himself, unwrapping a brand new pair of Adidas running shoes.

He painstakingly laced up the sneakers, then stood up and signalled to the kids. They seized a sack of rice and dragged it over to a dirt trench next to the fire. With a plastic scoop, Israel picked up a quantity of rice and poured it into the trench, then began carefully padding on the rice with his new shoes. Like some backwoods Minister of Finance, Israel had purchased a new pair of shoes for bringing in the crop. A pole was nailed to a pair of trees on either side of the trench. Like a game but gimpy ballet dancer, he gripped the pole as he moon-walked back and forth on the rice. We stood there watching.

Then Israel nodded towards the kids and said something to them in Ojibway. They each seized a corner of the tarpaulin, hauled the rice out of the trench, and carried it down to the water. Like a bunch of classmates giving their friend the bumps, they tossed the rice up and down, sending clouds of chaff skittering away on the breeze. They continued doing this until most of the chaff was gone. Finally all that remained in the tarp was five or ten pounds of glossy black kernels.

Israel directed them to bring the rice up to the fire, where he heated some cooking oil in a large frying pan. Squatting on his heel, Israel tossed several handfuls of rice into the hot oil. The kernels bubbled and jumped, bursting like popcorn. After a few moments, he scooped the rice out with a strainer and dried it in paper towel. He seasoned it with butter and salt, then gave each of us a sample, wrapped in tin foil. It was better than the best popcorn I've ever eaten.

"Do you eat a lot of rice in the winter?" I asked him.

"We eat it every day," he said. "Take more." As we stood there on the banks of the river, wolfing down the delicious rice, with the warm sun on our bare arms and the aromatic woodsmoke on the air, Stan lowered himself onto one heel and chatted with Israel in Ojibway. Roy, hampered by artificial legs, couldn't lower himself down next to them. But he stood there in his white shirt and slacks, and fired off an occasional remark anyway, speaking rapid-fire in that many-vowelled language that is so difficult to learn. The two city boys, Trevor Manywounds and Jim Calumet, stood alongside Roy, listening intently. Trevor was a Lakota, not an Ojibway, so he couldn't understand what

they were saying. And Jim Calumet, the native studies professor, whose authentic native beaded vest, turquoise jewellery,
and melodramatic long, plaited ponytail marked him as the
sort of Indian who'd probably never spent a night in the bush in
his life, listened to their jabbered conversation with obvious
pained incomprehension. Finally Stan stood up and tugged at
the brim of his Caterpillar hat. "Okay," he said. "Let's go for a
little drive."

Now we had to find Harriet, who was at another rice camp,
about forty miles away. Stan drove hard and we arrived there at
sundown. This camp consisted of only four tents. An old man
was squatting by the campfire, brewing coffee. He told us that
Harriet was down by the point. We walked down to a grove of
oak trees overlooking the river. Not far away we saw an old lady
moving through the woods, bending over, here and there, as if
picking objects off the ground. She had her back to us. And in
the interest of gently announcing our presence, Stan called out a
greeting. "*Boozhoo!*"

Harriet turned and faced us. "*Boozhoo,*" she replied.
"*Aaniish na.*"

She was a plump, small, old woman with large eyes, a
smooth pretty face, and silvery hair gathered back in a bun. Stan
introduced each of us. When it was my turn, I shook her hand,
which was soft and warm, and said it was a pleasure to meet her.
Harriet said that she was gathering medicinal plants. She held up
a willow leaf and handed it to me. "This is *kinnick-kinnick,*"
she said, with a tone of gravity and sorrow. "It's for the fever."

She had other plants, folded into a beaded deerhide purse on
her shoulder, and she showed us each one of them. I wished that
I'd brought along my notebook to make sketches. Harriet said
that she wanted to use the last few minutes of daylight, so we

walked alongside her, watching her as she stooped and sorted through the undergrowth. Jim Calumet was intrigued and kept stalking through the brush on his long thin legs and returning with plants he'd selected himself, asking Harriet to identify them. He seemed to have a knack for selecting diarrhea remedies.

When you stood beside Harriet, you couldn't accept how tiny she was. She was perhaps only four feet high. Her voice was tiny also, like the voice of a three-year-old girl. But she exuded a presiding matriarchal calmness that made you feel that if you stayed right by her side, it was entirely possible that nothing bad might ever happen to you ever again. In my turn, along with the others, I asked her questions about the plants. But I didn't really care what we discussed. I just wanted to hear her voice.

When I was a small kid in Winnipeg, walking home from school on grey winter afternoons, I would often feel discouraged about my life – the treeless barren of my neighbourhood, the intractable lousiness of my hockey skills, the unattainable per-fection of Teresa, the certainty that I would some day die and go to Hell or at least spend a couple of hundred years burning in Purgatory, and so on. Sometimes, however, when I walked in the back door of my house, the aroma of Player's cigarette smoke filled my nostrils, and I'd realize that my beloved white-haired grandmother was visiting. Kicking off my boots, I would run up the stairs and into the living room, eager to see my nanny and convinced, suddenly, that life was excellent after all. No matter how many things I'd failed at, my grandmother was totally and unequivocally in my corner. And although I didn't know Harriet, she seemed to project that same aura of support.

As we were walking, a tree branch suddenly cracked off in the woods and a black bear appeared behind an oak tree. Standing on its hind legs, the bear looked at us, then climbed the tree. It was a large bear, with a glossy pelt and a hefty rear end, but it went up the tree as lightly as a monkey. It didn't seem afraid of us. Once the bear had gained the crown of the tree, it gathered a limb in its powerful arms and bit at the acorns. It was about forty yards away. "Boy, that's a nice mukwa," said Roy. "I guess he likes acorns."

"We see many mukwa here," said Harriet.

And indeed we saw more bears, about five or six of them. I'd never seen a gathering of bears like this, except in a garbage dump, and judging by the enthusiastic exclamations, I don't think the other guys had either. It was like all the bears that ever there were had gathered here together because there were so many acorns. And until we arrived, Harriet had been here by herself, moving unconcernedly among them.

When it became too dark to gather plants we returned to the tents, where Stan sat down at the campfire next to Harriet and spoke to her in Ojibway for fifteen or twenty minutes. Occasionally we interrupted, firing questions at Stan, which he relayed to Harriet. Apparently she knew about the scroll. She knew it was hidden there. On two different occasions, she'd visited the cliff and burned sweet grass there and studied the scroll. She didn't know how old it was, but she said "those old people" put it there. "What's actually written on the scroll?" I asked.

Stan asked her my question. She answered him in her own language. Stan looked at me. "She says it gives lessons about healing."

"So it's a medical scroll?"

He put the question to her. She talked for several minutes. "She says the scroll is for healing, but not the sort of healing the doctors do, at the hospital. . . ."

Harriet talked some more, and Stan listened. Judging by the way he scrutinized her every gesture, I wondered if he didn't have a full grasp of her dialect. "It's the healing of the chest," he said. "She says there are four levels of nature – the earth mother, the plants, the animals, and the people. They can't exist without each other. If the hoop is broken between the four parts, it causes a sickness in the chest."

"What sort of sickness?"

Stan conveyed the question. I knew that I shouldn't be quite so assertive with my questions, but Stan didn't seem to mind.

Stan finally said, "She says it cures the sickness of the heart."

Roy asked a few questions, then Trevor. Jim finally asked the big question. "Will she let us see it?"

Stan conveyed the question. He listened to her answer, then finally stood up. He looked, if not unhappy, then manfully involved in an effort not to look unhappy. He said we should have a meeting. We thanked Harriet and got back in our trucks. We drove all the way back to Vermilion Bay, went to the Bigfoot Café, ordered some burgers, and sat there for a few minutes before Stan finally gave us the verdict. "Harriet wants the scroll to stay where it is. She says it belongs to her people."

Jim said, "She's not worried about it getting stolen?"

"She says it's been there for many years. Nobody's ever found it before."

Trevor spoke so infrequently that it startled me, hearing his gruff voice. "Did she say if we can look at it?"

Stan chuckled. "Well . . . she says the instruction scroll is like a medicine plant. If you use a medicine too many times, it loses its power. And then some day, when people really need it, the medicine is used up."

Roy was nodding. "I think she's right." He looked around the table. "Don't you think she's right?" Roy always seemed cheered up by bad news. Getting run over by a freight train had made him a hard man to discourage.

"So what are we going to do?" asked Trevor.

Stan said, "I would like to talk to her again tomorrow."

Jim asked, "Do you get the sense she'll change her mind?"

Stan leaned back in the booth, adjusted his beat-up old Caterpillar hat. "No," he said, "but I'd still like to talk to her."

He looked at Roy. "What are you going to do, Chief?"

Roy shrugged. "I'll stay for another day or two."

"Mr. Calumet?"

"I've been going so hard these last few days," Jim confessed. He sounded discouraged. "Maybe I'd better sleep on it."

"I better go home," said Trevor. "I gotta get back to work."

Stan looked at me. "And you?"

I said, "I guess I'll hit the trail too."

Stan nodded. He didn't seem to care. We finished our dinner, paid our bills, and went outside. It was a dark night. There was a smoky scent of autumn in the air. We exchanged handshakes, promised to keep in touch, and went our separate ways. I gassed up the van, found *As It Happens* on CBC radio, and hit the road. After two days of pounding up and down gravel roads, it was a relief to be on a highway again, feeling that smooth asphalt humming under the tires.

I was disappointed about the way the search had concluded. But that seemed to be the way life goes. You never reach the exact conclusion you wanted, but let's face it, sometimes the conclusion you do reach is the better one. All my life, ever since I was a kid camping out at Rosena Lake, I'd half-seriously wanted to be an Indian. I'd researched Indian culture, memorized Indian terms, tacked posters of long-dead Indian chiefs on my bedroom wall, and studied books about Indian mysticism – all in the hope that old native people like Harriet knew something I needed to know. And maybe my instincts were right, in the sense that I was slowly being cured of a certain foolishness. If we'd climbed up that cliff tonight and pulled the scroll out of its cedar cylinder, its pictographic symbols no doubt would have spelled a different message for each of us. Mine might have said: *You are not an Indian. Why don't you get a life of your own?*

∾

No matter how many times you do it, it's always a lonely experience, coming home in the middle of the night.

It's late, very late. The lights are off and the town is asleep. Minaki Lodge is boarded up and looks like the House of Usher. It's being renovated, and the owners are finding deep-seated problems that are far more serious than anyone expected. The renovation job has stalled, and no one knows when the lodge will open again.

Passing the lodge's black silhouette, I coast down the hill to Murray's Camp, park the Econoline, and sling my knapsack over my shoulder. Welcome home. It's cold and late, and I need a bed. The planks of the dock are wet from late-night dew, and clouds of moths are twirling around the lights. Stepping down into my boat, stowing my knapsack in a dry place up under the bow, I prime the motor and yank the cord five or six times. Finally it bursts to life, coughs and rattles for a while, then settles down into a rough idle. Untying the ropes, I steer out onto the glassy water.

Entering this river on a moonless night is an exercise in faith. It's so dark I can't see the hand in front of my face, so I switch over to the Winnipeg River that branches and forks like a black oak through my memory. The external river, the real one, is of course not perfectly represented by the version in my mind. But I've spent so many years exploring its crooks and limbs that even at times like this, driving blind, I can hypothesize my position with the same kind of approximate accuracy you use in your own home, when you descend a darkened stairway and put your hand out to touch a wall that you assume is still there.

Steering through the serpentine narrows at Orde's Island, I get the boat up and speeding, folding my wool Mackinaw jacket collar over my face to provide some cover from the blast of night air. On either side of the boat, invisible reefs and rocky shoals sprint past like cats in the dark. It's interesting to inhabit a river so intimately that your life depends on your familiarity with it. But in the end, how does that information serve you? Lately, I've wondered if the knowledge I've acquired while living in this country is only taking me farther and farther away from what I actually need in life. As the lights of town recede, there's only blackness all around, and nothing overhead but the cold stars. When I finally pull up to the dark houseboat, I can't help wishing I were returning to the glow of a lantern, and someone curled up in bed, waiting for me to come home.

My driver's licence lists my comical address as "Houseboat, Minaki, Ontario, POX 1J0." Last winter, the enumerator for the Federal Census Bureau arrived at my door wearing snowshoes. I'm supposed to be the sole occupant of this building. But when I walk in the door and throw my knapsack on the bed, I can hear all the little rustlings in the darkness, my room-mates. Living in the city, people get used to being the only living organism in their homes. They get ticked off if they find a spider in their bathroom sink. And if they detect the presence of a skunk under their porch or a raccoon in their attic, it's a cause for war. The last time I was in Winnipeg, my sister saw a mouse in her kitchen and announced that she was selling her house. But here in the bush, the balance of power tips in favour of the critters. Here, they own the place. I'm the visitor.

Lighting a candle, I kick off my jeans and consider rigging up a mousetrap. I killed off all the mice when I left, four or five days ago, but they're such persistent little critters they've probably moved in again. I climb into the soft bed and pull the flannel blanket to my chin. Through my bedroom window, the brightest object in the sky is Mars. It tracks from east to west across the night sky. Right now it's well past the centre of the window, which means it's getting on to two or two-thirty in the morning. People prefer to sleep at night, but animals are most active in the darkness, so this time of night there are always lots of sudden noises. You can lie in the dark and listen to your tenants. A big *clunk* under the floor means that a good-sized animal has just climbed into the flotation. It sounds like the arrival of a flesh-eating swamp creature, but it's just a beaver.

When I first came to the Shield, years ago, I brought along illustrated guidebooks to all the flora and fauna. I was thinking of Nature writ large – the timber wolves, eagles, bears, etc. – and didn't think it would be all that difficult to become an armchair expert on each of them. After all, how many species were on the list? You had your big showy trees, like the white pines, the red pines, the jackpines, the spruces, and your lesser deciduous trees, represented by maybe a dozen hardwoods. You had to learn your birds – your ducks and grouse, which in fact I already knew; your birds of prey, which you had to divide into falcons, buteos, and accipiters. And although the catalogue got a little more confusing when you got down to the insects, dragonflies, midges, and so on, that's what made it challenging. Compared to a tropical forest, the Shield seemed like a stripped-down, minimalist sort of ecosystem. It was like a big three-chord Neil Young ballad that covered half the country. Pine trees and granite, big skies, blue waters. Its beauty was in its simplicity. In total, I couldn't imagine that there'd be more than a hundred species to learn. In fact when I first got here, the bush seemed almost devoid of life.

But just because you can't see things doesn't mean they aren't there. The place was actually teeming with creatures; I just wasn't aware of them. Some animals forage in darkness, and you have to be a bit of a forensic investigator to detect their presence. You might never see the fierce and silent horned owl, although it's very common, but you'll find neat regurgitated packets of compressed fur and bones under a tall tree. Fishers are common too. They're low-slung and serpentine, like a lady's fur wrap sprung to life, and they know a special mongoose-like move that enables them to kill a porcupine without getting jabbed by quills. Fishers are ubiquitous all through the Shield country, but they're so furtive you'll rarely meet anyone who's seen one.

Some predators hunt with their ears, tilting their heads back and forth to focus on the source of a sound. And that makes sense, given that you tend to hear more animals than you see. When I'm lying in bed, the action never ceases. I can hear deer mice skittering up and down the walls, trying to find an entry that isn't plugged with steel wool. Outside the screened window, a soft but distinct *cheep* indicates the aerial passage of a brown bat, issuing its regular echo locator as it zooms around hunting mosquitoes. A loud thump on the roof, followed by a scrabble of claws, means that a flying squirrel has come to visit. It has to be a flying squirrel because it's the only squirrel active at night. They have immense liquid eyes and a kind of furry parachute that folds up into their underarms. Trappers say the best bait for catching them is a red rubber ball.

When I first arrived here most of my neighbours were hiding in plain sight. One day I watched a dragonfly patrol a quadrant of air in front of the houseboat. Her patrol zone was about a hundred feet square, and she went back and forth across it like a NATO helicopter, clipping insects that wandered into it and rushing other dragonflies that violated her boundaries. She was a big one, the common type known as the green darner. Most dragonflies die in the fall but green darners are strong enough to migrate south, like birds. Her labours continued all day, and when evening arrived, she was still zipping back and forth. When I lit the barbecue, I felt that I should be shouting a greeting at her, my neighbour.

Ants have lives too. Most ants are based in a central colony, but each travels up to a mile a day, searching for food. The old horror movies equate brutality with size. We assume that a beast isn't really scary unless it's capable of overturning a police car. But in nature, the downsized world seems the more savage one. Compare solemn and gentle creatures like the whale and the elephant to the bloodthirsty mouse, which thinks nothing of eating its own babies if there are no groceries in the house. Ants, with their mandible jaws and military alliances, end up serving as cannon fodder for some pampered queen. And if you follow a solitary ant for a few hundred yards, across open granite and through heavy forest, you can see that it has to face more dangers than one of the ancient warriors of Xenophon.

I have no idea how many ants live on this island, but they deserve to be on the census, as do the flying insects, whose numbers are legion. In this one houseboat alone, how many paper wasps live in that nest under the eaves? How many spiders inhabit the rafters, the walls, or the crannies along the windows? How many midges hold mating dances around the window boxes, and collapse in furry piles that must comprise tens of thousands? When I first came here I thought I was alone. But on nights like this, lying in my flannel bed, listening to all those scampering feet and tiny wings, I feel like I'm lying on my back in the marketplace of some bustling, alien city.

The world gets more crowded as you descend the food chain. Myriad tiny minnows live under the houseboat, and I've given up trying to identify them. When I tie up the boat and aim a flashlight at the water, they swarm through the down-slanting bomb of light. Some nights there are thousands of them; other nights there are none. I have no idea where they go, or where they've been. They apparently eat tiny shrimp and water bugs, which in turn prey on the zooplankton, which are tiny predators themselves.

Zooplankton hunt at night. They lurk in the depths of the lake until sundown, when they rise to the surface to hunt their cousins, the phytoplankton. Phytoplankton extract energy from sunlight and are simple-minded enough to be considered plants. Even smaller than the phytoplankton are the nematodes – microscopic wormlike creatures that should be counted on the census too. Beneath my bed, in the silt that covers the lake bottom, or in the dark soil that gives root to the bulrushes along the nearby shore, there are swarming colonies of nematodes. Nematodes in turn are massive compared to microbes, which are too numerous to count. In one cup of soil there are more microbes than all the people on earth.

∾

When Charles Darwin published *The Origin of Species* in 1859, he articulated a number of simple and aesthetically perfect ideas. Perhaps the most useful of these, from a layperson's point of view, is that success is determined by adaptability. The earth is covered with various landscapes. If animals succeed in adapting to a landscape, they survive. If they don't, they die. The map of Canada is dominated by the lakes, forests, and rocky outcrops of the Shield. It's a harsh landscape, with very little soil and pronounced swings of temperature from one season to the next. Virtually every corner of it is raked by wildfire every few decades, and it's populated by hordes of biting insects that can literally drain the blood from an exposed living body. If you're going to make a living on the Shield, you have to adapt to it. The Shield is not going to adapt to you.

When I lie in bed, listening to the sounds of the night, I often wonder how I'm ever going to fit in here. Ever since I was a kid I've wanted to live here, or at least somehow make a place for myself. But so far, it's been like digging at granite with a wooden spoon. I work as a fishing guide, which is an interesting and quirky sort of job, but no serious person would mistake it for a lifelong career. I have several cardboard boxes full of handwritten, unpublished fiction stuffed under my bed. But I'm only

beginning to get a grasp of the novelist's craft – plot development, characterization, and so on. I've been reading books on
the architecture of fiction, books like John Gardner's famous
text, and I'm beginning to appreciate that my laborious novels
are mostly just rambling disconnected stories with no noticeable
beginning or end.

I still have my night job at the police station. But that's not a
promising career either, and it doesn't have much to do with the
wilderness. I came here on a kind of quest. I wanted to learn
this country's secrets, or at least engage it in some kind of dialogue. But the country is ignoring me. Lying here, watching
Mars inch minutely across the window, I can dispassionately
look at my life without vested interest, as a book critic might,
and say that the stakes are definitely rising. In conventional
novels, the character usually emerges triumphant in the final
chapter. But the Canadian backwoods is inherently anti-heroic.
Around here, the only thing that's going to emerge triumphant
is the landscape.

Tomorrow night is Friday night, which means I'll have two
choices for spending the evening – staying home, or going to the
beer parlour. The beer parlour sits in the centre of town, luring
bachelors like me from far and wide with its glowing windows.
To hell with the wilderness, let's get drunk. All the bachelors are
hoping to meet a woman, a special woman with a pretty face
and a great personality who perhaps has a good job, owns a new
pick-up truck, and enjoys a bit of moose hunting. Everyone's
head swivels as if on gimbals every time the door opens, hoping
it's Miss Perfect, but she never walks in. Like every other
Canadian backwoods town, Minaki suffers from a permanent
shortage of women. Every autumn, as the north starts to empty

out, men outnumber women by a factor of about ten to one. On a typical night at the pub, there might be a dozen people drinking beer and playing pool. And the only woman in the whole place might be Susan, the bartender.

In the beer parlour at night, women are so absent that their absence becomes a kind of presence. Their absence imparts gravity to the most mundane of moments. Standing in the bathroom, washing your hands, glancing in the mirror for a moment to comb your hair, you suddenly realize, I have no one. Playing a game of snooker, working on your fifth ponderous glass of beer, the most banal Elton John ballad seems to have taken on remarkable artistic insight and emotion. Out at the snooker table, or along the sombre rows of men at the bar, there are never any conversations about women. The bachelors don't have to talk about women. Women are already the topic of every conversation they aren't having.

Years ago, a lot of young people came here in search of Utopia. But no one is young any more, and there's a widespread feeling that the party is ending. The community is fragmenting into tribes. The Married Tribe is composed of people who are settling down, building houses, and having children. As much as I grumble about my friends getting old and getting married, I have to admit that my resentment is fuelled partially by envy. Kelly and Sally are building a swanky lodge on the shores of Gun Lake. They've got their pilot's licences and have purchased a float-equipped airplane. Pete and Trout are building a tourist operation with neat cabins they rent out for $1,000 per week. (The resort is known locally as Tax Dodge Lodge.) My friend Dave has become a wilderness outfitter. He likewise flies his own float plane, guides an exclusive clientele of wealthy hunters and fishermen, and is beginning to rack up a collection of true-life adventures, some of which have even been documented in magazines like *Reader's Digest* ("Flight Into Danger!"). For the Married Tribe, moving to this little town in the northern Ontario bush was the best thing they ever did. Instead of soldiering away at some faceless corporation in the city, they're launching remarkable and highly individual lives. They're building splendid homes with floor-to-ceiling windows looking out on the wilderness. They're installing outdoor Jacuzzis on their multi-levelled cedar sundecks and growing their own produce out back. I'm glad they've figured out some perfect formula for unlocking the secret of this country, but I haven't. And I can feel the pressure incessantly rising, as though we were all back at university, in final exams. They've handed in their papers and waltzed out. But I'm still sitting here, stuck.

My comrades are the ones who are left behind: the Bachelor Tribe – a loosely knit group of oddballs, old-timers, fishing guides, carpenter's helpers, away-from-home railway workers, drunks, bush pilots with voided licences, know-it-alls, vagrants, and disheartened puppy-dog police constables who still can't quite figure out how they got posted to this hick town. They tend to gather every night at the beer parlour to commiserate, shoot pool, and tell absurd stories. (One of the new cops, for example, claims he's engaged to Miss Canada.) I like them all well enough. In fact, they're the most entertaining group in town. But I'm not quite ready to develop a serious drinking problem. So I spend most of my evenings at home, reading or writing, listening to the radio. Or else every couple of days, at about four in the afternoon, I dress warmly, load the boat, and cruise out to explore the wilderness, which is why I came here in the first place.

In the autumn, once the water gets cold, the risk of falling overboard and dying of exposure adds a kind of religious zest to boat travel, and I like heading down the river, banging across the charcoal-dark waves into the biting wind. Once I've caught a limit of fish (catching walleyes is easy in the fall), I pull up the boat on the shore and spend the last few hours of the day hunting for grouse. Walking along a forest ridge in some far-flung dead end of the river, you wonder if any human being has ever stepped on these granite hills. The last big thing that happened around here was the Pleistocene ice age, ten thousand years ago. Compared to four and a half billion years of planetary history, ten thousand years is not a long time. And it's not even a long time in human terms. If you consider that an average human life lasts seventy-two years, the ice age ended only 138 lives ago. You could in fact quite easily throw a party that included someone from every generation in human history. You could hold the party in the Grand Rotunda at Minaki Lodge; it would be the ultimate masked ball. Marie Antoinette and Cleopatra would be comparing notes in one corner, while outside, Ernest Hemingway might be watching Turok, the Son of Stone, sketch a giant Pleistocene lion on the patio with a piece of chalk.

These hills are like the halls of time. Environmentalists are worried that the so-called greenhouse effect will trigger a catastrophic increase in the earth's temperature. But a smaller group of scientists argues for a more dramatic and frightening scenario. They've been drilling core samples in the Greenland ice cap and have discovered that ice ages are a normal aspect of the planet's weather cycle. Cold periods last about ninety thousand years; warm periods last about ten thousand years. We're just coming to the end of a ten-thousand-year-long warm period. But that's not the scary part. The onset of an ice age is usually preceded by a pronounced warm spell. The temperature of the planet goes up and down, but it stays within a manageable limit, regulated by ocean currents, which function as the earth's natural thermostats. In the Atlantic the Gulf Stream, which pumps warm air into the northern hemisphere, shuts off if the weather gets too warm. During the 1600s, a prolonged hot dry spell caused the Gulf Stream to slow down, which plunged Europe into its well-documented "Little Ice Age," in which the Thames froze. Over in the Pacific Ocean, the Christ Child or El Niño current functions as a temperature thermostat for much of North America. But that's not the scary part either. What the scientists have discovered is that the onset of an ice age may be much more sudden than we formerly believed. Ice core samples suggest that ice ages are preceded by a steady rise in temperatures, followed by a pronounced correction: a cooling-off period that may actually bring on an ice age within a short period of time. Not millennia, not centuries, but *decades*.

Glaciers never go away. They just retreat. You can look at them on the maps, great packs of them positioned in staging areas across the north. They respond quickly to small variations in weather. Whenever the weather cools down, snow begins to fall. Under falling snow a glacier gathers mass, and its outer edges push outward. You'd think that a glacier's rate of travel would be slow – "glacial" – but once they get moving they grumble and creak like bulldozers, grinding forward at an alarming rate, up to a hundred yards per day. Their undersides are crusted with frozen rock. During the last ice age, the glaciers that covered most of Canada and the northern United States were about a mile thick. Pressed down by such an enormous slab of ice, the raspy undersurface works away granite like a belt-sander works wood. This repeated rasping by glaciers is what creates the undulant granite contours of the Shield. And if you think your own life is a temporary thing, go for an autumn walk in the bush country and you'll be forcefully reminded of the ephemeral quality of all living things. Everywhere on the smooth ground are the glacial striations, long parallel grooves resembling claw marks.

So even though I enjoy walking in the bush more than sitting in the beer parlour, it definitely reinforces the suspicion that time is not my ally. One cool October night I hooked an extraordinarily strong fish. It took five minutes to bring it to the side of the boat, and when I finally scooped it into the net I recognized it as a whitefish, a silvery thing with buggy eyes and clownish lips. I'd never caught a whitefish before and had no idea how to cook one, so I slipped it back into the water. The hook had cut its velvety gills and it was bleeding profusely. I shut off the motor and did a bit of CPR, pumping it back and forth in the numbingly cold water until it finally thrashed its tail and disappeared into the depths. A few minutes later, it floated back up to the surface, trembling, dead.

In the darkness of the autumn evening I carried the fish through town, trying to give it away. It was a big one, a five-pounder. But no one else knew how to cook a whitefish either, and with its overlapping scales it looked vaguely carplike and inedible. Finally I thought of The Prince, a well-liked but impoverished handyman who often strolled around town in a ruined navy blazer and beat-up yachting cap. The Prince was an active member of the Bachelor Tribe and probably needed a girlfriend even more than I did. He was living proof of the fact that men don't do well alone. Women get along fine alone. They somehow acquire a proper place to live, decent furniture, and a nice little imported automobile. But men tend to drop through the floor of the world and keep going.

I knew that The Prince lived on the edge of town in a camper van. Being a van owner myself, I'd always felt curious about his setup, so I walked over to offer him the fish. It was getting dark. I picked my way through the weeds to the back of the community hall, where I found an extension cord plugged into the back wall. By following the yellow cord through the darkened woods, I eventually came to a grassy clearing and a Volkswagen van. Its windows were illuminated with the blue glow of a television, which explained the extension cord.

I knocked on the door and The Prince appeared. He was pleased to accept the fish. ("Well, I'll make use of it for my Thanksgiving dinner! Thank you very much!") He had polish. He had manners and, like many people occupying the lower end of the economy, didn't seem to have a care in the world. He no doubt came from a good community somewhere, where he might have stayed and lived a normal life. But just like me, he'd rolled around the country until he'd wound up here. While I stood there talking to him it occurred to me that I didn't know his real name, and I felt embarrassed by that. What if he died some day? How would we commemorate him? Would we just sharpen his feet and pound him into the swamp? Perhaps no one else knew his real name either. That was the way it was, in this town. If I stayed here much longer, I'd probably lose my real identity too.

We bantered for a few minutes and then he showed me his van. It was small, and I just peered in the doorway. It contained a rumpled bed and a massive Sony television. He'd rigged up a little wood heater in the corner, with a crooked chimney that fed up through a hole in the roof, and it was so hot inside that the side windows were half-open.

I declined The Prince's dinner invitation and wished him luck with the fish. As I walked back out to the road, I glanced back at his campsite. The blue glow of the television filled the wooded clearing. He was back inside the van, and his bare legs were hanging out the window.

∾

That autumn, I enrolled in a creative writing class.

On Thursday afternoon, I'd make the long drive into the city with my briefcase full of dog-eared foolscap. The class took place at the University of Manitoba, in a gothic old hulk called the Tier Building. Walking into the Tier Building made me feel sheepish. I was the prodigal son, crawling back home as they always do.

If the highway was slippery I'd get to class a bit late, with snowflakes in my hair and the reek of woodsmoke on my sweater. "Oh good," my classmate Sandra Birdsell would announce, "our token wilderness writer is here."

Some writers feel that you can't learn to write in a classroom. And in truth, the very notion of studying "creative writing" seems to verge on the cornpone, like studying guitar by the Mel Bay Method. But our instructor was Robert Kroetsch, a man who wrote novels and had actually won a Governor General's Award, so I thought I might learn something. At the very least, I'd meet some other writers.

The bearded, frowning Kroetsch was a patient teacher. He listened to our stories and suggested approaches we might take to improve our technique. As soon as he made a suggestion, I usually realized he was right. And that structural problem, or error of syntax, or whatever it was, joined the list of mistakes I resolved to never make again. Just like playing a violin, writing requires arduous work, and it was exciting to learn new tricks.

When class was over, everyone adjourned to the campus pub, except for me. It was a three-hour drive home, and I didn't feel up to tackling a slippery highway after half a dozen beers. This habit of leaving at the end of class turned me, undeservedly, into a man of mystery, and I almost enjoyed teasing my classmates by refusing their invitations. "Can't you come for just one beer?" Kroetsch would ask, scowling with fatherly concern. "Gotta run," I'd say with a smile, lifting my glove in farewell. "Miles to go before I sleep."

I was working on a story called "Two Yellow Pails," a tale about a doomed romance between a white schoolteacher and a young native woman on the reserve north of Minaki. My classmates made some good suggestions for this story and I reworked it, then sent it off to a Toronto literary magazine called *Descant*. A few months later, I got a note in the mail. To my shock, they said they wanted to publish it, and furthermore, they'd pay me $85. It was my first publication, and in fact the first publication in our class. And since it was really my classmates' analysis that had made the story publishable, I went to the bar that night and picked up the tab, which with this hard-partying crew turned out to be more than I was getting paid for the story.

That night in the bar, I sat next to one of the married women in the class. We'd become quite a friendly and close-knit group, and perhaps out of sisterly empathy, she proposed to "fix me up" with one of her friends. This never works out, of course, but my datebook wasn't exactly filled with engagements so I agreed. On our first meeting, at a dinner party at my friend's house, my blind date, whose name was Mandy, didn't show up. She turned out to be sick, and I was glad she was. I knew she wouldn't like me and I wouldn't like her. I'd been on only a couple of blind dates in my life but they'd worked effectively as aversion therapy. During the dinner, my friend did the hard sell, told me what an attractive woman Mandy was. She said Mandy was a divorcée, who before her divorce had lived with her husband in a lovely antique farmhouse near Riding Mountain. "She's very interested in the fact that you live in a houseboat."

The next time, it was my turn to stand Mandy up. My van broke down and I was unable to drive to the city. Then spring came, the class ended, we all moved on with our lives. That summer, I worked again as a guide and spent a lot of time doing renovations on the houseboat. Renovations usually fall into one of two categories – maintenance or improvements. These definitely weren't improvements. They weren't even mainte-nance. They were last-ditch efforts to keep the place floating. Five or six years of freeze-ups and violent thaws had played hell with my flotation. The sixteen oil drums upon which the house-boat rested – substandard flotation at the best of times – had rusted, cracked, and shipped water. The floor was now only a few inches above the waterline, and the whole building heeled over alarmingly when I walked from one side to the other. I tried pushing long billets of Styrofoam under the deck, but each billet had about eight hundred pounds of flotation force, and it required a lot of planning to get one under the building.

I went to the pub and enlisted the help of four or five buddies. They jammed the nose of the billet under the building and then stood on the foam, trying to weigh it down, gripping each other by the waist, looking like nervous bachelors in a conga line, while I backed off with the boat and gently charged the billet, butting it repeatedly, forcing it under a few inches at a time. This method worked pretty well until the foam billet fetched up against a half-flooded drum. When I butted the billet, it slewed sideways. In slow motion my helpers waved their arms, rolled their eyes, grabbed at each other, then keeled over into the water.

Some of them suggested that I needed to remove the goddamn drums before inserting the foam. The drums still contained enough air to make such removal problematic, so I tried punching holes in them by hand. This was cold and difficult work. Climbing into the cold water, crawling around in the lily pads, I banged on the greasy steel with a hammer and chisel. But the holes didn't do much good if they were above the waterline, and hammering under water is a mug's game. Furthermore, some of the barrels were hidden under the floor, and for these, I had no choice but to blast holes in them with a .308 rifle, fired right through the floor. It wasn't the first time that I was forced to tackle some tricky repair problem with firearms, and although it may sound entertaining, it's actually fairly unpleasant work which calls for a thick towel around the head to preserve the old eardrums.

Attracted by loud gunfire, which even in Minaki was unusual in the middle of town, Larry Willot showed up in the OPP boat and asked me what in god's name I was doing. After I explained the problem, he offered to help out, and drifted down the side of the houseboat and blasted away at the rusty drums with his .38 revolver. Still, the barrels were slow to die. Some of them wallowed free, barely afloat, and I rolled them ashore. In the vacant spaces under the houseboat I jammed in blocks of foam, sawing them to fit. It was a makeshift repair, and by the time September arrived, the water became too cold to work in, and the houseboat was more waterlogged than ever.

I had a vague notion that freeze-up would solve everything. Once the houseboat was locked into the ice, I'd pry it up with hydraulic jacks, lay timbers under it, and lower it onto a fresh new foundation constructed of special marine foam and pressure-treated lumber. Once spring came, the houseboat would descend through the melting ice, and I'd get a few more years out of it.

Eventually I'd build a real house. That was my long-term scheme. You can't live in the backwoods without a scheme. Eventually, I planned to build a log house, which this time would be a real pleasure dome. I'd even selected the property: a handsome peninsula with access by bush road. I'd found out that you could get a government permit to harvest your own beautiful white pine logs. My house would have a huge stone fireplace, big windows overlooking the lake, and a log-buttressed cathedral ceiling with iron chandeliers. I wanted to have stained-glass windows in the bathroom, and I wanted to make them myself. If you lived in a place like that, the girl of your dreams would turn up. She would materialize automatically, as in a science project. Just visualize the scene – a stunning log home with cedar-shingled roof and a wide veranda, a nicely restored red 1956 Chevy pick-up truck in the driveway, a vintage wooden boat, and a Piper Cub float plane tied up at the dock. Now try to imagine the guy who lives in that place not having a great girl-friend. It's just not imaginable. I was quite sure that once I got started on the house, all kinds of chips would fall into place. But before I bought the property and built the house, I needed to raise some money. And I couldn't concentrate on raising money as long as I was dealing with petty day-to-day annoyances like my house going to the bottom of the lake.

My friend Kelly owned a skidder, which is a large insectoid tractor used for hauling logs out of the bush. A skidder is an impressive machine. With its huge wheels and steel claws it will plough through any forest, no matter how dense. The skidder used big inner tubes in its tires. Kelly suggested that I go to Winnipeg and buy some tubes, which could be had for about $25 apiece. Each one of them would float several thousand pounds. "Put one under each corner of the deck," he said. "Pump them up with an air compressor, and Bob's your mother's brother."

This was a perfect Minaki solution: cheap and temporary. I went to Winnipeg on the Thanksgiving weekend, bought some patched-up skidder tubes, and visited my parents. As always, my father wanted to know if I'd seen anything on the way, meaning wildlife. As always, my mother did my laundry and fed me great helpings of roast chicken and mashed potatoes, followed by tea and lemon meringue pie, my favourite. It was always pleasant to come home, eat a hot meal, and pretend to be fourteen years old again, and I'm sure my mother would have been happy if I'd just announced that I was moving back into my old bedroom. But my houseboat was sinking. So I bid them adieu and carried on.

On the way out of town I stopped to see my old friend Douglas. He told me he was going to a party. It was a serious party, with a bluegrass band, and he urged me to come. I wanted to keep moving and get back to Minaki, but I decided to follow the old tried-and-true rule – if there's a party, attend it. The party was at a large fancy house along the river, and there were lots of interesting people there. I ended up staying until two in the morning. When I left, I encountered a solitary woman in the front yard, smoking a cigarette. "Going home already?" she asked, in a deadpan tone.

I said something in return, and we fell into conversation. It was a chilly night, with a big moon above the treetops. She wore fine black leather gloves and some kind of dark woollen cape that made her look like she was on her way to a festival of witches. She had long dark hair and intelligent eyes. When I asked her why she was out here alone, she said she was in a foul mood because it was a full moon, and she missed her home in the country. It turned out, of course, that she was Mandy. And after we had a few chuckles about meeting at last, she grilled me about the houseboat, the country around Minaki, and where she could buy a copy of *Descant*.

After talking at length about Nature, music, wild creatures, the moon, and the effect of coincidence on human affairs, I accompanied her to her car, which was a respectable-looking Volvo four-door with a blue jay feather suspended from the rear view mirror. She climbed in and sat for a moment with the engine running, looking at me through the open window.

I leaned against the car. "Would you like to come and visit me at the lake?"

"When?"

"I don't know, tomorrow?"

"Where would we stay?"

"In my houseboat."

"Hmm. . . ." She pretended to tighten her gloves. She wore a pensive smile, as if considering a smart crack. She was the sort of woman who enjoyed a bit of fencing. "Could we have a fire before bed?"

"We can do whatever we want."

She gave me a direct look. "What time are you picking me up?"

❧

Even before the plane came into sight you could tell it was a Norseman. Like a vintage Indian motorcycle, an old Norseman produces an unmistakable guttural bawl as it flies past.

It was a lovely Saturday afternoon, sunny and warm, with the hills aflame with dying leaves and the glassy river as blue as a flag. Full moons seem to produce this kind of idyllic weather, and I couldn't have picked a better weekend to introduce my little town to someone like Mandy. We stood at the end of the dock at Holst Point and watched the Norseman glide in, bounce onto the water, then come taxiing towards us.

It took several minutes for the plane to taxi up to the dock, and Mandy seemed uncertain as to why we were standing there. I know that many human beings of the female persuasion aren't ordinarily fascinated by flying machines, but the fact is, I needed a few minutes to think.

I was very satisfied, so far, with the progress of our date. We'd had a leisurely drive up here and talked about everything under the sun. Since our arrival, there'd been only one small problem. She hated the houseboat. In my absence, the door had blown open, and the floor was covered with aspen leaves. There were tools all over the bed, sawed-up chunks of Styrofoam protruding from under the deck, and rusted barrels stacked along the shoreline. She didn't even want to go aboard. When we walked inside, the building rolled in such a sickening way that she actually yelped in alarm.

"We can't stay here," she said.

I apologized for the mess and explained that I would have had the place better prepared but I hadn't expected a guest. Whatever the reason, she said she simply wasn't going to spend the night there. And since everything else was going well, I silently forgave her for being fussy, and she probably silently forgave me for living in a shack. We got in my little wooden boat, which she admired, thank God, and went for a cruise down the river. I showed her the majestic and boarded-up Minaki Lodge, which was an even bigger mess than my houseboat. Then I took her for a bite of lunch in the rustic, log-walled dining room at the Point. We didn't mention the houseboat again, which was fine; I just didn't know where we would spend the night.

So I was glad to have a few minutes of silence as we watched the Norseman come sputtering up to the dock. When the pilot climbed out, I was pleasantly surprised to see my old buddy Dave come climbing out after him. Dave greeted us warmly, and I introduced him to Mandy. He said he'd been guiding moose hunters north of the seventh baseline and was glad to have a break and come home for the weekend. He asked us what we were doing that night. He said there was a big Thanksgiving party, and he strongly advised us to come. I told him my houseboat was a bit disorganized, with all the construction work, and we might end up driving back to Kenora and getting a hotel room for the night. "That's stupid," he said. "Use my place."

"Where are you going to stay?"

He said he would stay with his girlfriend. "I was planning to stay there anyway."

This was quite an offer. But for politeness' sake I took a moment or two to think it over. Dave's houseboat was an impressive dwelling. It was the second one he'd built, and it was much nicer than his first. He was a gifted designer, and since his father was a professional woodworker, Dave had access to all kinds of exotic, kiln-dried woods. He'd hand-crafted every detail, and it was beginning to look like it belonged on the cover of *Architectural Digest*. For the last couple of years, we'd moored our houseboats next door to each other out at Virgin Island, and I'd watched him gradually put the place together. He'd done a better job than I had of making a place for himself in this country. He was getting ahead. I was getting nowhere, but still, we were like brothers. Late at night, whoever came home last would swoop past the other person's house at full speed, kicking a big wave into the building and practically knocking the other guy out of bed. During midnight electrical storms, I'd hear a far-off cowboy gee-haw between crashes of thunder. And there were always the minor adventures that come with a life in the bush. One night, for example, a bear started climbing in my kitchen window, so I shooed him over to Dave's place, where he attempted to do the same thing. Some mornings, when it was rainy and depressing and he wasn't home, I'd go over and make myself a cup of tea and just sit in his houseboat. It boasted all the conveniences of a normal house. I could push a button and *Morningside* would issue from the ceiling. I could sit by the hanging plants in the sunroom and look out through the windows at the rainy lake, thinking that maybe some day I'd have a place like this. His houseboat offered an idealized glimpse of what life in this Shield country could be like. So I didn't consider his offer for too long before accepting.

When we arrived at Dave's place we unloaded our gear and got settled. Mandy was impressed with our lodgings, and while I sorted through the music cassettes, she unpacked her bag and laid her nightclothes on the bed. We both knew that we would be sleeping together, and that unspoken understanding imparted a delicious tension to every move we made, every comment. There was only about an hour of daylight left, so we took a walk around the island, climbing the high lichen-encrusted granite ledges. As we climbed the rocks, Mandy wondered aloud if we were walking on ancient "lava." I told her that it was actually igneous granite, the oldest rock on earth. "Certain parts of the Shield are almost as old as the universe," I said.

"How do you know?"

I explained that when I was taking the creative writing course at the University of Manitoba, I often visited the library and borrowed textbooks about botany, geology, and so forth. I explained that I was trying to develop some kind of general comprehension of this country; and not just Minaki, but the Shield country as a whole. "After all, it's our country, and we barely know anything about it."

"And what did you learn?" she asked. She actually seemed interested, so as we walked along through the woods, I told her that, in truth, I hadn't learned much. I'd never been any good at science and could never remember numbers or statistics. But after you read enough geology, you looked at the land differently. It was like removing the wrapper. When you walked these granite ridges you could almost visualize the last ice age, and what the land must have looked like when the glaciers pulled out. There was an old volcanic eruption site about thirty miles southwest of here, and when I drove through the highway rock cuts near there, I found myself picturing the event – the smoking volcano, the flocks of wheeling pterodactyls, and so on. You could never fully separate scientific fact from imagination, and the pictures in my mind were probably erroneous. But at least I was seeing the land in a context. When I was a kid I would have looked at it and thought, Hmm, rocks.

I said that a long time ago, back in Deep Time, 4.5 billion years ago, all the planets and stars had just coalesced, and the earth was an immense globule of molten nickel.

Lighter stuff floated to the top and cooled, forming a membrane like the skin on the surface of a cup of hot chocolate. It grew and thickened into granite, and formed itself into a huge ragged island called Pangea. After quite a while – I didn't know exactly how long – a large part of that super-continent split away and formed into the huge plaque of rock we now call the Canadian Shield. This rocky slab drifted west until it smashed into another immense structure called the Pacific Plate. For a while the two plates butted heads. But the Shield was harder and tougher, and eventually the Pacific Plate began "subducting," or slipping under the larger plate. That subduction process is still happening and causes the earthquakes that shake the west coast today.

In its original form, the Shield had jagged highlands like those we now see on the surface of the moon. They were rasped down by both rain and glaciers. Rain seeped into cracks in the granite and every night, when temperatures plunged, the rock crumbled, producing gravel, which washed off and produced wide alluvial flatlands, which stretched off for thousands of miles, which eventually turned into sedimentary rocks. It's important to realize that the Shield made our continent viable. It's the bedrock upon which North America was built. All the successful continents – Australia, Africa, and the others – have granite Precambrian rock as their foundation. Without a solid foundation of Precambrian rock, a continent can't survive.

I told her that the deeper nickel mines, like the ones in Sudbury, were warm at the bottom. And if you drilled only twenty-two miles down, you'd hit the Mohorovičić Discontinuity, which marked the edge of the planet's core, or if you will, its brain, which is fire. My throat was getting dry from all this talking and hiking, and judging by Mandy's amused silence, she'd heard enough geology for one day, so we walked back to the houseboat, arriving just before dark. We lit some candles, opened a bottle of wine, and went outside to watch the moon come up.

We sat on the slope of the island and toasted the evening, which was perfect. It was calm and warm, there were no mosquitoes, and the lake was a stained-glass window. Even the lunar cycle was perfect. The best night to watch the moonrise isn't on the night of the full moon (when it rises at the same time the sun goes down), but on the evening afterwards, when it comes up forty minutes after nightfall. For perhaps the entire time we sat there – from the moment that the first bulge of light appeared on the horizon, until perhaps half an hour later, when the moon hung like a Jack o' Lantern above the distant trees – we didn't say a word. But Mandy was curled up behind me, like a schoolgirl getting ready to ride a sled downhill, and her breath was soft on my neck. When the show ended I twisted around and kissed her, laying her flat on the rock and slipping my hand into the warmth under her sweater, feeling her heart banging beneath mine. "Are we going to bed now?" she asked. "Or are we going to the party?"

Her voice had that breathy sound of someone wanting to know if it's okay to let the dogs off the leash. If we went to bed now, there wasn't much chance that we'd be going anywhere, and I really wanted her to experience Minaki in its fullness, including a good party with lots of music and laughter. So I suggested we remain resolute and go to the party, at least for a while. "Good idea," she said, standing up and hauling on my hand. "This is going to be fun."

We blew out all the candles. Or at least we thought we blew out all the candles. Then we put on our jackets and headed off. The party was at Pete and Trout Barber's house, alias Tax Dodge Lodge. (Pete, being a scrupulous sort of guy and careful bookkeeper, didn't think the name was all that funny.) Pete was a little older than I was, and when I was growing up back in Winnipeg, he was one of those cool guys who ran the school dances and hung out with guys like Neil Young. Now he lived in Minaki, had a pretty wife, lots of business on the go, and was the unofficial mayor of the village. When Mandy and I arrived, fifty or sixty people were already milling about on the back deck and in the party room indoors. The food was a potluck affair, based on a theme of local bounty, and there was lots of smoked fish, venison loin roast, bannock, roast partridge, fresh pickerel, moose casserole, wild rice pilaf, baked lake trout, and mallard *à l'orange*. Mandy elbowed me in the ribs, embarrassed that we hadn't brought any food. But I reminded her that we hadn't known about the party until this afternoon. And in any case, these people were like family. When you go to a party at your family's house, you don't have to bring anything; you just have to wear a clean shirt.

Later, there was dancing and music. Kelly was playing the saxophone. Dave was dancing with a bunch of women, and Mandy was having a fine time too, working the room without any help from me. It was well past midnight before I finally coaxed her to come outside for a minute, on the ruse of sharing a cigarette. Once we got outside, I gave her her jacket. "Let's go."

"Why?"

"Ssshh . . ." I whispered. "They'll catch us."

"It's a good party."

"It's always a good party." I pulled her behind the bushes and kissed her. Her mouth tasted like wine. She pulled me into the shadow of the house and we necked for a few minutes, grappling and jostling against the wall.

"Okay, you've convinced me," she whispered.

My boat was down the road, parked at the marina. Once we climbed into the cockpit, I told Mandy to close her eyes. "I've got a present for you."

She closed her eyes, and I drove out of Town Bay, past the myriad lights that slurred the surface of the slick water. When the lights of town fell behind us, I shut off the motor and coasted to a stop. "Okay, there it is."

She opened her eyes and murmured in amazement.

High above us, the stars glowed and flickered like a million birthday candles. We drifted in total silence for a few minutes, gazing up at them. I said, "You can see six thousand stars on an average night around here."

"Did you count them?"

"Yes," I lied. "Every single one."

"If I lived here I'd learn the stars too," Mandy allowed. "They're just so bright."

We were both speaking in whispers. With my arm around her, and her head tilted back against my shoulder, we watched the sky slowly rotating above us. She asked me if I'd included astronomy on my home-study course. I said I had, but couldn't remember many of the details. She said, "Give me the Coles Notes version."

I told her that, according to current science, it all started fifteen billion years ago. Fifteen billion years ago there was Nothing. Floating in the middle of this Nothingness was a "cosmic egg." The egg was very dense, because it was packed with all the material in the universe. Abruptly, the egg exploded. Scientists aren't sure why it exploded, but their best guess sounds pretty much like the Book of Genesis:

> Darkness was upon the face of the deep; and the spirit
> of God moved over the waters. And God said: Be light
> made. And light was made.

And a flash of light bigger than any supernova – so big in fact that scientists abandoned all hope of capturing it with elevated language and simply called it "the Big Bang" – sent hot gases flying in all directions. As the burning shrapnel blasted through space, some of it congealed into tiny burning droplets called stars, and the smaller ones cooled down and formed planets.

Here and there, particularly thick clouds of stellar dust formed galaxies. Our galaxy, the Milky Way, contains about two hundred billion stars, give or take a hundred billion.

(Scientists can't count them properly because they can't stand outside the galaxy to get a look.) There are hundreds of millions of other galaxies like the Milky Way, but we can't see them with the naked eye. Back in 1927 the astrophysicist Edwin Hubble determined that the universe is still expanding. And later, two astronomers named Arno Penzias and Robert Wilson discovered that the shock wave of the Big Bang is still out there, rolling away like a thunderclap. With highly specialized measuring equipment, you can hear it.

All the scientists pretty much agree on how the universe started. But they differ on how it will all end. Some hold with fire; others with ice. Some scientists say the universe will keep expanding until it runs out of energy and dies. The fire buffs argue that the universe will eventually slow down, as gravity overcomes the momentum of the Big Bang. Then each star will pause, like a burning arrow at the top of its arc, and begin to rush back towards a terrific pile-up that collapses every wooden boat, highway, mountain, planet, star, and galaxy into one super-compressed tiny super-hot particle. Stephen Hawking says the particle – another cosmic egg – will be about the size of an atom. Then what? Maybe the process will begin again. The cosmic egg may flash to life again with another great bang. Even if we're not around to enjoy it, a fiery rebirth seems like a more encouraging version than a universe that runs out of energy and dies with a whimper.

The only trouble with star-gazing is that it's a bit of a conversation stopper. I'd read every book on this country, gone from the end to the beginning, but I still hadn't figured out the answer to anything. So before we got too chilled and disheartened, I fired up the motor and we carried on. I was looking forward to climbing into bed with Mandy, snuggling under flannel sheets and warm quilts. But when we came around the corner, I saw something. I stopped the boat. A scarf of white smoke was drifting out of Dave's chimney.

"What's the matter?" she said.

"The houseboat is on fire."

"What are you talking about?"

"The house must be full of smoke. Look at the smoke going up the chimney."

I sped up the boat and we carefully approached the door. The windows were black, and we had to be wary of opening the door and causing a backdraft explosion. Standing off to one side, we wrenched the door open and smoke belched out. We ducked inside. The houseboat's interior was like a demonic chapel, dark and smoky, illuminated by a hundred tiny flames. In such a fire, the upper layers of the room fill with carbon monoxide, and if you take a lungful you lose consciousness. So we stayed low, grabbed a couple of plastic buckets from under the sink, and dashed outside. Filling the buckets, we began throwing water on every exposed flame. Fresh air was now coming into the building, and the fire was starting to roll. Mandy and I argued about tactics. She thought I should go and get the fire department. I told her it was too late. She was flinging water like a madwoman and screaming that I should go for help. So I made her promise not to go in the building, then I jumped into the boat and sped for town.

As I burst in the door, the party was still in full swing. Dave and several women were doing the hokey-pokey. I accosted him. "Dave! Your houseboat is on fire."

"Oh sure."

"I'm serious! We need to go! Right now!"

He put his left foot in and his left foot out. "Was it burning when you left?"

"Yeah!"

"Then it's too late."

I got his jacket and pushed him towards the door. He wasn't drunk. He was just refusing to let a little thing like total disaster ruin his evening. We got in the boat and drove across Town Bay. Past the corner of Muncer's Reef the whole sky was lit up with the horrid orange glow of fire. When we arrived at the island the houseboat was encased in a gel of flames forty feet high. I was worried about Mandy, but I could see her standing up on a granite ridge, well back from the heat of the flames. We parked the boat and climbed up to join her. She was crying. Her face gleamed with tears, and gasping wails tore from her throat. Dave stood at my side, slapping me on the shoulder consolingly, as though it were my place and not his.

"Look at her go," he kept murmuring, almost in admiration. The building was cracking and mewing in the terrible heat. He'd built it from Quebec pine, cypress from Florida, and mahogany from Honduras. They were kiln-dried woods and the building burned as fiercely as if it had been soaked in gasoline. There was a sudden explosive boom as the big propane tank on the rear deck blew. Hissing like a huge furious reptile, it spat a dragon's breath of flame twenty feet sideways. Then the roof started falling in. Other boats were now arriving, people climbing the rock to stand here beside us. The women were crying. The men stood there with bottles of beer in their hand. There was nothing to say.

The walls fell in. Soon there was nothing but a burning skeleton on the deck. A barge came steaming around the corner, with its light flashing, and as it drew closer we could see that it was the rescue party – the Minaki Volunteer Fire Department. Assistant fire chief Nick Grogan and about five other volunteers had come to fight the fire. Nick Grogan was a local mechanic, a bachelor who lived quietly in a little house and was probably an alcoholic. At any party, it was about ten minutes worth of entertainment watching him trying to climb a set of stairs. He and the other firemen had all been at the party, and for some reason they'd allowed Nick to drive the barge. As the barge approached, it became apparent that Nick was frozen at the wheel. His eyes were wide, as if mesmerized by the flames, and he held the throttle with a fierce grip right up to the moment when the barge hit the burning houseboat.

It collided at an angle, so instead of being thrown onto the flames, the fire fighters tumbled into the water. The water was shallow enough that they were able to stand up. One of them wallowed through chest-deep water and punched Nick Grogan in the head. Nick snapped out of his daze and returned the roundhouse blow, sputtering and swearing. Soon four of five of them were wrestling and punching each other. Up on the rock, the onlookers barely paid any attention to the donnybrook. In the midst of this sad disaster, it was not only unfunny but too predictable to deserve comment.

That night, Mandy and I stayed at Holst Point. We felt so bad about the fire that we stayed in separate rooms. We probably blamed each other. I suspected that Mandy had left one of her cigarettes on the couch or the bed, and she probably thought I'd done something wrong with the candles. I don't know what she thought, because early the next morning she went back to the city on the train.

Constable Larry Willot came to my room at Holst Point and interviewed me for the police report. I told him we might have left a cigarette or neglected to blow out a candle. Or it might have been a short circuit in the wiring of the houseboat; I just didn't know. He kept nodding in feigned sympathy as he filled out the report. I didn't need any sympathy because I already knew it was my fault. After all, Mandy was just a visitor. And we might have gotten back to the houseboat in time, if I hadn't been holding forth on the universe.

Dave rented a little shack across the road from the bait shop and settled in for the winter. I went to see him to apologize for the fire, but he was annoyed that I even brought it up. "Forget it," he said. "You want a coffee?" The shack was about the size of an ice-fishing hut. It had a plywood table, a Coleman camp stove, and a little closet-type bathroom with a plastic pail for a toilet. The houseboat hadn't been insured, so he had to start all over again. He got a job at a construction site, driving a rock wagon. It was a rough, boring job, driving up and down pot-holed roads all day. But he never said a critical word, not to me or to anyone else, not once.

I would have offered him my houseboat but it would have been an insult. The flotation was so bad that every time I walked to one side it began to tip over. When I fell asleep I dreamed it was turning topsy-turvy, furniture and chairs clattering down from the ceiling, black water pouring in the doors like the end of the world.

Kelly Gibson believed that we could fix the flotation if we pulled the houseboat up on shore with his skidder. Kelly's skidder was an astoundingly rude and uncalled-for sort of machine with immense scarred tires and a winch that was capable of pulling trees out of the ground. Kelly was always entertaining himself with it, and pulling the houseboat up on the beach at Murray's Camp seemed like an interesting experiment. So we wrapped the cable around the base of the houseboat. It was a late October day, very cold. Gusts of wind were tumbling in off the lake like broken sheets of glass, and the ragged steel cable was so cold that our hands kept clenching up into paralytic claws. Finally the jerry-rigged towing harness looked ready, and Kelly climbed onto the skidder. The skidder dug in and spat pieces of lawn. The houseboat screamed as the cable came tight. Most of the building hopped and wiggled onto shore. But a good portion of it remained – a grisly wreckage of rusted drums and broken planks half-submerged in water.

Kelly jumped off and we stood there looking at the mess. The houseboat looked like it had been in a car accident. I knew what he was thinking. We'd been in a lot of adventures together, and I knew he was a proponent of cutting your losses and moving on.

I finally said, "Okay, let's destroy it."

"Where will you live?"

"I don't know."

Kelly climbed back onto the skidder and hauled the building the rest of the way out of the water. He opened the skidder's great mandibles and crushed the walls. Within half an hour the houseboat was reduced to heap of broken lumber. I poured a few gallons of heating oil onto the wreckage and lit the match. We stood there watching, warming our hands on the ripping flames. I kept looking at individual parts of the fire: pieces of shelving that I'd built, a trapezoidal window with melting shards of glass, a window box burning, its soil on fire too. Each tangled object seemed to be creaking and writhing in the heat, giving off hundreds of memories that rose into the flames and tore away on the wind.

By nightfall there was nothing left of the houseboat but a broad scorch mark on the beach. I loaded the van with the things I'd salvaged and headed for the highway. I didn't tell anyone I was leaving. Sometimes it's better to just slip away. It was snowing and flurries hooked sideways out of the darkness and bombed into the headlights. It's wearisome work, driving on snow-packed slippery roads, and I was happy when the storm finally ceased. After three hours of driving I finally saw the city, glowing like a scatter of embers on the horizon.

∾

I rented a bachelor apartment in the Osborne Village and started all over again. My old friend Paul Craft was a contractor, and he charitably hired me to work as a carpenter, a job for which I couldn't have been less qualified. We hammered nails all day, and in the evenings I worked on the latest novel. Writing seemed to be the string of yarn that kept my life intact. My apartment was below ground level, and from my desk I could see bicycle wheels and legs going by. Living in the city made me feel like I'd been exiled from my own country, and all those memories of working as a guide and living in the wilderness lent poignancy to the writing process. I was working on a story that never happened but very well could have. It felt like important work, like recording the lives of people who had never lived. I'd written almost three novels now and amused myself by thinking that I'd eventually become a lesser Kilgore Trout, the unpublished oddball of the Vonnegut novels.

Still, I missed my ducks. On hot early mornings in high summer, when it was already broad daylight at five o'clock in the

morning, the wild ducks from the neighbourhood would swim
back and forth in the lily pads outside my bedroom, rapping at
the wall to request breakfast.

When you're living in the city, it seems like there's time for
only a bit of work, a few meetings, and then the day is over. But
the island occupied its own time zone. If it was my day off, I'd
write in the morning, then do some work outside. There was
always decking to be repaired or boat seats that needed varnish-
ing, and it was so silent, on those hot afternoons with no one
around, that each single day seemed to go on forever. I often
went up on the roof to fiddle with my antennae, trying new
configurations to clarify my radio reception, and I liked working
up there with my shirt off, feeling the heat pouring up off the
asphalt roof, sweating in the afternoon heat, and then walking
over to the south side of the roof and stepping off, dropping
twelve feet straight down into the water.

Dusk too stretched on. The sun entered the northwesterly
horizon at such a shallow angle that it was still twilight at ten-
thirty. My bed was like a captain's bunk with an open screen
window through which the night air breathed. The antennae on
the roof was for maintaining contact with CBC radio, my lifeline
to the outside world, and I always listened to *Book Time*, a show
that featured readings of great novels, and later on, Big Al
McFee, who with his pet mouse finished off the night with music
and poetry. During one of those late-night broadcasts I heard
someone interviewing the writer Alice Munro. She said that a
short story should provide a kind of illumination at its ending,
which ideally is one we hadn't expected.

I finally reached a kind of illumination too. Ever since I was
a kid, exploring the forests north of Laclu, I'd fantasized about

living permanently in the woods. The whole time I lived in Minaki, all I really wanted was a relationship with the wild lakes and forests of the Canadian Shield. I thought it would be like having a summer vacation that never ended. I finally found that relationship, more or less, but it took a few years, and I found it in the last place I would have looked: in the city.

One Saturday morning, I called Larry Krotz and asked him if he wanted to have lunch. Larry was a freelance writer, the only person I'd ever met who actually made a living from writing, and I was so impressed by this that I'd resolved to make him a friend. Larry told me that he couldn't have lunch because he had another commitment, with a woman named Lynn Cunningham. He told me that she was from Toronto, and that she edited a general-interest magazine called *Quest*. Apparently she was travelling across the country, taking the pulse of the nation, and looking for fresh new writers. He said, "Why don't you join us?"

Riding the elevator up to the restaurant, I tried to think up some story ideas. We had a very pleasant lunch. She seemed interested in the fact that I'd worked as a fishing guide. She wanted to hear some stories. I told her about the many characters I'd met, both the good and bad ones. Afterwards, she asked me to write an article about it. "Have some fun with it," she suggested.

I went home. Be careful what you wish for. I'd never written a magazine article before, and now I had to actually do it. But I got busy, and by midnight, I'd completed the piece. I mailed it off in the morning and awaited her reply. There was no reply. A week passed, then a month. Fearing the worst, I phoned her in Toronto and asked if she'd had a chance to look at it. "Of course!" she said. "I loved it. Your cheque should be on its way. Is a thousand dollars all right?"

Apart from publishing my story, she was offering to pay me one-fifth of my annual salary, so yes, it was all right. A few weeks later, I managed to get another piece of short fiction accepted. And that same week, a local publisher phoned me up and told me she wanted to publish my novel. I felt lucky, ridiculously lucky, but I had to remind myself that I'd been working at this for a long time. When my cheque arrived from *Quest* magazine, I told my contractor buddy Paul Craft that I was going to conduct an experiment. I was going to deposit the $1,000 in a separate bank account and for the next three months do nothing else but write. I'd write every morning and every night, and send stories off in every direction. I'd conduct my life as a business. I'd get a bunch of fresh white paper, some new typewriter ribbons, and even a swivel chair.

Three months later, I'd made some withdrawals from the bank account, but I'd also made some deposits, and the principal amount was still hovering around a thousand bucks. At tax time that year, I put "writer" on my tax form and haven't had a job since.

∽

Many years before I mutated into a writer, years in fact before I quit university and hit the open road with that old canoe on the roof, I was cruising down Academy Road one day in a red Triumph sports car piloted by one of my university friends, a good-time Charlie named Glen Harvey.

It was one of those warm, sunny autumn days when the slightest waft of warm breeze sends operatic chords of yellow leaves cascading down from the big elm trees, and you can't imagine being stuck in class or doing anything else that involves being indoors. I was trying to find some music on the radio when Glen suddenly locked up the brakes and we skidded to a stop. "Oh my God," he said. "Did you see that?"

From the panicked sound in his voice I thought he'd just witnessed someone being hit by a car. But as he downshifted into first gear and pulled a fast U-turn, I realized that he'd only spotted a girl. He pulled to a stop at the street corner, where the girl was standing there alone, waiting for a bus. She was a knockout, all right, with long wavy chestnut hair and the sort of large, heavy-lashed brown eyes that cartoonists draw when they want to render some impossibly luscious stereotype of the female face. This wasn't my sort of thing, to hail women at bus stops, so I just sat there and kept quiet while Glen delivered the routine. He was a good talker who wrote his own mottoes in the margins of his schoolbooks ("Never be afraid to ask for the sale"), and to my surprise, she agreed to accept a ride. Moments later, we were speeding along with our new friend somehow jammed into the tiny space between us.

We went to Glen's basement and listened to his new Country Joe and the Fish record, then went to the university pub for a drink. I had my dad's car and followed them over to the campus. It was my assumption that she was with Glen. He was the guy with the patter. But as we sat in the pub, she spent most of the time talking to me, about poetry and stuff, which turned out to be among her interests. Glen's tolerance for heartfelt conversation was minimal, and he soon wandered off. Later that night, when I dropped Carolyn off at her house, I asked her if I could take her to a movie sometime. She informed me that she had a boyfriend, but as she climbed out of the car she kissed me on the cheek and said that she'd enjoyed herself.

Ten years passed. I rented the basement apartment and started a new life as a self-employed writer. Early in the evening, I often walked over to the Safeway to buy my groceries. At about six o'clock every night, the store was busy with stylishly dressed young professionals on their way home from work. One night I bought a platter of chicken breasts, took them home, and discovered they were rancid. Was it worth walking all the way back to the store for a lousy three dollars and fifty cents? I decided that it was the principle of the thing. Back at the supermarket, the manager tried to explain the various ways that the rotten chicken was in fact my fault. I was arguing with him when who should go walking by but Carolyn. In spite of the ten years passing, I recognized her immediately. I chased her and said hello. She was cordial enough, and we chatted a bit. It turned out we were even neighbours. She lived right across the street from me. She didn't, however, share my opinion that this was all an amazing and fortuitous coincidence. I asked her if she wanted to go for coffee, but she declined.

A few days later, I phoned her to see if she'd changed her mind. She hadn't changed her mind, so I gave her a few more days and checked again. Finally, I realized that she didn't want to go for coffee. Several weeks later, in one of those great wheel-of-fate coincidences that seem improbably geared to our lives, Glen Harvey showed up at my door. He was driving a Mercedes coupe and wearing a raccoon coat. He smelled like Giorgio Armani. After planting a big smooch on my cheek, he suggested we go out looking for chicks.

We were no longer teenagers but Glen was still the same. We exchanged a few stories of the old days, and I told him I'd bumped into Carolyn just a while ago. He suggested that I call her, "for old times' sake." I told him I'd already tried that. He badgered me. He urged me to call both Carolyn and her fetching sister, and we'd take them out for drinks. Finally I gave up and called Carolyn, and this time she was annoyed. It was a short, curt conversation, and I hung up wishing that I hadn't done it. Glen swept off into the night.

Minutes later, the doorbell rang. It was Carolyn, looking furious. She shook her finger in my face and asked why I was "harassing" her. I apologized and explained that it was because Glen had dropped over. Glen was the sort of guy it was easy to blame things on. She somehow ended up staying for a cup of tea. She told me that she worked as an RN, and when Paul Craft had been in a bad car accident, she'd taken care of him. When she left my apartment that night, it seemed like we'd agreed to be friends. A month later, she came to the launch party for my first novel. I'd sent her an invitation, but hadn't really expected her to show up. When the party was winding down, I asked her if she wanted to catch a movie sometime. A week later we went to see *Lady and the Tramp*. We got married in the spring, and our daughter was born on Valentine's Day.

We purchased an old three-storey house with big elms in the yard. I organized an office in the porch, and while I tapped at my old IBM Executive, our infant daughter Caitlin would lie snoozing across my knees in her bumblebee pyjamas. When Carolyn came home from work at midnight, she sometimes had just finished wrapping a dead body. All she asked was that I put on a good TV show and rub her feet. There seemed to be a lot of writing work around, and we bought a new apple-red Cherokee. We had lots of friends and enjoyed speeding off to see a movie at the last minute. We had the traffic lights timed so that we could careen downtown, park, and walk into the theatre with our popcorn just as the curtains were opening. We did this at least twice a week. Hollywood couldn't keep up with us. We had a good life. But I'd often lie awake at night, listening to the wind in the trees outside our window, missing the lake country.

One day the phone rang. It was Kelly and Sally, my old friends from Minaki. They said that there'd been a big auction at Minaki Lodge. They'd bought a dismantled building – the old pro shop, a beautifully designed octagonal structure with massive fir beams in the ceiling. They'd intended to make it into a cabin, but changed their minds. Did Carolyn and I want to turn it into a houseboat? I sat down with Carolyn and we discussed the idea. She could see that I needed to do this and agreed to go ahead with it.

I went down to Minaki on the Ides of March, and with the help of Kelly and Dave and a few other guys, we framed it right on the ice, using sixty pieces of foam for flotation. That summer I spent a lot of time in Minaki, finishing the place up. Carolyn didn't always come. She liked the city just fine and didn't feel the same zest for rough backwoods living. I often brought Caitlin though. She was the size of a small tree lemur, and would clamber up onto my chest when she saw something she didn't like. She had her own room in the houseboat, but it was full of dangers. I'd moved the houseboat out to Virgin Island, and during the night thunderclaps would shake the building. Caitlin would climb into my bed, mumbling that there was "a short fat witch" in her bedroom. Then in the morning she would wake up ready to go, eager to go outside and look for minnows.

Just as mysteriously as we had drifted together, her mum and I began to drift apart. You never know why a marriage unravels. You might be attracted to someone because they're smart, funny, sexy, or wealthy, or because it's time you got married and they look like a good person to make a baby with. It's complicated, and doubly so when you blend together two personalities. When a marriage goes sideways, everyone wants to hear a simple explanation, so you come up with something. The truth is, you don't really know what happened, and you never will. After six years together, Carolyn and I decided to split up. We agreed to remain partners in raising Caitlin and expressed our determination to keep our relationship civilized. I found a big old rambling apartment with gleaming woodwork and a fireplace. It had a big bedroom for Caitlin. On weekends and holidays, we headed off to the houseboat, which was gradually turning into the place I'd always wanted, a floating piece of architectural fancy that looks a bit like a Japanese mountain pagoda. Fishermen were always stopping to take pictures of it, and when my tiny niece Helen first saw it, she scrambled aboard and asked, "Is this a fairy house?"

Being single again, or at least single some of the time, I was now free to pursue the mission that had taken me to the Shield in the first place. Being a freelance writer, I found that some publication or magazine was always willing to pick up the tab for my travels, as long as I came back with a good story. I used my freelance journalism work to subsidize the time I spent writing fiction and managed to put out a novel or a book of short stories every couple of years. Life never delivers exactly what we want, but the irony that foils one plan sometimes delivers a better one. When I was growing up, I'd imagined that I'd live in the Shield country and become a hunter-gatherer. As it worked out, I became a hunter-gatherer of stories. My job took me from one end of the Shield to the other, from top to bottom and from east to west. It's a place so full of stories, fabulous scenery, roaring waterfalls, teeming wildlife, self-made people, and heart-stopping vistas of uninhabited wilderness that it would be foolish to try to summarize them. But eventually, I figured out a sort of rough translation of its enigmatic message.

The discovery of the message didn't occur in a dramatic way. And I didn't find it in some far-flung arctic river valley, secreted under a rock. Rather, it just kind of sank in with the passing of the years. Literary critics like Northrop Frye and Margaret Atwood have made the point that the Canadian psyche is shaped by the belief that Nature still prevails. And that's an interesting idea, but it's just an idea. It doesn't sink in until you feel it, and feel it with every step you take.

The old-timers in Minaki knew the truth. Even when they were spinning yarns, it shaped every word that they said. One hot summer night after a long day of fishing I was sitting on the dock with the other fishing guides, and the topic came around to the afterlife. What kind of animal would you like to be?

The young guides voted for all the usual poster animals – the big charismatic creatures with impressive talons and teeth. "I'd like to be a timberwolf," said one. "I'd like to be an eagle," said another. An old Indian named Mitchell Muckle was sitting quietly at the picnic table, with cigarette smoke wafting up from his beat-up hands. He said, "I'd like to be a mouse."

I'd spent all these years trying to develop a big overview of this country. But maybe Mitchell was right. Maybe the mouse, with its sense of smell and its close-up view of every blade of grass, saw the world as it really was. As in any investigation, God is in the details. And although I'd always presumed that you acquired wisdom by acquiring knowledge, I was beginning to wonder if the path to understanding wasn't so much a learning curve as a de-learning curve. The answer wasn't in knowing more, but in knowing less.

One winter afternoon, for example, I wanted to ski over to Virgin Island and visit the houseboat. I wasn't sure if the ice was safe, so I went and visited Jack Stevens, a richly entertaining and hatchet-faced old-timer who was locally known as The Wedge. Jack's trapline included Virgin Island, and he knew more about the ice than anyone. "When is the ice safe?" I asked him. "Never," he said. I'd half-expected him to do this, to bait me with some provocative and playful answer. But he wasn't kidding. "The ice is never safe," he said. "No matter what the weather. And anyone who thinks it's safe is a fool."

He seemed a bit brusque, as though I shouldn't have been asking such a question. He had been travelling and working on the ice all his life. And he'd done it with the terrible knowledge that his life could be taken from him at any moment. We're all travelling on thin ice, of course. But for him the ice wasn't a metaphor; it was real, and walking on it every day had made him a wise man. His point was, nobody knows anything about this country. We're not in charge, Nature is. And it was high time I understood that.

We're lucky enough to inhabit a country where Nature still prevails. In the words of Northrop Frye, the Shield is not merely hostile, but "indifferent to human values." It was here billions of years before we came, and will still be here billions of years after we're gone. It provokes us into admitting that we are nothing. It obliges us to build our own values, invent our own identities. Our country may be a land of snow, a land of chilly lakes, haunted trees, and granite ridges rolling off into the distance like ribs of time, but it makes us who we are.

When my daughter was fourteen years old, she went on a wilderness canoe trip organized by the YMCA. It was an expensive vacation, but her mother and I were convinced that she needed to see the wilderness face to face. The canoe trip turned out to be long and miserable, and the bugs were bad. They dodged bears, waded shin-deep through mucky swamps with heavy canoes and packs on their backs, and paddled so hard their hands bled. It rained heavily, and they slept on the ground in sodden sleeping bags. One night they found a rotted, fallen-down trapper's cabin with skunk turds on the floor and bats crawling around in its broken rafters. But they were as excited as if it was a Four Seasons Hotel. It meant they could sleep on a wooden floor! When they paddled back to camp, the counsellors prepared a welcoming celebration. The girls beached their canoes, kneeled, clasped their sacred paddles to their hearts, bowed their heads, and received the traditional voyageur's benediction. They had left the camp as girls and returned as women.

The Shield has a different effect on everyone who spends time there. For some, it's a tool for growing up. For others, it's a frontier, a place to discard old identities and start anew. In the United States, the cowboy hat and the pick-up truck are symbols of the American heartland. But Canada's symbols are the symbols of the Shield – the beaver, the snowshoe, the checkered jacket, and the float plane. The Shield can be a place that poses an insoluble puzzle, or it can be a place to drink beer at the cottage and relax. God knows there's nothing wrong with that. As one old fisherman told me, "People ask me why I spent so much of my life at the lake. I've thought about it, and decided it's because I enjoyed it." I enjoyed the Shield so much that I tried to live there and proved to my satisfaction that I couldn't. But it's an addictive landscape, and I return to it time and time again.

It's my own unwritten page, a blankness where my own story begins and ends.

One spring night, several years ago, I was staying in the Park Plaza hotel in Toronto, trying to decide whether to go to a birthday party or just stay in my room and watch television. I didn't feel like going to a party. I was listless. It was a rainy night and my immense expense-accounted hotel room was vaguely depressing. But the rule is, always attend the party. So I went, and met Ann, who was alone, like me. She was a smart, attractive blonde, a talented writer, and I'd admired her work for many years. We stayed up late and went back to her house for a nightcap. While she fixed our drinks, I looked at the art in her living room. She owned quite a few landscapes. They were oil paintings, originals, and I was surprised to see A.Y. Jackson's name written in the bottom right-hand corner. "We called him Uncle Alec," she said. "He wasn't really our uncle, but he spent so much time at our cottage in Georgian Bay that he was like a member of the family. When I was a little girl I'd sit on his knee at the table and wipe the marmalade off his sweater. I'd sometimes go with him when he went out sketching."

Ann loved the north country, like me. How could we not love the north country? Summer was coming. We were Canadians. We'd grown up at the lake and we knew how to make love in a canoe. It took some doing, but I persuaded her to be my girlfriend. She came to Minaki and we looked at the stars. I took her out to my old camping spot at Tower Island, which, as always, was like a green cathedral. The moss was soft underfoot and the great pines stirred in the wind.

We drove to Kenora a few days later to buy groceries. On the way, we stopped at Laclu so that I could show her the old cottage. My father had been crippled by a severe stroke and was in a veteran's hospital in Winnipeg. He'd probably never come to the lake again. My mother still came for a weekend when one of my brothers or sisters found the time to bring her, but the cottage was no longer the busy, happy, family meeting place it had once been.

We parked the truck next to the old shed. The lawn was high and unkempt. The front door of the cottage was padlocked, so I couldn't show Ann the interior. But it was fine to walk around outside. My father had planted all these trees when I was a kid, but now they were as tall as the trees in a forest, and busy with hundreds of songbirds. It was nesting season, and the wooded yard was so full of chirping, warbling cries that it was like walking through a Montreal Jazz Festival of birds.

We stopped under a big apple tree to look at one of the decrepit birdhouses that my father had built so many years ago. Then we walked down the hill to look at the water.